Study Guide

for

Fundamental Accounting Principles
VOLUME 2 – CHAPTERS 12-25

Twentieth Edition

John J. Wild
University of Wisconsin at Madison

Ken W. Shaw
University of Missouri at Columb

Barbara Chiappetta
Nassau Community College

Prepared By
Barbara Chiappetta
Nassau Community College

Patricia Walczak
Lansing Community College

McGraw-Hill Irwin

Study Guide for
FUNDAMENTAL ACCOUNTING PRINCIPLES, VOLUME 2 – CHAPTERS 12-25
John J. Wild, Ken W. Shaw, and Barbara Chiappetta

Published by McGraw-Hill/Irwin, an imprint of The McGraw-Hill Companies, Inc., 1221 Avenue of the
Americas, New York, NY 10020. Copyright © 2011, 2009, 2007, 2005, 2002, 1999, 1996, 1993, 1990, 1987, 1984, 1981, 1978,
1975, 1972, 1969, 1966, 1963, 1959, 1955 by The McGraw-Hill Companies, Inc. All rights reserved.

1 2 3 4 5 6 7 8 9 0 QDB/QDB 1 0 9 8 7 6 5 4 3 2 1 0

ISBN: 978-0-07-733817-6
MHID: 0-07-733817-0

www.mhhe.com

TO THE STUDENT

is study guide is provided as a learning tool for your study of *Fundamental Accounting Principles* by John Wild, Ken W. Shaw and Barbara Chiappetta. You should understand that the material provided is not ended to substitute for your textbook. Instead, the objectives of this guide are as follows:

1. To summarize important information that is explained in the text. For example, the **chapter outline** of each chapter identifies important topics in the chapter. In reading the outline, you should ask yourself whether or not you understand each of the topics listed. If not, you should return to the appropriate chapter in *Fundamental Accounting Principles* and read carefully the portions that explain the specific outlined topics about which you are unclear.

2. To provide you with copies of **visuals** that your instructor may use in class to introduce selected topics. Even if not used in class, these visuals serve as useful study tools.

3. To provide you with a quick means of testing your knowledge of the chapter. If you are unable to correctly answer the **problems** that follow the chapter outline, you should again return to the appropriate chapter in *Fundamental Accounting Principles* and review the sections about which you are unclear.

ur best approach to the use of this booklet out of class is:

- **First,** read the learning objectives and the related summary paragraphs. Then, ask whether your understanding of the chapter seems adequate for you to accomplish the objectives.

- **Second,** review the chapter outline, taking time to think through (describing to your self) the explanations that would be required to expand the outline. Use the notes column to indicate your questions or weaknesses. Return to *Fundamental Accounting Principles* to answer questions and cover areas of weakness.

- **Third**, review visuals if provided in the chapter. These will reinforce major concepts of the chapter.

- **Fourth,** answer the requirements of the problems that follow the chapter outline. Then, check your answers against the solutions that are provided after the problems.

- **Fifth,** return to *Fundamental Accounting Principles* for further study of any material you have not fully mastered.

ou may also find it helpful to **bring outlines and visuals to class**. In class you can use a highlighter to mark eas your instructor emphasizes. Use the note section for additional notes and/or to indicate the numbers of levant quick studies or exercises from the text that were worked in a notebook or on working papers during ass. You can then refer back to these when studying with the outline later.

e next page is provided to recommend an **overall approach to succeeding** in an accounting course.

HOW TO SUCCEED IN YOUR ACCOUNTING COURS

A. **Stay Up-To-Date**

Accounting is a unique discipline in that learning takes place in "building blocks." The best analogy is that it is almost impossible to learn to read without learning the sounds of the letters in the alphab It is almost impossible for you to learn topics in accounting without having a level of understanding of the previously addressed topic. Accounting is the language of business, and like any language, it learned through a developmental process.

Staying up-to-date includes completing all assignments on a timely basis. This allows you to take fu advantage of classroom assignment check. The best insurance for staying up-to-date is to use good time management skills. This means plan a regular study schedule for the week—and stick to it! Staying up-to-date will give you the foundations to learn and ***succeed!***

B. **Know How to Use Your Textbook**

1. Overview the chapter

   a. Preview the learning objectives and mark those that the instructor has listed in the course outline or mentioned in class.

   b. Read title page which provide a very brief look at chapter contents, as well as a look back a ahead. This allows you to see the links or building blocks you will put in place.

   c. Read the Summary of Learning Objectives found at the end of the chapter as well as in this study guide. This first pass on summaries is just to get a broad perspective of the contents. I not expect to understand all that you read at this point.

2. Read the chapter

   a. Using a highlighter as you read will keep you mentally alert. Writing is a proven vehicle for learning. Use the wide text margins to note key concepts as well as your questions. This wil clarify your thoughts as you read.

   b. Use Quick Checks. These are brief questions interspersed throughout the chapter. Use them to check whether you are grasping essential concepts. Guidance answers are found at the en of the chapter.

   c. Reread the Summary of Learning Objectives. Make sure you thoroughly understand those specified by the instructor.

3. Use the demonstration problems

   Don't miss these! Students find these most helpful in learning how to solve accounting problem They address all major topics of the chapter. An approach to planning the solution is offered. Complete solutions are also provided.

C. **Get Involved**

1. The more actively involved you are in the learning process, the more you will understand and retain. Ask questions that arose while you were reading the chapter. Fully participate in all classroom activities.

2. Form a study group or a learning team. Meet regularly outside class. Support each other's learning. Teaching others is proven to be the most effective way of reinforcing your learning an increasing your retention. All students benefit from collaborating in the learning process.

TABLE OF CONTENTS

CHAPTER 12
ACCOUNTING FOR PARTNERSHIPS

Learning Objective C1:

Identify characteristics of partnerships and similar organizations.

Summary

Partnerships are voluntary associations, involve partnership agreements, have limited life, are not subject to income tax, include mutual agency, and have unlimited liability. Organizations that combine selected characteristics of partnerships and corporations include limited partnerships, limited liability partnerships, "S" corporations, and limited liability companies.

Learning Objective A1:

Compute partner returns on equity and use it to evaluate partnership performance.

Summary

Partner return on equity provides each partner an assessment of his or her return on equity invested in the partnership.

Learning Objective P1:

Prepare entries for partnership formation.

Summary

A partner's initial investment is recorded at the market value of the assets contributed to the partnership.

Learning Objective P2:

Allocate and record income and loss among partners.

Summary

A partnership agreement should specify how to allocate partnership income or loss among partners. Allocation can be based on a stated ratio, capital balances, or salary and interest allowances to compensate partners for differences in their service and capital contributions.

Learning Objective P3:

Account for the admission and withdrawal of partners.

Summary

When a new partner buys a partnership interest directly from one or more existing partners, the amount of cash paid from one partner to another does not affect the partnership total recorded equity. When a new partner purchases equity by investing additional assets in the partnership, the new partner's investment can yield a bonus to either existing partners or to the new partner. The entry to record a withdrawal can involve payment from either (1) the existing partners' personal assets or (2) from partnership assets. The latter can yield a bonus to either the withdrawing or remaining partners.

<u>Learning Objective P4:</u>

Prepare entries for partnership liquidation.

Summary

When a partnership is liquidated, losses and gains from selling partnership assets are allocated to the partners according to their income-and-loss-sharing ratio. If a partner's capital account has a deficiency that the partner cannot pay, the other partners share the deficit in their relative income-and-loss-sharing ratio.

I. **Partnership Form of Organization**—An unincorporated association of two or more people to pursue a business for profit as co-owners.

A. Characteristics of Partnerships

1. Voluntary association.

2. Partnership contract (called *articles of copartnership*)—should be in writing but may be expressed orally.

3. Limited life—death, bankruptcy, or expiration of the contract period automatically ends a partnership.

4. Taxation—not subject to tax on income—partners report their share of income on personal income tax return.

5. Mutual agency—each partner is an agent of the partnership and can enter into and bind it to any contract within the normal scope of its business.

6. Unlimited liability—each general partner is responsible for payment of all the debts of the partnership if the other partners are unable to pay a share.

7. Co-ownership of property—assets are owned jointly by all partners but claims on partnership assets are based on their capital account and the partnership contract.

B. Organizations with Partnership Characteristics

1. Limited Partnership (LP or Ltd.) has two classes of partners, general (at least one) and limited. The general partners assume unlimited liability for the debts of the partnership. The limited partners assume no personal liability beyond their invested amounts and cannot take active role in managing the company.

2. Limited Liability Partnership (LLP) is designed to protect innocent partners from malpractice or negligence claims resulting from the acts of another partner. Generally, all partners are personally liability for other partnership debts.

3. "S" Corporation has 100 or fewer stockholders, is treated as a partnership for income tax purposes but otherwise is accounted for as a "C" corporation.

4. Limited Liability Company (LLC or LC) owners are called members, are protected with the limited liability feature of corporations and can assume an active management role. The LLC has a limited life and is typically classified as a partnership for tax purposes.

C. Choosing a Business Form
Factors to be considered include: taxes, liability risk, tax and fiscal year-end, ownership structure, estate planning, business risks, and earnings and property distributions.

II.   **Basic Partnership Accounting**—Same as accounting for a proprietorship except for transactions directly affecting partners' equity. Use separate capital and withdrawal accounts for each partner. Allocates net income or loss to partners according to the partnership agreement.

   A.   Organizing a Partnership
        Each partner's investment is recorded at an agreed upon value, normally the market value of the assets and liabilities at their date of contribution.

   B.   Dividing Income and Loss

        1.   Any agreed upon method of dividing income or loss is allowed. If there is no agreement, the net income or loss is divided equally.

        2.   Common methods of dividing partnership earnings use:

             a.   Stated ratio.

             b.   Allocation on capital balances.

             c.   Allocation on service, capital, and stated ratio—salary and interest allowances, and a fixed ratio are specified—when income exceed allowances, the remainder is allocated to individual partners using a fixed ratio and added to their individual planned allowance. But when allowances exceed the income, the negative amount or shortage is allocated using the ratio and applied *against* each partner's total allowance.

        3.   Salaries to partners and interest on partners' investments are not partnership expenses; they are allocations of net income.

        4.   Partners may agree to salary and interest allowances to reward unequal contributions of services or capital.

   C.   Partnership Financial Statements
        Similar to a proprietorship except:

        1.   The statement of partners' equity usually shows changes for each partner's capital account, including the allocation of income.

        2.   The balance sheet generally lists a separate capital account for each partner.

III. **Admission and Withdrawal of Partners**

    A. Admission of a Partner—two means:

       1. Purchase of partnership interest.

          a. The purchase is a personal transaction between one or more current partners and the new partner.

          b. Purchaser does not become a partner until accepted by the current partners.

          c. Involves a reallocation of current partners' capital to reflect the transaction.

       2. Investing assets in a partnership.

          a. The transaction is between the new partner and the partnership. Invested assets become partnership property.

          b. New partner's equity recorded for assets invested may be equal to, less than, or greater than investment.

          c. When the recorded new partner's equity differs from investment, there is a bonus to new or old partner's equity.

          d. Bonuses to old partners are allocated based on their income and loss sharing agreement.

    B. Withdrawal of a Partner—two means:

       1. Withdrawing partner sells his or her interest to another person who pays cash or other assets to the withdrawing partner.

       2. Cash or other assets of the partnership can be distributed to the withdrawing partner in settlement of his or her interest.

          a. Withdrawing partner may accept assets equal to, less than, or greater than his/her equity.

          b. When the withdrawing partner's equity differs from assets withdrawn, there is a bonus to remaining or withdrawing partner's equity.

          c. Bonuses to remaining partners are allocated based on their income and loss sharing agreement.

    C. Death of a Partner

       1. Dissolves a partnership.

       2. Deceased partner's estate is entitled to receive his or her equity. Contract usually calls for closing of the books and determining current value of assets and liabilities to update equity.

       3. Settlement of the deceased partner's equity can involve selling the equity to remaining partners or to an outsider, or it can involve withdrawing assets.

IV.   **Liquidation of a Partnership**

   A. Involves four basic steps:

      1. Noncash assets are sold for cash and a gain or loss on liquidation is recorded.

      2. Gain or loss on liquidation is allocated to partners using their income-and-loss ratio.

      3. Pay or settle liabilities.

      4. Distribute any remaining cash to partners **according to their capital account balances.**

   B. Allocating gains or losses on liquidation may result in:

      1. No capital deficiencies—all partners' have a zero or credit balance in their capital accounts the totals or which are equivalent to final distribution of cash.

      2. Capital deficiencies—when at least one partner has a debit balance in his/her capital account.

         a. Partners with a capital deficiency must, if possible, cover the deficit by paying cash into the partnership.

         b. When a partner is cannot pay the deficiency, the remaining partners with credit balances absorb the unpaid deficit according to their income-and-loss ratio. Inability to cover deficiency does not relieve partner of liability.

V.   **Global View—Compares U.S.GAAP to IFRS**

   A. Both systems include broad and similar guidance for partnership accounting.

   B. Different legal systems can impact partnership agreements.

VI.   **Decision Analysis—Partner Return on Equity**

   A. Evaluates partnership success compared with other opportunities.

   B. Computed separately for each partner.

   C. Computed by dividing partner's share of net income by that partner's average partner equity.

Problem I

The following statements are either true or false. Place a (T) in the parentheses before each true statement and an (F) before each false statement.

1. ( ) Partnership accounting is exactly like that of a single proprietorship except for transactions affecting the partners' equities.

2. ( ) Although a partner does not work for either a salary or interest, to be fair in the distribution of partnership earnings, it is often necessary to provide allowances for services and investments.

3. ( ) In the liquidation of a partnership, after selling all assets and paying all debts, the partners share any remaining cash equally.

4. ( ) When a partner withdraws from a partnership, that partner always withdraws assets equal to his equity.

5. ( ) Partners return on equity is computed by dividing a partner's average investment by that partner's share of net income.

Problem II

You are given several words, phrases, or numbers to choose from in completing each of the following statements or in answering the following questions. In each case select the one that best completes the statement or answers the question and place its letter in the answer space provided.

_____ 1. Reggie and Veronica began a partnership by investing $28,000 and $20,000, respectively, and during its first year the partnership earned a $42,000 net income. What would be the share of each partner in the net income if the partners had agreed to share by giving a $16,400 per year salary allowance to Reggie and an $18,000 per year salary allowance to Veronica, plus 10% interest on their beginning-of-year investments, and the remainder equally?

   a. Reggies' share, $20,600; Veronica's share, $21,400.

   b. Reggies' share, $22,200; Veronica's share, $19,800.

   c. Reggies' share, $21,400; Veronica's share, $20,600.

   d. Reggies' share, $24,500; Veronica's share, $17,500.

   e. Reggies' share, $21,000; Veronica's share, $21,000.

_____ 2. Red and White operate a partnership in which they have agreed to share profits and losses in a ratio of 3:2 respectively. They have agreed to accept Blue as a partner, offering him a 25% share for an $80,000 investment. Prior to his investment the combined equity of Red and White totals $120,000. The admission of Blue as a partner will result in

   a. a bonus of $30,000 to Blue.

   b. a bonus of $18,000 to Red and $12,000 to White.

   c. a bonus of $30,000 each to Red and Blue.

   d. a bonus of 15,000 each to Red and Blue.

   e. no bonus for any of the parties.

Problem III

Many of the important ideas and concepts discussed in Chapter 12 are reflected in the following list of key terms. Test your understanding of these terms by matching the appropriate definitions with the terms. Record the number identifying the most appropriate definition in the blank space next to each term.

_____ C corporation	_____ Partner return on equity
_____ General partner	_____ Partnership
_____ General partnership	_____ Partnership contract
_____ Limited liability company (LLC)	_____ Partnership liquidation
_____ Limited liability partnership (LLP)	_____ S Corporation
_____ Limited partners	_____ Statement of partners' equity
_____ Limited partnership	_____ Unlimited liability
_____ Mutual agency	

1. Partners who have no personal liability for partnership debts beyond the amounts they have invested in the partnership.

2. Partnership in which all partners have mutual agency and unlimited liability for partnership debts.

3. A partnership that has two classes of partners, limited partners and general partners.

4. Partner who assumes unlimited liability for the debts of the partnership; the general partner in a limited partnership is responsible for its management.

5. Legal relationship among partners whereby each partner is an agent of the partnership and is able to bind the partnership to contracts within the scope of the partnership's business.

6. Agreement among partners that sets terms under which the affairs of the partnership are conducted.

7. Legal relationship among general partners that makes each of them responsible for partnership debts if the other partners are unable to pay their shares.

8. Unincorporated association of two or more persons to pursue a business for profit as co-owners.

9. Corporation that does not qualify for and elect to be treated as a partnership for income tax purposes and therefore is subject to income taxes.

10. Partnership in which partner is not personally liable for malpractice or negligence unless that partner is responsible for providing the service that resulted in the claim.

11. Dissolution of a business partnership by (1) selling noncash assets and allocating the gain or loss according to partners' income-and-loss ratio, (2) paying liabilities, and (3) distributing any remaining cash according to partners' capital balances.

12. Corporation that meets special tax qualifications so as to be treated as a partnership for income tax purposes.

13. Financial statement that shows the total capital balances at the beginning of the period, any additional investment by partners, the income or loss of the period, the partners' withdrawals, and the ending capital balances; also called *statement of partners' capital*.

14. Form of organization that combines corporation and limited partnership features; provides limited liability to its members (owners), and allows members to actively participate in management.

15. Partner net income divided by average partner equity.

Problem IV

Complete the following by filling in the blanks.

1. A _____ (limited, general) partnership has two classes of partners.

2. Blake and Dillon are partners who have always shared incomes and losses equally. Hester has sued the partners on a partnership debt and obtained a $12,000 judgment. The partnership and Dillon have no assets; consequently, Hester is attempting to collect the entire $12,000 from Blake. Blake has sufficient assets to pay the judgment but refuses, claiming she is liable for only one-half of the $12,000. Hester _____ (can, cannot) collect the entire $12,000 from Blake because _____.

3. Since a partnership is a voluntary association, an individual _____ (can, cannot) be forced against his will to become a partner; and since a partnership is based on a contract, its life is _____.

4. Partners work for partnership _____ and not for a salary. Furthermore, when a partnership agreement calls for an interest and/or salary allowance, these allowances are only used to calculate the allocation of _____.

5. The phrase mutual agency, when applied to a partnership, means _____
    _____
    _____.

6. The four steps in the liquidation of a partnership are:
    _____
    _____
    _____
    _____.

7. If the allocation of loss from sale of the assets results in a deficit balance in a partner's capital account, that partner is responsible for making up the negative amount. If the partner fails to make up the negative then the other partners _____
    _____.

Problem V

Flip and Flop began a partnership by investing $14,000 and $10,000, respectively, and during its first year the partnership earned a $21,000 net income. Complete the tabulation below to show, under the several assumptions, the share of each partner in the $21,000 net income.

		Flip's Share	Flop's Share
1.	The partners failed to agree as to the method of sharing............	_____	_____
2.	The partners had agreed to share in their beginning-of-year investment ratio...	_____	_____
3.	The partners had agreed to share by giving an $8,200 per year salary allowance to Flip and a $9,000 per year salary allowance to Flop, plus 10% interest on their beginning-of-year investments, and the remainder equally	_____	_____

Solutions for Chapter 12

Problem I

1. T
2. T
3. F
4. F
5. F

Problem II

1. A
2. B

Problem III

9	C corporation		15	Partner return on equity
4	General partner		8	Partnership
2	General partnership		6	Partnership contract
14	Limited liability company (LLC)		11	Partnership liquidation
10	Limited liability partnership		12	S Corporation
1	Limited partners		13	Statement of partners' equity
3	Limited partnership		7	Unlimited liability
5	Mutual agency			

Problem IV

1. limited
2. can, each partner has unlimited liability for the debts of the partnership
3. cannot, limited
4. profits, or earnings, profits or earnings (net income also correct)
5. each partner is an agent of the partnership and can bind it to contracts
6. (1) Noncash assets are sold for cash and a gain or loss on liquidation is recorded; (2) gain or loss on liquidation is allocated to partners using their income-and-loss ratio; (3) liabilities are paid; and (4) remaining cash is distributed to partners based on their capital balances.
7. must absorb the negative amount according to their ratio for sharing income or loss.

Problem V

1. $10,500, $10,500

2. $12,250, $8,750

3. $10,300, $10,700

Learning Objective C1:

Identify characteristics of corporations and their organization.

Summary

Corporations are legal entities whose stockholders are not liable for corporate debts. Stock is easily transferred and the life of a corporation does not end with the incapacity of a stockholder. A corporation acts through its agents, who are its officers and managers. Corporations are regulated and are subject to income taxes. Authorized stock is the amount of stock that a corporation's charter authorizes it to sell. Issued stock is the portion of authorized shares sold. Par value stock is a value per share assigned by the charter. No-par value stock is stock *not* assigned a value per share by the charter. Stated value stock is no-par stock to which the directors assign a value per share.

Learning Objective C2:

Explain characteristics of, and distribute dividends between common and preferred stock.

Summary

Preferred stock has a priority (or senior status) relative to common stock in one or more areas, usually (1) dividends and (2) assets in case of liquidation. Preferred stock usually does not carry voting rights and can be convertible or callable. Convertibility permits the holder to convert preferred stock to common. Callability permits the issuer to buy back preferred stock under specified conditions. Preferred stockholders usually hold the right to dividend distributions before common stockholders. When preferred stock is cumulative and in arrears, the amount in arrears must be distributed to preferred before any dividends are distributed to common.

Learning Objective C3:

Explain the items reported in retained earnings.

Summary

Stockholders' equity is made up of (1) paid-in capital and (2) retained earnings. Paid-in capital consists of funds raised by stock issuances. Retained earnings consists of cumulative net income (losses) not distributed. Many companies face statutory and contractual restrictions on retained earnings. Corporations can voluntarily appropriate retained earnings to inform others about their disposition. Prior period adjustments are corrections of errors in prior financial statements.

Learning Objective A1:

Compute earnings per share and describe its use.

Summary

A company with a simple capital structure computes basic EPS by dividing net income less any preferred dividends by the weighted-average number of outstanding common shares. A company with a complex capital structure must usually report both basic and diluted EPS.

Learning Objective A2:

Compute price-earnings ratio and describe its use in analysis.

Summary

A common stock's price-earnings (PE) ratio is computed by dividing the stock's market value (price) per share by its EPS. A stock's PE is based on expectations that may prove to be better or worse than eventual performance.

Learning Objective A3:

Compute dividend yield and explain its use in analysis.

Summary

Dividend yield is the ratio of a stock's annual cash dividends per share to its market value (price) per share. Dividend yield can be compared with the yield of other companies to determine whether the stock is expected to be an income or growth stock.

Learning Objective A4:

Compute book value and explain its use in analysis.

Summary

Book value per common share is equity applicable to common shares divided by the number of outstanding common shares. Book value per preferred share is equity applicable to preferred shares divided by the number of outstanding preferred shares.

Learning Objective P1:

Record the issuance of corporate stock.

Summary

When stock is issued, its par or stated value is credited to the stock account and any excess is credited to a separate contributed capital account. If the stock has neither par nor stated value, the entire proceeds are credited to the stock account. Stockholders must contribute assets equal to the minimum legal capital of a corporation or be potentially liable for the deficiency.

Learning Objective P2:

Record transactions involving cash dividends, stock dividends, and stock splits.

Summary

Cash dividends involve three events. On the date of declaration, the directors bind the company to pay the dividend. A dividend declaration reduces retained earnings and creates a current liability. On the date of record, recipients of the dividend are identified. On the date of payment, cash is paid to stockholders and the current liability is removed. Neither a stock dividend nor a stock split alters the value of the company. However, the value of each share is less due to the distribution of additional shares. The distribution of additional shares is done according to individual stockholders' ownership percent. Small stock dividends ($\leq 25\%$) are recorded by capitalizing retained earnings equal to the market value of distributed shares. Large stock dividends ($>25\%$) are recorded by capitalizing retained earnings equal to the par or stated value of the distributed shares. Stock splits do not yield journal entries but do yield changes in the description of stock.

Learning Objective P3:

Record purchases and sales of treasury stock and the retirement of stock.

Summary

When a corporation purchases its own previously issued stock, it debits the cost of these shares to Treasury Stock. Treasury Stock is subtracted from equity in the balance sheet. If treasury stock is reissued, any proceeds in excess of cost are credited to Paid-in Capital, Treasury Stock. If the proceeds are less than cost, they are debited to Paid-in Capital, Treasury Stock to the extent a credit balance exists. Any remaining amount is debited to Retained Earnings. When stock is retired, all accounts related to the stock are removed.

I.   **Corporate Form of Organization**—An entity created by law that is separate from its owners. Owners are called *stockholders*. A *publicly held* corporation offers its stock for public sale (organized stock market) whereas a *privately held* corporation does not.

     A.   Characteristics of a Corporation—Advantages

        1.   Separate legal entity—a corporation, through its agents (officers and managers), may conduct business affairs with the same rights, duties, and responsibilities of a person.

        2.   Limited liability of stockholders—stockholders are not liable for corporate debt or corporate acts.

        3.   Transferable ownership rights—transfer of shares generally has no effect on corporation operation.

        4.   Continuous life—life is indefinite because it is not tied to physical life of owners.

        5.   Lack of mutual agency for stockholders—stockholders do not have the power to bind the corporation to contracts.

        6.   Ease of capital accumulation—Buying stock is attractive to investors and enables a corporation to accumulate large amounts of capital.

     B.   Characteristics of a Corporation—Disadvantages

        1.   Governmental regulation—must meet requirements of a state's incorporation laws.

        2.   Corporate taxation—corporate income is taxed; and when income is distributed to shareholders as dividends, it is taxed a second time as personal income (*double taxation*).

     C.   Corporate Organization and Management

        1.   Incorporation—A corporation is created by obtaining a charter from a state government. A charter application, signed by prospective stockholders (*incorporators or promoters*) must be filed with the state and fees must be paid.

        2.   Organization Expenses (*organization costs*)—include legal fees, promoters' fees, and amounts paid to obtain a charter. Expensed as incurred.

        3.   Management of a Corporation

           a.   Stockholders have ultimate control through vote to elect board of directors.

           b.   Board of directors (BOD) has final managing authority, but it usually limits its actions to setting broad policy.

       c. Executive officers (appointed by the BOD) manage the day-to-day direction of corporation. President is often the chief executive officer (CEO) unless one person has the dual role of chairperson of the BOD and CEO, then the president is the chief operation officer (COO).

D. Stockholders of Corporations

  1. Rights of Stockholders—*Specific* rights are granted by the charter and *general* rights by state laws. State laws vary but common stockholders general rights usually include right to:

    a. Vote at stockholders' meeting.

    b. Sell or otherwise dispose of their stock.

    c. Purchase their proportional shares of any common stock later issued. (called *preemptive right*).

    d. Receive the same dividend, if any, on each common share of the corporation.

    e. Share equally, on a per share basis, in any assets remaining after creditors and preferred stockholders are paid in liquidation.

    f. Receive timely financial reports.

  2. Stock Certificates and Transfer

    a. Stock certificate is sometimes received as proof of share ownership.

    b. Certificates show the company name, stockholder name, number of shares and other crucial information.

  3. Registrar and Transfer Agents—if stock is traded on a major exchange, the corporation must have both a registrar and transfer agent (usually large banks or financial institutions).

    a. *Registrar*—person who keeps stockholder records and prepares official lists of stockholders for stockholders' meetings and dividend payments.

    b. *Transfer agent*—person who assists with purchases and sales of shares by receiving and issuing certificates as necessary.

E. Basics of *Capital Stock*—shares issued to obtain capital (owner financing).

  1. Authorized stock—the total amount of stock that the charter authorizes for sale.

    a. Outstanding stock refers to issued stock held by stockholders.

    b. Corporation must apply for a change in its charter if it wishes to issue more shares than previously authorized.

  2. Issuing stock—can be sold directly/indirectly to stockholders.

3. Market value of stock—the price at which a stock is bought or sold.

    a. Influenced by expected future earnings, dividends, growth, and other company and economic events.

    b. Current market value of previously issued shares does not impact that corporation's stockholders' equity accounts.

4. Classes of stock

    a. Common—the name of stock when all classes have same rights and privileges.

    b. Preferred stock—gives its owners a priority status over common stockholders in one or more ways.

    c. Additional classes—corporation may issue more than one class of common and/or preferred stock.

5. Par value stock—a class of stock that is assigned a value per share by the corporation in its charter.

    a. Printed on the stock certificate.

    b. In many states, used to establish minimum legal capital.

6. No-par value stock—*not* assigned a value per share by the corporate charter.

7. Stated value stock—no-par stock that is assigned a "stated" value per share by the directors. This value becomes minimum legal capital par value.

8. Stockholder's Equity—has two parts:

    a. Paid-in capital—the total amount of cash and other assets received by the corporation from its stockholders in exchange for stock.

    b. Retained earnings—the cumulative net income (and loss) retained by a corporation.

II. **Common Stock**—Issuance of stock affects only paid-in capital accounts, not retained earnings accounts.

A. Issuing Par Value Stock

1. At par for cash—debit Cash and credit Common Stock (both for the amount received which is the total *par value* of the shares issued).

2. Issuing par value stock at a premium. *(Premium on stock is an amount paid in excess of par by the purchasers of newly issued stock.)*

    a. Debit Cash (for amount received or issue price).

    b. Credit Common Stock (for par value).

    c. Credit Paid-In Capital in Excess of Par Value, Common Stock (for the amount of the premium).

        3.   Issuing par value stock at a discount—*Discount occurs when a corporation sells its stock for less than its par value* (prohibited by most states).

          a.   Debit Cash (for amount received or issue price).

          b.   Credit Common Stock (for par value).

          c.   Debit Discount on Common Stock, a contra to the common stock account (for the amount of the discount).

          d.   When allowed, the purchasers usually become contingently liable to the corporation's creditors for the amount of the discount.

  B. Issuing No Par Value Stock
When no-par stock is not assigned a stated value, the entire amount received becomes legal capital and is recorded as Common Stock.

  C. Issuing *Stated Value* Stock
Stated value becomes legal capital and is credited to a no-par stock account. If stock is issued at an amount in excess of stated value, this excess is credited to Paid-In Capital in Excess of Stated Value, Common Stock.

  D. Issuing Stock for Noncash Assets

        1.   Issuing par value stock for other assets

          a.   Record the transaction at the market value of the noncash asset as of the date of the transaction.

          b.   Record par value or stated value of stock issued in stock account.

          c.   Record amount the market value exceeds par value or stated value of stock in the Paid-In Capital in Excess account.

        2.   Issuing par value stock for organizational cost—stock is issued in exchange for services (from promoters, lawyers, accountants) in organizing the corporation

          a.   Record the transaction at the market value of the services received debiting this amount to *Organization Expense*.

          b.   Record par or stated value of shares issued in stock account and any value received above this in Paid-In Capital in Excess account.

III.   **Dividends**

  A. Cash Dividends—decision to pay these dividends rest with BOD and is based on evaluating the amounts of retained earning and cash as well as many other factors.

        1.   Accounting for cash dividends involves three important dates. The dates of:

          a.   Declaration—date the directors vote to pay a dividend (legal liability created).

       b.   Record—date specified for identifying stockholders (owners on this date will receive dividend).

       c.   Payment—date corporation makes payment.

  2. Cash Dividend Entries—reduce in equal amounts both cash and the retained earnings component of stockholders' equity.

       a.   At declaration—Debit Retained Earnings and credit Dividends Payable.

       b.   At payment—Debit Dividends Payable and credit Cash.

  3. Deficit and Cash Dividends—a debit (abnormal) balance for retained earnings.

       a.   Arises when cumulative losses and/or dividends are greater than total profits earned in prior years.

       b.   Deducted on the balance sheet.

       c.   In cases of deficit, some states allow a *liquidating cash dividend* where paid-in capital accounts are debited instead of retained earnings because this is returning part of original investment back to investors.

B. Stock Dividends—Distribution of additional shares of stock to stockholders without receipt of any payment in return. They do not reduce assets or *total* equity, just the components of equity.

  1. Reasons for a stock dividend

       a.   To keep the market price of stock affordable.

       b.   To provide evidence of management's confidence that the company is doing well.

  2. Accounting for stock dividends—transfers a portion of equity from retained earnings to contributed capital (called *capitalizing* retained earnings)

       a.   *Small stock dividend* is 25% or less of the issuing corporation's previously outstanding shares; the market value of the shares to be distributed is capitalized.

       b.   *Large stock dividend* is more than 25% of the shares outstanding before the dividend; only the legally required minimum amount (par or stated value of shares) must be capitalized.

       c.   Declaration entry—Debit Retained Earnings (full *capitalized* amount), credit Common Stock Dividend Distributable (par value of dividend shares) and credit Paid-in Capital in Excess of Par (any capitalization above par).

       d.   Payment entry—Debit Common Stock Dividend Distributable and credit Common Stock (to transfer par).

C. Stock Splits

The distribution of additional shares of stock to stockholders according to their percent of ownership. Involves "calling in" the outstanding shares of stock and replacing them with a larger number of shares that have a lower par value.

1. Reason for stock splits is similar to those for stock dividends.

2. Only a memorandum entry is required.

3. Splits do not affect any equity accounts or any individual stockholder's percentage of ownership.

4. Reverse stock splits reduce number of shares and increase par value.

IV. **Preferred Stock**—Has special rights that give it priority over common stock in one or more areas such as preference for receiving dividends and for the distribution of assets if the corporation is liquidated. Usually does not have right to vote.

A. Issuance of Preferred Stock

Usually has a par value; can be sold at a price different from par.

1. Separate contributed capital accounts are used to record preferred stock.

2. Preferred Stock account is used to record the par value of shares issued.

3. Paid-in in Excess of Par Value, Preferred Stock is used to record any value received above the par value.

B. Dividend Preference of Preferred Stock

Preferred stockholders are allocated their dividends before any dividends are allocated to common stockholders.

1. Cumulative or Noncumulative Dividend

a. Cumulative preferred stock has a right to be paid both current and all prior periods' unpaid dividends before any dividend is paid to common stockholders. These unpaid dividends are referred to as *dividends in arrears*.

b. Noncumulative preferred stock confers no right to prior periods' unpaid dividends if they were not declared.

c. Full-disclosure principle requires that the amount of preferred dividends in arrears be reported as of the balance sheet date, normally in a note to the financial statements. Undeclared dividends are not a liability.

      2. Participating or Nonparticipating Dividend

        a. Nonparticipating—dividends are limited each year to a maximum amount determined by applying the preferred percentage to the par value. Any remaining declared dividend amounts are received by common stockholders.

        b. Participating—gives its owners the right to share in dividends in excess of the stated percentage or amount after common stockholders have received the same rate.

   C. Convertible Preferred Stock

      1. Gives holders the option of exchanging their preferred shares into common shares at a specified rate.

      2. Offers investors a higher potential return.

   D. Callable Preferred Stock

      1. Gives the issuing corporation the right to purchase (retire) this stock from its holders at specified future prices and dates.

      2. Amount paid to call and retire a preferred share is its call price, or *redemption value,* and is set when stock is issued.

      3. Dividends in arrears must be paid when stock is called.

   E. Reasons for Issuing Preferred Stock

      1. To raise capital without sacrificing control of the corporation.

      2. To boost the return earned by common stockholders on corporate assets. Called *financial leverage* or *trading on equity*.

V.   **Treasury Stock**—A corporation acquires their own shares for several reasons such as to acquire another company, or to avoid a hostile takeover, or to use for employee compensation, or to maintain a strong market for their stock.

   A. Purchasing Treasury Stock

      1. Reduces the corporation's assets and stockholders' equity by equal amounts.

      2. Debit Treasury Stock (contra-equity) and credit Cash for full cost. (reduces total assets and total equity).

      3. The equity reduction is reported by subtracting Treasury Stock account balance from the total of Paid-in Capital accounts and Retained Earnings on the Balance Sheet.

      4. Places a restriction on retained earnings.

    B. Reissuing Treasury Stock

        1. Sale at cost—Treasury stock is reduced (credited) for the *cost* of the reissued shares and Cash is debited for the amount received.

        2. Sale above cost—the amount received in excess of cost is credited to Paid-in Capital, Treasury Stock.

        3. Sale below cost—entry depends on whether the Paid-in Capital, Treasury Stock account has a balance. If it has no balance, the excess of cost over sales price is debited to Retained Earnings. However, if the Paid-in Capital, Treasury Stock account exists, then it is debited for the excess of the cost over the sales price, not to exceed the balance in the account.

    C. Retiring Stock—results in a reduction in assets and equity equal to the amount paid for the retired stock. Reduces the number of issued shares.

        1. When stock is purchased for retirement, all capital amounts (from original issuance) that relate to the retired shares are removed from the accounts.

        2. Any excess of original issuance price over cost from the transaction should be credited to Paid-in Capital from Retirement of Stock.

        3. Any excess of cost over original issuance price from the transaction should be debited to Retained Earnings.

VI.   Reporting of Equity

    A. Statement of Retained Earnings—Retained Earnings is total cumulative amount of reported net income less any net losses and dividends declared since the company's inception. It is part of stockholders' equity (claim to the assets) and is *not* implying that any certain amount of cash or other assets actually exists.

        1. Restrictions and Appropriations

            a. Restricted retained earnings refers to both *statutory* and *contractual* restrictions.

            b. Appropriated retained earnings refers to a voluntary transfer of amounts from the Retained Earnings account.

      2. Prior Period Adjustments

         a. Corrections of material errors made in prior periods.

         b. Include arithmetic mistakes, unacceptable accounting, and missed facts.

         c. Reported in *statement of retained earnings* as corrections (net of income tax effects) to the beginning retained earnings balance.

         d. *Changes in Accounting Estimates* do not result in prior period adjustments, but are accounted for in current and future periods.

      3. Closing Process

         a. Close credit balances in revenue accounts to Income Summary.

         b. Close debit balances in expense accounts to Income Summary.

         c. Close Income Summary to Retained Earnings.

         d. Close Dividends account to Retained Earnings (if dividends were recorded in a Dividends account).

  B. Statement of Stockholders' Equity

      1. Provided by most companies rather than a separate statement of retained earnings; the statement of stockholders' equity includes changes in retained earnings.

      2. Lists the beginning and ending balances of each equity account and describes the changes that occurred during the period.

  C. Reporting Stock Options

      1. Stock options are rights to purchase common stock at a fixed price over a specified period of time. As stock prices rise above the fixed price, the option value increases.

      2. Stock options are said to motivate employees and managers.

VII. **Global View—Compares U.S. GAAP to IFRS**

  A. Accounting for Common Stock—both systems have similar procedures for issuing common. Rights and responsibilities and terminology, may differ due to legal and cultural differences.

  B. Accounting for Dividends—consistent under both systems for cash and stock dividends, and stock splits.

  C. Accounting for Preferred Stock—similar under both systems, but redeemable preferred stock is reported between liabilities and equity in U.S. GAAP balance sheets but as a liability in IFRS. Differences also exist in reporting convertible preferred stock.

  D. Accounting for Treasury Stock—Both systems are consistent as applied to treasury stock purchases, reissuances, and retirements.

VIII.   Decision Analysis

    A. Earnings per Share (EPS)

        1. Amount of income earned by each share of outstanding common stock; reported on the income statement.

        2. Basic earnings per share is computed by dividing the net income less preferred dividends by the weighted average number of shares outstanding.

    B. Price-Earnings Ratio (PE ratio)

        1. Used to gain understanding of the market's expected receipts for the stockholders.

        2. Calculated as market value per share divided by earnings per share.

        3. Can be based on current or *expected* EPS.

    C. Dividend Yield

        1. Used to determine whether a company's stock is an income stock (pays large and regular dividends) or a growth stock (pays little or no cash dividends).

        2. Calculated as annual cash dividends per share divided by market value per share.

    D. Book Value per Share—stockholders' claim to the assets on a per share basis.

        1. Book value per common share

            a. If only one class outstanding, equals total stockholders' equity divided by the number of common shares outstanding.

            b. If two classes of stock outstanding, equals the recorded amount of stockholders' equity applicable to common shares (total stockholders' equity less *equity applicable to preferred stock*—see section below) divided by the number of common shares outstanding.

        2. Book value per preferred share

            a. The stockholders' *equity applicable to preferred* shares equals the preferred share's call price (or par value if the preferred is not callable) plus any cumulative dividends in arrears. The remaining stockholders' equity is the portion applicable to common shares.

            b. Book value per preferred share equals *equity applicable to preferred* shares divided by number of preferred shares outstanding.

Problem I

The following statements are either true or false. Place a (T) in the parentheses before each true statement and an (F) before each false statement.

1. ( ) Par value has nothing to do with a stock's worth.

2. ( ) Final authority in the management of corporation affairs rests with its board of directors.

3. ( ) The life of a corporation may be unlimited.

4. ( ) To transfer and sell his or her interest in a corporation, a stockholder must secure permission from the corporation's secretary.

5. ( ) The chief executive officer of a corporation is usually elected by the stockholders at one of their annual meetings.

6. ( ) The president of a corporation is responsible to its board of directors for management of the corporation's affairs.

7. ( ) A discount on stock is the difference between market value and the amount at which stock is issued when the stock is issued at a price below its par value.

8. ( ) A small stock dividend should be recorded by capitalizing retained earnings equal to the book value of the stock to be distributed.

9. ( ) In most states, a corporation must have current net income in order to pay a cash dividend.

10. ( ) Since a stock dividend is payable in stock rather than in assets, it is not a liability of its issuing corporation.

11. ( ) A stock split has no effect on total stockholders' equity, the equities of the individual stockholders, or on the balances of any of the contributed or retained capital accounts.

12. ( ) Dividend yield is an estimate of how much one share of stock will yield in cash dividends per year.

13. ( ) A company with common stock having a market value of $45 per share and earnings of $5 per share has a price-earnings ratio of 9.

14. ( ) A cash dividend reduces a corporation's cash and its stockholders' equity, but a stock dividend does not affect either cash or total stockholders' equity.

15. ( ) A stock option is the right of a stockholder to convert common stock to preferred stock.

16. ( ) For companies with simple capital structures, earnings per share is calculated by dividing net income minus preferred dividends, if any, by the weighted-average number of common shares outstanding.

17. ( ) Hadley Corporation stock has a current market value of $16 and is expected to pay cash dividends of $1.20 during the next year. The expected dividend yield of Hadley stock is 7.5%.

Problem II

You are given several words, phrases, or numbers to choose from in completing each of the following statements or in answering the following questions. In each case select the one that best completes the statement or answers the question and place its letter in the answer space provided.

_____ 1. The difference between the par value of stock and its issue price when it is issued at a price above par value is the:

   a. Paid-In capital.

   b. Stock dividend.

   c. Minimum legal capital.

   d. Premium on stock.

   e. Discount on stock.

_____ 2. Vector Corporation has outstanding 3,000 shares of $100 par value, 7% cumulative and nonparticipating preferred stock and 10,000 shares of $10 par value common stock. Dividends have not been paid on the preferred stock for the current and one prior year. The corporation has recently prospered, and the board of directors has voted to pay out $49,000 of the corporation's retained earnings in dividends. If the $49,000 is paid out, how much should the preferred and common stockholders receive per share?

   a. $14.00 per share preferred, $0.70 per share common.

   b. $ 7.00 per share preferred, $2.80 per share common.

   c. $12.25 per share preferred, $1.23 per share common.

   d. $ 1.14 per share preferred, $4.56 per share common.

   e. $16.33 per share preferred, $ -0- per share common.

_____ 3. Vector Corporation has outstanding 3,000 shares of $100 par value, 7% noncumulative and nonparticipating preferred stock and 10,000 shares of $10 par value common stock. Dividends have not been paid on the preferred stock for the current and one prior year. The corporation has recently prospered, and the board of directors has voted to pay out $49,000 of the corporation's retained earnings in dividends. If the $49,000 is paid out, how much should the preferred and common stockholders receive per share?

   a. $ 1.14 per share preferred, $4.56 per share common.

   b. $9.33 per share preferred, $2.10 per share common.

   c. $ 7.00 per share preferred, $2.80 per share common.

   d. $14.00 per share preferred, $0.70 per share common.

   e. $12.25 per share preferred, $0.23 per share common.

_____ 4. Participating preferred stock is:

a. Preferred stock that can be exchanged for shares of the issuing corporation's common stock at the option of the preferred stockholder.

b. Preferred stock on which undeclared dividends accumulate annually until they are paid.

c. Preferred stock on which the right to receive dividends is forfeited for any year that the dividends are not declared.

d. Preferred stock that the issuing corporation, at its option, may retire by paying a specified amount to the preferred stockholders plus any dividends in arrears.

e. Preferred stock that gives its owners the right to share in dividends in excess of the stated percentage or amount.

_____ 5. Stated value of stock is:

a. One share's portion of the issuing corporation's net assets as recorded in the corporation's accounts.

b. An arbitrary amount assigned to stock by the corporation's board of directors which is credited to the stock account when the stock is issued.

c. The difference between the par value of stock and its issue price when it is issued at a price below or above par value.

d. The market value of the stock on the date of issuance.

e. The price at which a share of stock can be bought or sold.

_____ 6. Bartlett Company had a weighted-average of 20,000 shares of common stock outstanding for the year. Assume the company earns $140,000 net income for the year and declared $40,000 in dividends on its non-cumulative preferred stock. What is the basic earnings per share on the common stock?

a. $6.00

b. $9.00

c. $7.00

d. $5.00

e. $4.00

_____ 7. The Poseidon Corporation issued $10 par value common stock for $15, with the premium being credited to Paid-In Capital in Excess of Par Value; Common Stock. Later, 500 shares of this stock was repurchased and retired at a cost of $17. The entry to record the retirement is as follows:

a. Common Stock 5,000.00

    Paid-In Capital in Excess of Par Value, Common Stock 2,500.00

    Retained Earnings 1,000.00

      Cash 8,500.00

b. Common Stock 5,000.00

    Paid-In Capital in Excess of Par Value, Common Stock 2,500.00

    Paid-In Capital from the Retirement of Common Stock 1,000.00

      Cash 8,500.00

c. Common Stock 5,000.00

    Paid-In Capital in Excess of Par Value, Common Stock 3,500.00

      Cash 6,500.00

d. Common Stock 5,000.00

    Paid-In Capital in Excess of Par Value, Common Stock 2,500.00

      Cash 6,500.00

      Paid-In Capital from the Retirement of Common Stock 1.000.00

e. Treasury Stock 8,500.00

      Cash 8,500.00

_____ 8. Captan, Inc issued 2,000 shares of $100 par value common stock for $130 per share. The entry to record the issue is as follows:

a. Common Stock 200,000

    Paid-In Capital in Excess of Par Value, Common Stock 60,000

      Cash 260,000

b. Cash 260,000

      Common Stock 200,000

      Paid-In Capital in Excess of Par Value, Common Stock 60,000

c. Common Stock 260,000

      Cash 260,000

d. Cash 5,000.00

      Common Stock 6,500.00

e. Cash 260,000

      Common Stock 60,000

      Paid-In Capital in Excess of Par Value, Common Stock 200,000

_____ 9. The statement of stockholders' equity is:

    a. A financial statement that discloses the inflows and outflows of cash during the period.

    b. A financial report showing the assets, liabilities, and equity of an enterprise on a specific date.

    c. A financial statement showing revenues earned by a business, the expenses incurred in earning the revenues, and the resulting net income or net loss.

    d. A financial statement that lists the beginning and ending balances of each equity account and describes all the changes that occurred during the year.

    e. None of the above.

_____ 10. On December 15, RTA Corporation declares a $.75 per share cash dividend on its 4,000 outstanding shares. Payment date is January 15. On December 15, RTA should make the following entry related to the cash dividend:

    a. Cash Dividends Declared 3,000
          Retained Earnings 3,000

    b. Common Dividend Payable 3,000
          Cash Dividends Declared 3,000

    c. Retained Earnings 3,000
          Cash Dividends Declared 3,000

    d. Retained Earnings 3,000
          Common Dividend Payable 3,000

    e. No entry should be made on December 15 related to the cash dividend.

Problem III

Many of the important ideas and concepts discussed in Chapter 13 are reflected in the following list of key terms. Test your understanding of these terms by matching the appropriate definitions with the terms. Record the number identifying the most appropriate definition in the blank space next to each term.

_____ Appropriated retained earnings	_____ Noncumulative preferred stock
_____ Authorized stock	_____ Nonparticipating preferred stock
_____ Basic earnings per share	_____ No-par value stock
_____ Book value per common share	_____ Organization expense
_____ Book value per preferred share	_____ Paid-in capital
_____ Callable preferred stock	_____ Paid-in capital in excess of par value
_____ Call price	_____ Participating preferred stock
_____ Capital stock	_____ Par value
_____ Changes in accounting estimates	_____ Par value stock
_____ Common stock	_____ Preemptive right
_____ Complex capital structure	_____ Preferred stock
_____ Convertible preferred stock	_____ Premium on stock
_____ Corporation	_____ Price-earnings (PE) ratio
_____ Cumulative preferred stock	_____ Prior period adjustment
_____ Date of declaration	_____ Proxy
_____ Date of payment	_____ Restricted retained earnings
_____ Date of record	_____ Retained earnings
_____ Diluted earnings per share	_____ Retained earning deficit
_____ Dilutive securities	_____ Reverse stock split
_____ Discount on stock	_____ Simple capital structure
_____ Dividend in arrears	_____ Small stock dividend
_____ Dividend yield	_____ Stated value of stock
_____ Earnings per share	_____ Statement of stockholder's equity
_____ Financial leverage	_____ Stock dividend
_____ Large stock dividend	_____ Stockholders' equity
_____ Liquidating cash dividend	_____ Stock option
_____ Market value per share	_____ Stock split
_____ Minimum legal capital	_____ Treasury stock

1. Total amount of cash and other assets received from stockholders in exchange for stock.

2. Unpaid dividend on cumulative preferred stock; must be paid before any regular dividends on preferred stock and before any dividends on common stock.

3. Preferred stock on which the right to receive dividends is lost for any dividends period which are not declared.

4. Total amount of stock that a corporation's charter authorizes it to sell.

5. Preferred stock that the issuing corporation, at its option, may retire by paying the call price to the preferred stockholders plus any dividends in arrears.

6. Preferred stock on which undeclared dividends accumulate until paid; common stockholders cannot receive dividends until cumulative dividends are paid.

7. Earning of a higher return on common stock by paying dividends on preferred stock or interest on debt at a rate that is less than the return earned with the assets from issuing preferred stock or debt.

8. Stock dividend that is more than 25% of the previously outstanding shares.

9. Ratio of a company's market value per share to its earnings per share.

10. Occurs when a corporation calls in its stock and replaces each share with less than one new share; increases both the market value per share and the par or stated value per share.

11. Equity applicable to preferred shares [equals the preferred share's call price (or par value if the preferred is not callable) plus any cumulative dividends in arrears] divided by the number of preferred shares outstanding.

12. Amount that must be paid to call and retire a preferred share.

13. Amount of assets defined by law that stockholders must invest and leave invested in a corporation; usually defined as a par value of the stock; intended to protect the corporation's creditors.

14. Corporations own stock that it reacquired and is still holds.

15. Price at which stock is bought or sold.

16. Capital structure that consists of only common stock and non-convertible preferred stock; but no dilutive securities.

17. Preferred stock on which dividends are limited to a maximum amount each year.

18. Stock dividend that is 25% or less of a corporation's previously outstanding shares.

19. Cumulative net income a corporation retains.

20. A corporation's basic stock; usually carries voting rights for controlling the corporation.

21. Debit (abnormal) balance in Retained Earnings; occurs when cumulative losses and dividends exceed cumulative income.

22. Right to purchase common stock at a fixed price over a specified period of time.

23. Financial statement that lists the beginning and ending balances of each equity account and describes all changes in amounts.

24. Retained earnings not available for dividends because of legal or contractual limitations.

25. Corporation's distribution of its own stock to its stockholders without the receipt of any payment.

26. Correction of an error in a prior year reported in the statement of retained earnings (or statement of changes in stockholder's equity) net of any income tax effects.

27. Difference between the par value of stock and its issue price when issued at a price below par value.

28. Preferred stock giving the option to exchange it for common shares at a specified rate.

29. Stock class that has not been assigned a par value by the corporate charter.

30. A distribution of assets that returns part of the original investment to the stockholders; these distributions are charged to contributed capital accounts.

31. Legal document giving a stockholder's agent the power to exercise the stockholder's voting rights.

32. Retained earnings reported separately as a way of informing stockholders of funding needs.

33. Date directors vote to pay a dividend.

34. Ratio of the annual amount of cash dividends distributed relative to the common stock's market value (price).

35. Class of stock assigned a par value by the corporate charter.

36. Recorded amount of equity applicable to common shares divided by the number of common shares outstanding.

37. Date specified by the directors for identifying stockholders to receive dividends.

38. Amount of income earned by each share of a company's outstanding common stock; also called net income per share.

39. Stock that gives its owners a priority status over common stockholders in one or more ways, such as paying of dividends or distributing assets.

40. Preferred stock feature that allows it to share with common holders any dividends paid in excess of the percent stated on the preferred stock.

41. Occurs when a corporation calls in its stock and replaces each share with more than one new share; decreases both the market value per share and the par or stated value per share.

42. No-par stock assigned a stated value by a corporation's directors; this amount is recorded in the stock account when the stock is issued.

43. Difference between the par value of stock and its issue price when issued at a price above par value.

44. Corrections to previous estimates of future events and outcomes accounted for in the current and future periods.

45. Earnings per share calculation that requires dilutive securities be added to the denominator of the basic EPS calculation.

46. Stockholders' right to maintain their proportionate interest in a corporation by having the first opportunity to buy additional shares issued.

47. Corporation's equity also called shareholders' equity or corporate capital.

48. Value assigned a share of stock by the corporate charter when the stock is authorized.

49. Securities having the potential to increase common shares outstanding; examples are options, rights, convertible bonds and convertible preferred stock.

50. Net income minus preferred dividends divided by the weighted-average common shares outstanding.

51. Capital structure that includes outstanding rights or options to purchase common stock or securities that are convertible into common stock.

52. Date the corporation makes the dividend payment.

53. Costs (legal fees, promoter fees, and state fees to secure the charter) to bring an entity into existence.

54. General term referring to a corporation's stock used in obtaining capital (owner financing).

55. Entity created by law and separate from its owners.

56. Premium that is accounted for separately from par value.

Problem IV

Complete the following by filling in the blanks.

1. When a corporation gives shares of stock to promoters in exchange for their services in organizing the corporation, the corporation records increases to _____ and _____ accounts. The transaction is evaluated at the _____ _____.

2. Laws establishing minimum legal capital requirements were written to protect _____ _____, with the protection resulting from making illegal the payment of any dividends that reduce stockholders' equity below _____.

3. When stock is issued at a price above its par value, the difference between par and the price at which the stock is issued is called a _____.

4. Advantages claimed for no-par stock are: (a) It may be issued at any price without _____. (b) Uninformed persons buying such stock are not misled as to the stock's worth by a _____ printed on the certificates.

5. Laws setting minimum legal capital requirements normally require stockholders to invest, in a corporation, assets equal in value to minimum legal capital or be contingently liable to _____ for the deficiency.

6. A preferred stock is so called because of the preferences granted its owners. The two most common preferences are a preference as to_____ _____and a preference _____ _____.

7. In many jurisdictions when a corporation issues par value stock, it establishes for itself a _____ equal to the par value of the issued stock.

8. In addition to its separate legal existence, other characteristics of a corporation as a form of business organization are _____ _____ _____ _____ _____.

9. A corporation is said to be a separate legal entity; this phrase means that in a legal sense a corporation is _____ _____.

10. When a corporation purchases treasury stock, a portion of its retained earnings equal to the cost of the treasury stock becomes _____ and unavailable for _____.

11. If treasury stock is reissued at a price above cost, the amount received in excess of cost is credited to _____. If treasury stock is sold below cost the difference between cost and the sale price is debited to either _____ or _____.

12. A stock dividend enables a corporation to give its shareholders some evidence of their interest in its retained earnings without reducing the corporation's _____ _____.

13. Issued stock that has been reacquired by the issuing corporation is called _____ _____.

14. If the book value of a share of common stock before the declaration and distribution of a 20% stock dividend was $90, the declaration and distribution of the dividend changed the book value to $_____.

15. If a corporation has sufficient cash to pay a dividend, it must also have sufficient _____ _____ before it pays that dividend.

16. A small stock dividend contains a number of shares amounting to _____% or less of the previously outstanding shares.

Problem V

The stockholders' equity section from Sonar Corporation's balance sheet shows the following:

Capital Stock And Retained Earnings

Preferred stock, $100 par value, 8% cumulative and nonparticipating, issued and outstanding 2,000 shares..	$200,000	
Common stock, $10 par value, issued and outstanding 25,000 shares.......	250,000	
Total Paid-In capital		$450,000
Retained earnings		230,000
Total stockholders' equity		$680,000

1. If there are no dividends in arrears, the book value per share of the corporation's preferred stock is

   $_____ and the book value per share of its common stock is

   $_____.

2. If a total of two years' dividends are in arrears on the preferred stock, the book value per share of the preferred stock is $ _____ , and the book value per share of the common stock is $_____.

Problem VI

On August 10 Mainline Corporation purchased for cash 2,000 shares of its own $25 par value common stock at $27 per share. On October 3 it sold 1,000 of the shares at $30 per share. Complete the entries below to record the purchase and sale of the stock.

DATE	ACCOUNT TITLES AND EXPLANATION	P.R.	DEBIT			CREDIT		
Aug. 10								
	Purchased 2,000 shares of treasury stock.							
Oct. 3								
	Sold 1,000 shares of treasury stock.							

Problem VII

The May 31 balance sheet of Eastwood Corporation carried the following stockholders' equity section:

Stockholders' Equity

Common stock, $10 par value, 25,000 shares authorized, 20,000 shares issued........	$200,000
Retained earnings...	44,000
Total stockholders' equity..	$244,000

On the balance sheet date, with the common stock selling at $12 per share, the corporation's board of directors voted a 2,000-share stock dividend distributable on June 30 to the June 20 stockholders of record.

1. In the space below give without explanations the entries to record the declaration and distribution of the dividend.

DATE	ACCOUNT TITLES AND EXPLANATION	P.R.	DEBIT			CREDIT		

2. Harold Jax owned 2,000 shares of the corporation's common stock before the declaration and distribution of the stock dividend; as a result, his portion of the dividend was _____ shares. The total book value of Jax's 2,000 shares before the dividend was $ _____ ; the total book value of his shares after the dividend was $ _____ ; consequently, Jax gained $ _____ in the book value of his interest in the corporation.

Problem VIII

Retained earnings and shares issued and outstanding for Endel, Incorporated, are as follows:

	Retained Earnings	Shares Issued and Outstanding
December 31, 2011	$475,000	35,000
December 31, 2012	$447,000	38,500

On April 3, 2012, the board of directors declared a $0.775 per share dividend on the outstanding stock. On August 7, while the stock was selling for $17.50 per share, the corporation declared a 10% stock dividend on the outstanding shares to be issued on November 7. Under the assumption that there were no transactions affecting retained earnings other than the ones given, determine the 2012 net income of Endel, Incorporated.

Solutions for Chapter 13

Problem I

1.	T	10.	T
2.	T	11.	T
3.	T	12.	F
4.	F	13.	T
5.	F	14.	T
6.	T	15.	F
7.	F	16.	T
8.	F	17.	T
9.	F		

Problem II

1.	D	6.	D
2.	A	7.	A
3.	C	8.	B
4.	E	9.	D
5.	B	10.	D

Problem III

32	Appropriated retained earnings	45	Diluted earnings per share
4	Authorized stock	49	Dilutive securities
50	Basic earnings per share	27	Discount on stock
36	Book value per common share	2	Dividend in arrears
11	Book value per preferred share	34	Dividend yield
5	Callable preferred stock	38	Earnings per share
12	Call price	7	Financial leverage
54	Capital stock	8	Large stock dividend
44	Changes in accounting estimates	30	Liquidating cash dividend
20	Common stock	15	Market value per share
51	Complex capital structure	13	Minimum legal capital
28	Convertible preferred stock	3	Noncumulative preferred stock
55	Corporation	17	Nonparticipating preferred stock
6	Cumulative preferred stock	29	No-par value stock
33	Date of declaration	53	Organization expense
52	Date of payment	1	Paid-in capital
37	Date of record	43	Paid-in capital in excess of par value

40	Participating preferred stock	21	Retained earning deficit
48	Par value	10	Reverse stock split
35	Par value stock	16	Simple capital structure
46	Preemptive right	18	Small stock dividend
39	Preferred stock	42	Stated value of stock
56	Premium on stock	23	Statement of stockholder's equity
9	Price-earnings (PE) ratio	25	Stock dividend
26	Prior period adjustment	47	Stockholders' equity
31	Proxy	22	Stock option
24	Restricted retained earnings	41	Stock split
19	Retained earnings	14	Treasury stock

Problem IV

1. Organization Expense, Stock (Equity), market value of services received

2. corporation creditors, minimum legal capital

3. premium

4. (a) discount liability, (b) par value

5. corporation creditors

6. the payment of dividends, in the distribution of assets if the corporation is liquidated

7. minimum legal capital

8. lack of stockholder liability, ease of transferring ownership rights, continuity of life, stockholders are not agents, ease of capital assembly, increased governmental regulation, and double taxation

9. an individual body, separate and distinct from its stockholders

10. restricted, dividends

11. Paid-in capital, Treasury Stock; Paid-in capital, Treasury Stock; Retained Earnings

12. cash or other assets

13. treasury stock

14. $75

15. retained earnings

16. 25

Problem V

1. $100, $19.20

2. $116, $17.92

Problem VI

Aug. 10	Treasury Stock, Common	54,000	
	Cash		54,000
Oct. 3	Cash	30,000	
	Treasury Stock, Common		27,000
	Paid-in Capital Treasury Stock..		3,000

Problem VII

1.

May 31	Retained Earnings	24,000	
	Common Stock Dividend Distributable......................................		20,000
	Paid-in capital in Excess of Par Value, Common Stock		4,000
June 30	Common Stock Distributable..	20,000	
	Common Stock		20,000

2.   200; $24,400; $24,400; $0

Problem VIII

Retained earnings as of December 31, 2012		$475,000
Reductions in retained earnings due to transactions:		
Dividends declared:		
April 3, on 35,000 shares	$27,125	
Retained earnings capitalized in stock dividend	61,250	
Total reductions...		88,375
Retained earnings balance before transfer of net income from Income		
Summary account		$386,625
Retained earnings, December 31, 2012, after transfer of net income		
from Income Summary account		$447,000
Deduct retained earnings balance before transfer of net income from		
Income Summary account		386,625
Net income		$ 60,375

CHAPTER 14
LONG-TERM LIABILITIES

Learning Objective C1:

Explain the types and payment patterns of notes.

Notes repaid over a period of time are called *installment notes* and usually follow one of two payment patterns: (1) decreasing payments of interest plus equal amounts of principal or (2) equal total payments. Mortgage notes also are common.

Learning Objective C2 (Appendix 14A):

Explain and compute the present value of an amount(s) to be paid at a future date(s).

The basic concept of present value is that an amount of cash to be paid or received in the future is worth less than the same amount of cash to be paid or received today. Another important present value concept is that interest is compounded, meaning interest is added to the balance and used to determine interest for succeeding periods. An annuity is a series of equal payments occurring at equal time intervals. An annuity's present value can be computed using the present value table for an annuity (or a calculator).

Learning Objective C3 (Appendix 14C):

Describe interest accrual when bond payment periods differ from accounting periods.

Issuers and buyers of debt record the interest accrued when issue dates or accounting periods do not coincide with debt payment dates.

Learning Objective C4 (Appendix 14D):

Describe the accounting for leases and pensions.

A lease is a rental agreement between the lessor and the lessee. When the lessor retains the risks and rewards of asset ownership (an *operating lease*), the lessee debits Rent Expense and credits Cash for its lease payments. When the lessor substantially transfers the risks and rewards of asset ownership to the lessee (a *capital lease*), the lessee capitalizes the leased asset and records a lease liability. Pension agreements can result in either pension assets or pension liabilities.

Learning Objective A1:

Compare bond financing with stock financing.

Bond financing is used to fund business activities. Advantages of bond financing versus stock include (1) no effect on owner control, (2) tax savings, and (3) increased earnings due to financial leverage. Disadvantages include (1) interest and principal payments and (2) amplification of poor performance.

Learning Objective A2:

Assess debt features and their implications.

Certain bonds are secured by the issuer's assets; other bonds, called *debentures,* are unsecured. Serial bonds mature at different points in time; term bonds mature at one time. Registered bonds have each bondholder's name recorded by the issuer; bearer bonds are payable to the holder. Convertible bonds are exchangeable for shares of the issuer's stock. Callable bonds can be retired by the issuer at a set price. Debt features alter the risk of loss for creditors.

Learning Objective A3:

Compute the debt-to-equity ratio and explain its use.

Both creditors and equity holders are concerned about the relation between the amount of liabilities and the amount of equity. A company's financing structure is at less risk when the debt-to-equity ratio is lower, as liabilities must be paid and usually with periodic interest.

Learning Objective P1:

Prepare entries to record bond issuance and interest expense.

When bonds are issued at par, Cash is debited and Bonds Payable is credited for the bonds' par value. At bond interest payment dates (usually semiannual), Bond Interest Expense is debited and Cash credited; the latter for an amount equal to the bond par value multiplied by the bond contract rate.

Learning Objective P2:

Compute and record amortization of bond discount.

Bonds are issued at a discount when the contract rate is less than the market rate, making the issue (selling) price less than par. When this occurs, the issuer records a credit to Bonds Payable (at par) and debits both Discount on Bonds Payable and Cash. The amount of bond interest expense assigned to each period is computed using either the straight-line or effective interest method.

Learning Objective P3:

Compute and record amortization of bond premium.

Bonds are issued at a premium when the contract rate is higher than the market rate, making the issue (selling) price greater than par. When this occurs, the issuer records a debit to Cash and credits both Premium on Bonds Payable and Bonds Payable (at par). The amount of bond interest expense assigned to each period is computed using either the straight-line or effective interest method. The Premium on Bonds Payable is allocated to reduce bond interest expense over the life of the bonds.

Learning Objective P4:

Record the retirement of bonds.

Bonds are retired at maturity with a debit to Bonds Payable and a credit to Cash at par value. The issuer can retire the bonds early by exercising a call option or purchasing them in the market. Bondholders can also retire bonds early by exercising a conversion feature on convertible bonds. The issuer recognizes a gain or loss for the difference between the amount paid and the bond carrying value.

Learning Objective P5:

Prepare entries to account for notes.

Interest is allocated to each period in a note's life by multiplying its beginning-period carrying value by its market rate at issuance. If a note is repaid with equal payments, the payment amount is computed by dividing the borrowed amount by the present value of an annuity factor (taken from a present value table) using the market rate and the number of payments.

©The McGraw-Hill Companies, Inc., 2011

I.   Basics of Bonds

Projects that demand large amounts of money often are funded from bond issuances.

A. Bond Financing

1. A **bond** is its issuer's written promise to pay an amount identified as the par value of the bond with interest.

a. Most bonds require the issuer to make periodic interest payments.

b. The **par value of a bond**, also called the *face amount* or *face value*, is paid at a specified future date known as the *maturity date*.

2. Advantages of bonds

a. *Bonds do not affect owner control.*

b. *Interest on bonds is tax deductible.*

c. *Bonds can increase return on equity.* A company that earns a higher return with borrowed funds than it pays in interest on those funds increases its return on equity. This process is called *financial leverage* or *trading on the equity.*

3. Disadvantages of bonds

a. *Bonds can decrease return on equity.* A company that earns a lower return with borrowed funds than it pays in interest on those funds decreases its return on equity.

b. *Bonds require payment of both periodic interest and par value at maturity.* Equity financing, by contrast, does not require any payments because cash withdrawals (dividends) are paid at the discretion of the owner (board).

B. Bond Trading

1. Bonds can be traded on exchanges including both the New York Stock Exchange and the American Stock Exchange.

2. A bond *issue* consists of a large number of bonds (denominations of $1,000 or $5,000, etc.) that are sold to many different lenders.

3. Market value (price) is expressed as a percentage of par (face) value. Examples: bonds issued at 103 ½ means that they are sold for 103.5% of their par value. Bonds issued at 95 means that they are sold for 95% of their par value.

C. Bond-Issuing Procedures
Governed by state and federal laws. Bond issuers also insure they do not violate any existing contractual agreements.

1. **Bond indenture** is the contract between the bond issuer and the bondholders; it identifies the obligations and rights of each party. A bondholder may also receive a **bond certificate** that includes specifics such as the issuer's name, the par value, the contract interest rate, and the maturity date.

2. Issuing corporation normally sells its bonds to an investment firm (the *underwriter*), which resells the bonds to the public.

3. A *trustee* (usually a bank or trust company) monitors the issuer to ensure it complies with the obligations in the indenture.

II. **Bond Issuances**

A. Issuing Bonds at Par—bonds are sold for face amount. Entries are:

1. Issue date: debit Cash, credit Bonds Payable (face amount).

2. Interest date: debit Interest Expense, credit Cash (face times bond interest rate times interest period).

3. Maturity date: debit Bonds Payable, credit Cash (face amount).

B. Bond Discount or Premium—bonds are sold for an amount different than the face amount.

1. **Contract rate**—(also called *coupon rate, stated rate*, or *nominal rate*) annual interest rate *paid* by the issuer of bonds (applied to par value).

2. **Market rate**—annual rate borrowers are willing to pay and lenders are willing to accept for a particular bond and its risk level.

3. When contract rate and market rate are equal, bonds sell at par value; when contract rate is above market rate, bonds sell at a *premium* (above par); when the contract rate is below market rate, bonds sell at a *discount* (below par).

C. Issuing Bonds at a Discount—sell bonds for *less* than par value.

1. The **discount on bonds payable** is the difference between the par (face) value of a bond and its lower issuance price.

2. Entry to record issuance at a discount: debit Cash (issue price), debit Discount on Bonds Payable (amount of discount), credit Bonds Payable (par value).

3. Discount on Bonds Payable is a contra liability account; it is *deducted* from par value to yield the **carrying (book) value** of the bonds payable.

    4. Amortizing a Bond Discount

       a. Total bond interest expense is the *sum* of the interest payments and bond discount (or can be computed by comparing total amount borrowed to total amount repaid over life).

       b. Discount must be systematically reduced (*amortized*) over the life of the bond to report periodic interest expense incurred.

       c. Requires crediting Discount on Bonds Payable when bond interest expense is recorded (payment and/or accruals) and increasing Interest Expense by the amortized amount.

       d. Amortizing the discount increases book value; at maturity, the unamortized discount equals zero and the carrying value equals par value.

    5. Straight-line method—allocates an equal portion of the total discount to bond interest expense in each of the six-month interest periods.

  D. Issuing Bonds at a Premium—sell bonds for *more* than par value.

    1. The **premium on bonds payable** is the difference between the par value of a bond and its higher issuance price.

    2. Entry to record issuance at a premium: debit Cash (issue price), credit Premium on Bonds Payable (amount of premium), credit Bonds Payable (par value).

    3. Premium on Bonds Payable is an adjunct liability account; it is added to par value to yield the carrying (or book) value of the bonds payable.

    4. Amortizing a Bond Premium

       a. Total bond interest expense incurred is the interest payments *less* the bond premium.

       b. Premiums must be systematically reduced (*amortized*) over the life of the bond to report periodic interest expense incurred.

       c. Requires debiting Premium on Bonds Payable when bond interest expense is recorded (payment and/or accruals) and decreasing Interest Expense by the amortized amount.

       d. Amortizing the premium decreases book value; at maturity, book value = face value.

    5. Straight-line method allocates an equal portion of the total premium to bond interest expense in each of the six-month interest periods.

    E. Bond Pricing

The price of a bond is the present value of the bond's future cash flows discounted at the current market rate. Present value tables can be used to compute price, which is the *combination of* the:

1. Present Value of a Discount Bond. Present value of the maturity payment is found by using single payment table, the market rate, and number of periods until maturity.

2. Present Value of a Premium Bond. Present value of the semiannual interest payments is found by using annuity table, the market rate, and number of periods until maturity.

3. Present values found in present value tables in Appendix B at the end of this book.

III.   **Bond Retirement**

    A. Bond Retirement at Maturity

1. Carrying value at maturity will always equal par value.

2. Entry to record bond retirement at maturity: debit Bonds Payable, credit Cash.

    B. Bond Retirement Before Maturity

1. Two common approaches to retire bonds before maturity:

    a. Exercise a call option—pay par value plus a call premium.

    b. Purchase them on the open market.

2. Difference between the purchase price and the bonds' carrying value is recorded as a gain (or loss) on retirement of bonds.

    C. Bond Retirement by Conversion

Convertible bondholders have the right to convert their bonds to stock. If converted, the carrying value of bonds is transferred to equity accounts and no gain or loss is recorded.

IV.   **Long-Term Notes Payable**

Notes are issued to obtain assets, such as cash. Notes are typically transacted with a single lender, such as a bank.

    A. Installment Notes—obligations requiring a series of periodic payments to the lender.

1. Entry to record issuance of an installment note for cash: debit Cash, credit to Notes Payable.

2. Payments include interest expense accruing to the date of the payment plus a portion of the amount borrowed (*principal*).

    a. Equal total payments consist of changing amounts of interest and principal.

    b. Entry to record installment payment: debit Interest Expense (issue rate times the declining carrying value of note), debit Notes Payable (for difference between the equal payment and the interest expense), credit Cash for the amount of the equal payment.

Chapter Outline	**Notes**

B. Mortgage Notes and Bonds

A **mortgage** is a legal agreement that helps protect a lender if a borrower fails to make required payments. A *mortgage contract* describes the mortgage terms.

1. Accounting for mortgage notes and bonds—same as accounting for unsecured notes and bonds.

2. Mortgage agreements must be disclosed in financial statements.

V. **Global View—Compares U.S. GAAP to IFRS**

1. Accounting for Bonds and Notes – The definitions and characteristics of bonds and notes are broadly similar for both GAAP and IFRS.

   a. Both systems allow companies to account for bonds and notes using **the fair value option** method. This method is similar to that applied to measuring and accounting for debt and equity securities.

   b. *Fair value* is the amount a company would receive if it settled a liability in an orderly transaction as of the balance sheet date.

   c. Companies can use several sources of inputs to determine fair value which fall into three classes:

      i. Level 1: observable quoted market price in active markets for identical items

      ii. Level 2: observable inputs other than those in Level 1

      iii. Level 3: observable inputs reflecting a company's assumptions about value.

2. Accounting for Leases and Pensions—Both GAAP and IFRS require companies to distinguish between operating leases and capital leases; the latter is referred to as *finance leases* under IFRS. Both systems account for leases in a similar manner. The main difference is the criteria for identifying a lease as a capital lease are more general under IFRS.

VI. **Decision Analysis—Debt Features and the Debt-to-Equity Ratio**

Collateral Agreements—reduce the risk of loss for both bonds and notes; unsecured bonds and notes are riskier because the issuer's obligation to pay interest and principal has the same priority as all other unsecured liabilities in the event of bankruptcy.

A. Features of Bonds and Notes

1. Secured or Unsecured

   a. **Secured bonds** and notes have specific assets of the issuer pledged (or *mortgaged*) as collateral.

   b. Unsecured bonds and notes also called *debentures*, are backed by the issuer's general credit standing. Unsecured debt is riskier than secured debt.

2. Term or Serial

   a. **Term bonds** and notes are scheduled for maturity on one specified date.

   b. **Serial bonds** and notes mature at more than one date (often in series) and are usually repaid over a number of periods.

3. Registered or Bearer

   a. **Registered bonds** are issued in the names and addresses of their holders. Bond payments are sent directly to registered holders.

   b. **Bearer bonds**, also called *unregistered* bonds, are made payable to whoever holds them (the bearer). Many bearer bonds are also **coupon bonds**; which are interest coupons that are attached to the bonds.

4. Convertible and/or Callable

   a. **Convertible bonds** and notes can be exchanged for a fixed number of shares of the issuing company's common stock.

   b. **Callable bonds** and notes have an option exercisable by the issuer to retire them at a stated dollar amount before maturity.

B. Debt-to-Equity Ratio

   1. Knowing the level of debt helps in assessing the risk of a company's financing structure.

   2. A company financed mainly with debt is riskier than a company financed mainly with equity because liabilities must be repaid.

   3. Debt-to-equity ratio measures the risk of a company's financing structure.

   4. Debt-to-equity ratio is computed by dividing total liabilities by total equity.

VII. **Present Values of Bonds and Notes (Appendix 14A)**

A. Present Value Concepts

   1. Cash paid (or received) in the future has less value now than the same amount of cash paid (or received) today.

   2. An amount borrowed equals the present value of the future payment.

   3. *Compounded interest* means that interest during a second period is based on the total of the amount borrowed plus the interest accrued from the first period.

   4. Present Value tables can be used to determine the present value of future cash payments of a single amount or an annuity.

    B. Present Value Tables (Complete tables in Appendix B)

        1. Present values can be computed using a formula or a table.

        2. Present value of $1 table is used to compute present value of a single payment.

        3. The column and row will intersect at the factor number.

        4. To convert the single payment to its present value, multiply this amount by the factor.

    D. Present Value of an Annuity (Complete tables in Appendix B)

        1. Determine the column with the interest rate.

        2. Determine the row with the number of periods.

        3. The column and row will intersect at the factor number.

        4. To convert the annuity to its present value, multiply the annuity amount by the factor.

    E. Compounding Periods Shorter than a Year

        1. Interest rates are generally stated as annual rates.

        2. They can be allocated to shorter periods of time.

VIII. **Effective Interest Amortization (Appendix 14B)**

    A. Effective Interest Amortization of a Discount Bond

        1. The straight-line method yields changes in the bonds' carrying value while the amount for bond interest expense remains constant.

        2. The **effective interest method** allocates total bond interest expense over the bonds' life in a way that yields a constant rate of interest.

        3. The key difference between the two methods lies in computing bond interest expense. Instead of assigning an equal amount of bond interest expense in each period, the effective interest method assigns a bond interest expense amount that increases over the life of a discount bond.

        4. Both methods allocate the same amount of bond interest expense to the bonds' life, but in different patterns.

        5. Except for differences in amounts, journal entries recording the expense and updating the Discount on Bonds Payable account balance are the same under both methods.

    B. Effective Interest Amortization of a Premium Bond

        1. As noted above, the **effective interest method** allocates total bond interest expense over the bonds' life in a way that yields a constant rate of interest.

        2. Except for differences in amounts between the two methods (that is, the straight-line and effective interest methods), journal entries recording the expense and updating the Premium on Bonds Payable account are the same under both methods.

IX. **Issuing Bonds Between Interest Dates (Appendix 14C)**

A. Procedure used to simplify recordkeeping:

1. Buyers pay the purchase price plus any interest accrued since the prior interest payment date.

2. This accrued interest is repaid to these buyers on the next interest date.

3. Entry to record issuance of bonds between interest dates: debit Cash, credit Interest Payable (for any interest accrued since the prior interest payment date), credit Bonds Payable.

4. Entry to record first semiannual interest payment for bonds issued between interest dates: debit Interest Payable (for amount accrued in entry above), debit Interest Expense (for interest accrued since issuance date), credit Cash.

B. Accruing Bond Interest Expense

1. Necessary when bond's interest period does not coincide with issuer's accounting period.

2. Adjusting entry is necessary to record bond interest expense accrued since the most recent interest payment and requires amortization of the premium or discount for this period.

3. Affects the subsequent interest payment date entry.

X. **Leases and Pensions (Appendix 14D)**

A. Lease Liabilities

A **lease** is a contractual agreement between a *lessor* (asset owner) and a *lessee* (asset renter or tenant) that grants the lessee the right to use the asset for a period of time in return for cash (rent) payments.

1. **Operating leases** are short-term (or cancelable) leases in which the lessor retains the risks and rewards of ownership.

a. Lessee records lease payments as expenses.

b. Lessor records lease payments as revenues.

2. **Capital leases** are long-term (or noncancelable) leases in which the lessor transfers substantially all risks and rewards of ownership to the lessee. The lease must meet *any one of the four* following criteria:

a. Transfer title of leased asset to lessee.

b. Contain a bargain purchase option.

      c. Have lease term of 75% or more of leased asset's useful life.

      d. Have present value of leased payments of 90% or more of leased asset's market value.Failure to meet one of the criteria results in *off-balance-sheet financing* (not recorded on the balance sheet).

      e. Capital leases are recorded as assets and liabilities. The asset is depreciated. At each lease payment date, the liability is amortized to record interest expense incurred.

B. Pension Liabilities

A pension plan is a contractual agreement between an employer and its employees for the employer to provided benefits (payments) to employees after they have retired.

    1. Employer records their payment into pension plan as a debit to Pension Expense and a credit to Cash.

    2. Based on contracted benefits, pension plans can be overfunded (resulting in plan assets) or underfunded (resulting in plan liabilities).

Problem I

The following statements are either true or false. Place a (T) in the parentheses before each true statement and an (F) before each false statement.

1. ( )   Interest expense on installment notes is calculated each period as the interest rate multiplied by the beginning-of-period principal balance.

2. ( )   Bondholders do not share in either management or earnings of the issuing corporation.

3. ( )   Bondholders are creditors of the issuing corporation.

4. ( )   If bonds are sold at par value, the entry to record the sale has a debit to Cash and a credit to Bonds Payable.

5. ( )   Investors will be willing to pay more than par (buy at a premium) for bonds when the market rate of interest is higher than the contract rate of interest.

6. ( )   To determine the price of bonds, the present value of the future cash flows is calculated by discounting the amounts to be received in the future at the contract rate of interest.

7. ( )   If the market rate of interest is 12%, it is 4% semiannually.

8. ( )   The straight-line method of amortizing bond premium allocates an equal portion of the premium to each interest period.

9. ( )   When the straight-line method is used to amortize bond premium or bond discount, interest expense as a percentage of carrying amount is the same each period the bonds are outstanding.

10. ( )   Callable bonds are bonds that can be redeemed at the option of the investor.

11. ( )   The debt-to-equity ratio is computed by dividing total liabilities by total equity.

12. ( )   The carrying amount of a payable decreases each year by the amount of discount amortized that year.

13. ( )   The process of allocating the interest on a noninterest-bearing note payable is called amortizing the discount.

14. ( )   (Appendix 14A) The concept of present value is based on the idea that the right to receive $1 a year from now is worth more than $1 today.

15. ( )   (Appendix 14A) Receiving $500 on June 30 and $500 on December 31 has the same present value as receiving $1,000 on December 31.

16. ( )   (Appendix 14A) If a note requires quarterly payments and the borrower could obtain a 12% annual rate of interest in borrowing money, a 3% quarterly interest rate should be used to determine the present value of the note.

17. ( )   (Appendix 14B) To calculate the amount of interest expense each period using the effective interest method, the beginning of-period carrying amount of the bonds must be multiplied by the market rate of interest at the time the bonds were issued.

18. ( )   (Appendix 14D) In a capital lease the lessor retains substantially all the risks and rewards of ownership.

19. ( )   (Appendix 14D) Based on contracted benefits, an overfunded pension plan will result in plan assets.

20. ( )   (Appendix 14D) Operating leases are generally short-term and cancelable.

Problem II

You are given several words, phrases, or numbers to choose from in completing each of the following statements or in answering the following questions. In each case select the one that best completes the statement or answers the question and place its letter in the answer space provided.

_____ 1. On December 31, the interest payment date, the carrying value of Taylor Company's issued bonds is $106,000. The bonds have a par value of $100,000. On January 1, Taylor buys and retires the outstanding bonds. The market price on this date is 103.5. The entry to retire the bonds includes a:

    a. $6,000 credit to Premium on Bonds Payable.

    b. $3,500 debit to Loss on Retirement of Bonds.

    c. $3,500 credit to Gain on Retirement of Bonds.

    d. $2,500 credit to Gain on Retirement of Bonds.

    e. $100,000 credit to Cash.

_____ 2. Commonly used payment patterns on installment notes include:

    a. Installment payments consisting of equal amounts of interest and equal amounts of principal.

    b. Installment payments of accrued interest plus equal amounts of principal.

    c. Installment payments that are equal in total amount and consist of changing amounts of interest and principal.

    d. A and C

    e. B and C

_____ 3. Unsecured bonds that are supported by only the general credit standing of the issuer are called:

    a. Callable bonds

    b. Sinking fund bonds

    c. Serial bonds

    d. Coupon bonds

    e. Debentures

_____ 4. (Appendix 14A) Indigo, Inc., is offered a contract whereby it will be paid $15,000 every six months for the next five years. The first payment will be received six months from today. What will the company be willing to pay for this contract if it expects a 16% annual return on the investment? [Use the appropriate present value table in the Appendix B.]

    a. $10,209.00

    b. $6,948.00

    c. $100,651.50

    d. $59,890.50

    e. Cannot be determined from information provided.

_____ 5. (Appendix 14A) On June 30, 2012, the DEF Corporation sold bonds with a face value of $100,000. The contract rate of bond interest was 9% with interest payments on December 31 and June 30. The bonds mature in 10 years. When the bonds were sold, the market rate of bond interest was 12%. How much money did the DEF Corporation receive when it sold the bonds? (Use the present value tables in Appendix B and round amounts to the nearest whole dollar.)

a. $119,252

b. $110,042

c. $100,000

d. $82,795

e. $83,052

_____ 6. (Appendix 14B) How is the interest expense for each period calculated when the effective interest method is used to amortize bond discount?

a. The par value of the bonds is multiplied by the contract rate of bond interest.

b. The par value of the bonds is multiplied by the market rate of bond interest which applied to the bonds at the time the bonds were issued.

c. The beginning balance of the bond liability is multiplied by the market rate of bond interest which applied to the bonds at the time the bonds were issued.

d. The beginning balance of the bond liability is multiplied by the contract rate of bond interest.

e. The total amount of discount at the time of issue is divided by the number of periods to maturity and added to the cash payment of interest.

_____ 7. (Appendix 14B) On June 30, 2012, the DEF Corporation sold bonds with a face value of $100,000. The contract rate of bond interest was 9% with interest payments on December 31 and June 30. The bonds mature in 10 years. When the bonds were sold, the market rate of bond interest was 12% and they were issued for $82,795. What is the entry to record the payment of interest on December 31, 2012? DEF uses the effective interest method of amortizing bond discount or premium.

a. Interest Expense 4,500.00
    Cash 4,500.00

b. Interest Expense 4,968.00
    Cash 4,500.00
    Discount on Bonds Payable...............................   468.00

c. Interest Expense 6,000.00
    Cash 6,000.00

d. Interest Expense 4,500.00
    Premium on Bonds Payable 1,500.00
    Cash 6,000.00

e. Interest Expense 4,500.00
    Cash 4,230.00
    Discount on Bonds Payable...............................   270.00

Problem III

Many of the important ideas and concepts discussed in Chapter 10 are reflected in the following list of key terms. Test your understanding of these terms by matching the appropriate definitions with the terms. Record the number identifying the most appropriate definition in the blank space next to each term.

_____ Annuity

_____ Bearer bonds

_____ Bond

_____ Bond certificate

_____ Bond indenture

_____ Callable bonds

_____ Capital leases**

_____ Carrying value of bonds

_____ Contract rate

_____ Convertible bonds

_____ Coupon bonds

_____ Debt-to-equity ratio

_____ Discount on bonds payable

_____ Effective interest method*

_____ Installment note

_____ Lease**

_____ Market rate

_____ Mortgage

_____ Off-balance-sheet financing**

_____ Operating leases**

_____ Par value of a bond

_____ Pension plan**

_____ Premium on bonds payable

_____ Registered bonds

_____ Secured bonds

_____ Serial bonds

_____ Sinking fund bonds

_____ Straight-line method

_____ Term bonds

_____ Unsecured bonds

* _Key term discussed in Appendix 14B._
** _Key term discussed in Appendix 14D._

1. Contract between the bond issuer and the bondholders; identifies the parties' rights and obligations.

2. Difference between a bond's par value and its lower issue price or carrying value; occurs when the contract rate is less than the market rate.

3. Interest rate borrowers are willing to pay and lenders are willing to accept for a specific debt agreement at its risk level.

4. Allocates interest expense over the bond life to yield a constant rate of interest; interest expense for a period is found by multiplying the balance of the liability at the beginning of the period by the bond market rate at issuance; also called _interest method_.

5. Bonds that bondholders can exchanged for a set number of the issuer's shares.

6. Bonds made payable to whoever holds them (the _bearer_); also called _unregistered bonds_.

7. Net amount at which bonds are reported on the balance sheet; equals the par value of the bonds less any unamortized discount or plus any unamortized premium; also called _carrying amount_.

8. Legal agreement that protects a lender by giving the lender the right to be paid from the cash proceeds from the sale of the borrower's assets identified in the mortgage.

9. Difference between bond's par value and its higher issue price or carrying value; occurs when the contract rate is higher than the market rate.

10. Bonds that require the issuer to make deposits to a separate account; bondholders are repaid at maturity from that account.

11. Bonds consisting of separate amounts that mature at different dates.

12. Bonds with interest coupons attached to their certificates; bondholders detach coupons when they mature and present them to a bank or broker for collection.

13. Bonds that give the issuer an option to retire them at a stated amount prior to maturity.

14. Interest rate specified in a bond indenture; multiplied by the bonds' par value to determine the interest paid each period; also called *coupon rate*, *stated rate*, or *nominal rate*.

15. Amount the bond issuer agrees to pay at maturity and the amount on which interest payments are based; also called *face amount* or *face value*.

16. Series of equal payments at equal intervals.

17. Measures the risk of a company's financing structure.

18. Method allocating an equal amount of interest expense to each period in the life of bonds.

19. Liability requiring a series of periodic payments to the lender.

20. Bonds owned by investors whose names and addresses are recorded by the issuer; interest payments are made to the registered owners.

21. Written promise to pay the bond's par (or face) value and interest at a stated contract rate; often issued in denominations of $1,000.

22. Bonds backed only by the issuer's credit standing; almost always riskier than secured bonds; also called *debentures*.

23. Bonds scheduled for payment (mature) at a single specified date.

24. Bonds that have specific assets of the issuer pledged as collateral.

25. Document containing bond specifics such as the issuer's name, bond par value, contract interest rate, and maturity date.

26. Contractual agreement between *lessor* and *lessee* that grants a lessee the right to use an asset for a period of time in return for cash payments.

27. Short-term (or cancelable) leases in which lessor retains risks and rewards of ownership.

28. Acquisition of assets by agreeing to liabilities not reported on the balance sheet.

29. Contractual agreement between an employer and its employees to provide benefits to employees after they retire.

30. Long-term leases in which the lessor transfers substantially all risk and rewards of ownership to the lessee.

Problem IV

Complete the following by filling in the blanks.

1. Two important rights given to the owner of a bond are:

    a. _____

    _____, and

    b. _____

    _____.

2. Often a corporation cannot obtain debt financing without providing security to the creditors by the issuance of a _____.

3. The rate of interest a corporation agrees to pay on a bond issue is called the _____ rate. This rate is applied to the _____ value of the bonds to determine the amount of interest that must be paid.

4. If a corporation offers to sell a bond issue when the contract rate of interest is below the market rate, the bonds will sell at a _____ and if it offers to sell bonds when the contract rate is above the market rate, the bonds will sell at a _____.

5. A $1,000 bond with a contract rate of bond interest of 9% would provide semiannual interest payments of $_____.

6. Bonds that may be redeemed at the issuing company's option are known as _____ bonds.

7. (Appendix 10C) When a corporation sells bonds between interest dates, it collects accrued interest from the purchasers. On the interest payment date, the accrued interest is _____ to the purchaser.

8. The accounting procedure for allocating a discount to each period in the life of a bond is called

    _____.

9. The terms of installment notes payable require one of two payment plans:

    a. _____

    _____, or

    b. _____

    _____.

10. When the issuing company retires bonds, it recognizes a gain or loss for the difference between the _____ and the retirement price.

11. (Appendix 14D) Capital leases must meet one of the following four criteria:

    a. _____

    b. _____

    c. _____

    d. _____

Problem V

(Appendix 14C) On December 15, 2012, Candida Corporation deposited a bond indenture with the trustee of its bondholders authorizing it to issue $1,000,000 of 10.2%, 20-year bonds dated January 1, 2012, and upon which interest is payable each June 30 and December 31. The bonds were issued at par plus accrued interest on February 1, 2013.

1.   Prepare the 2012 journal entries for this bond issue.

DATE	ACCOUNT TITLES AND EXPLANATION	P.R.	DEBIT			CREDIT		
2012 Feb. 1								
	Sold $1,000,000 of 10.2%, 20-year bonds at par plus							
	one month's accrued interest.							
June 30								
	Paid the semiannual interest on the bonds.							
Dec. 31								
	Paid the semiannual interest on the bonds.							

2.   Post to the T-account below the portions of the above entries that affect bond interest expense and then complete the statement that follows.

Bond Interest Expense

Candida Corporation's 2012 income statement should show $_____ of bond interest expense and its 2013 income statement should show $_____ of bond interest expense.

Problem VI

On January 1, 2011, a day on which the market rate of interest for Bullock Company's bonds was 10%, Bullock Company sold bonds having a $100,000 par value, a five-year life, and on which interest was to be paid semiannually at a 9% annual rate. The bonds were issued for $ 96,138.

1.   The buyer of these bonds received two rights:
   (a) the right to receive $_____ in interest at the end of each six-month interest period throughout the five-year life of the bond issue, and
   (b) the right to receive $_____ at the end of the bond issue's life.

2. Bullock Corporation's journal entry to record the sale of the bonds would be as follows:

DATE	ACCOUNT TITLES AND EXPLANATION	P.R.	DEBIT		CREDIT	
2011 Jan. 1						
	Sold bonds at a discount					

3. At the end of the first semiannual interest period Bullock Corporation calculated the number of dollars of interest to be paid to bondholders as follows:

   $ _____ x _____ % = $ _____

4. (Appendix 14B) Using the effective interest method, the company then calculated the amount of interest expense to be recorded at the end of the first semiannual interest period as follows:

   $ _____ x _____ % = $ _____

5. (Appendix 14B) Next, the company determined the amount of discount to be amortized with this calculation:

   $ _____ – $ _____ = $ _____

6. (Appendix 14B) After making these calculations, Bullock Corporation would record the interest paid its bondholders and the discount amortized with the following journal entry:

DATE	ACCOUNT TITLES AND EXPLANATION	P.R.	DEBIT		CREDIT	
2011 June 30						
	Paid the semiannual interest on the bonds and					
	amortized a portion of the discount					

7. (Appendix 10A) To prove that the issue price equaled the present value of the rights received, the buyer of the bonds should discount the rights at the _____ % (semiannual) market rate for bond interest prevailing on the day of the purchase.

8. (Appendix 14A) The calculations for determining the present value of the bond buyer's two rights, using the tables in Appendix B in the text are:

   Present value of $100,000 to be received _____ periods hence,
   discounted at _____% per period ($100,000 x _____) $ _____
   Present value of $ _____ to be received periodically
   for _____ periods, discounted at _____ %
   ($_____ x _____) ....   _____
   Price to pay for the bonds .... $ _____

Problem VII

On December 31, 2011, HX Company borrowed $60,000 by signing a 14% installment note that is to be repaid with six annual payments, the first of which is due on December 31, 2012.

a. Prepare the journal entry to record the borrowing of the money.

DATE	ACCOUNT TITLES AND EXPLANATION	P.R.	DEBIT	CREDIT

b. Assume that the payments are to consist of accrued interest plus equal amounts of principal. Prepare the journal entries to record the first and second installment payments.

DATE	ACCOUNT TITLES AND EXPLANATION	P.R.	DEBIT	CREDIT

c. Contrary to the assumption in (b) above, assume now that the note requires each installment payment to be $15,464. Prepare journal entries to record the first and second installment payments. (Round all amounts to the nearest whole dollar.)

DATE	ACCOUNT TITLES AND EXPLANATION	P.R.	DEBIT	CREDIT

Problem VIII (Appendix 14A)

1. Use the present value tables in the text (Appendix B) to calculate the following present values:
    a. $1 to be received 9 years hence, at 10%. $ _____
    b. $2,000 to be received 6 years hence, at 8%. $ _____
    c. $1 to be received at the end of each year for 10 years, at 4%. _____
    d. $1,000 to be received at the end of each year for 7 years, at 6%. _____

2. When the rate of interest on an investment is 8% compounded annually, the present value of $1,000 to be received three years hence is the amount of money that must be invested today that together with the 8% compound interest earned on the investment will equal $ _____ at end of three years. The amount is $1,000 x _____ = $ _____.

3. If the interest rate is changed from 8% to 5%, will the present value of $1 to be received in one year be increased or decreased? _____.

Solutions for Chapter 10

Problem I

1. T
2. T
3. T
4. T
5. F
6. F
7. F
8. T
9. F
10. F
11. T
12. F
13. T
14. F
15. F
16. T
17. T
18. F
19. T
20. T

Problem II

1. D
2. E
3. E
4. C
5. D
6. C
7. B

Problem III

16	Annuity	3	Market rate
6	Bearer bonds	8	Mortgage
21	Bond	28	Off-balance-sheet financing**
25	Bond certificate	27	Operating leases**
1	Bond indenture	15	Par value of a bond
13	Callable bonds	29	Pension plan**
30	Capital leases**	17	Pledged assets to secured liabilities
7	Carrying value of bonds	9	Premium on bonds payable
14	Contract rate	20	Registered bonds
5	Convertible bonds	24	Secured bonds
12	Coupon bonds	11	Serial bonds
17	Debt-to-equity ratio	10	Sinking fund bonds
2	Discount on bonds payable	18	Straight-line method
4	Effective interest method*	23	Term bonds
19	Installment note	22	Unsecured bonds
26	Lease**		

* *Key term discussed in Appendix 10B.*
** *Key term discussed in Appendix 10D.*

Problem IV

1. a. the right to receive periodic interest payments, and
   b. the right to receive the face amount of the bond when it matures

2. mortgage

3. contract; par

4. discount; premium

5. $45

6. callable

7. refunded

8. amortizing the bond discount

9. a. payments of accrued interest plus equal amounts of principal, or
   b. payments that are equal in total amount, consisting of changing amounts of interest and principal

10. carrying value of the bonds

11. a. Transfer title of leased asset to lessee.
    b. Contain a bargain purchase option.
    c. Have lease term of 75% or more of leased asset's useful life.
    d. Have present value of leased payments of 90% or more of leased asset's market value.

Problem V

1.   Feb. 1   Cash...   1,008,500.00

                        Bond Interest Payable 8,500.00

                        Bonds Payable..   1,000,000.00

                        ($1,000,000 x 0.102)/12 = $8,500

    June 30   Bond Interest Payable 8,500.00

               Bond Interest Expense 42,500.00

                        Cash..   51,000.00

                        ($1,000,000 x 0.102)/2 = $51,000

    Dec. 31   Bond Interest Expense...   51,000.00

                        Cash..   51,000.00

2.

Bond Interest Expense		
June 30	42,500.00	
Dec. 31	51,000.00	

    $93,500; $102,000

Problem VI

1.   (a) $4,500, (b) $100,000

2.   Jan. 1   Cash...   96,138.00

                Discount on Bonds Payable 3,862.00

                      Bonds Payable..   100,000.00

3. $100,000 x 0.045 = $4,500

4. $96,138 x 0.05 = $4,807 (rounded to the nearest whole dollar)

5. $4,807 – $4,500 = $307

6.   June 30   Bond Interest Expense...   4,807.00

               Discount on Bonds Payable..................................   307.00

               Cash..   4,500.00

7.   5

8.   Present value of $100,000 to be received 10 periods hence, discounted at 5%

        per period ($100,000 x 0.6139)... $61,390

        Present value of $4,500 to be received periodically for 10 periods, discounted

        at 5% ($4,500 x 7.7217)..   <u>34,748</u>

        Price to pay for the bonds (rounded to the nearest whole dollar) ....   <u>$96,138</u>

Problem VII

a. 2011
Dec. 31 Cash 60,000.00
                Notes Payable 60,000.00

b. 2012
Dec. 31 Interest Expense ($60,000 x 0.14)............................. 8,400.00
            Notes Payable 10,000.00
                Cash 18,400.00

   2013
Dec. 31 Interest Expense ($60,000 - $10,000) x 0.14 .... 7,000.00
            Notes Payable 10,000.00
                Cash 17,000.00

c. 2012
Dec. 31 Interest Expense ($60,000 x 0.14)............................. 8,400.00
            Notes Payable 7,064.00
                Cash 15,464.00

   2013
Dec. 31 Interest Expense ($60,000 - $7,064) x 0.14................ 7,411.00
            Notes Payable 8,053.00
                Cash 15,464.00

Problem VIII

1. a. $0.4241

   b. $2,000 x 0.6302 = $1,260.40

   c. $8.1109

   d. $1,000 x 5.5824 = $5,582.40

2. $1,000, $1,000 x 0.7938 = $793.80

3. increased

Learning Objective C1:

Distinguish between debt and equity securities and between short-term investments and long-term investments.

Summary

Debt securities reflect a creditor relationship and include investments in notes, bonds and certificates of deposit. *Equity securities* reflect an owner relationship and include shares of stock issued by other companies. Short-term investments in securities are current assets that meet two criteria. First, they are expected to be converted into cash within one year or the current operating cycle of the business, whichever is longer. Second, they are readily converted to cash, or *marketable*. All other investments in securities are long-term investments. Long-term investments also include assets not used in operations and those held for a special purpose, such as land for expansion. Investments in securities are classified into five groups: (1) trading securities, which are always short-term, (2) debt securities held-to-maturity, (3) debt and equity securities available-for-sale, (4) equity securities in which an investor has a significant influence over the investee, and (5) equity securities in which an investor has a controlling influence over the investee.

Learning Objective C2:

Describe how to report equity securities with controlling influence.

Summary

If an investor owns more than 50% of another company's voting stock and controls the investee, the investor's financial reports are prepared on a consolidated basis. These reports are prepared as if the company is organized as one entity.

Learning Objective C3^A:

Explain foreign exchange rates between currencies and record transactions listed in a foreign currency.

Summary

A foreign exchange rate is the price of one currency stated in terms of another. An entity with transactions in a foreign currency when the exchange rate changes between the transaction dates and their settlement will experience exchange gains or losses. When a company makes a credit sale to a foreign customer and sales terms call for payment in a foreign currency, the company must translate the foreign currency into dollars to record the receivable. If the exchange rate changes before payment is received, foreign exchange gains or losses are recognized in the year they occur. The same treatment is used when a company makes a credit purchase from a foreign supplier and is required to make payment in a foreign currency.

Learning Objective A1:

Compute and analyze the components of return on total assets.

Summary

Return on total assets has two components: profit margin and total asset turnover. A decline in one component must be met with an increase in another if return on assets is to be maintained. Component analysis is helpful in assessing company performance compared to that of competitors and its own past.

Learning objective P1:

Account for trading securities.

Summary

Investments are initially recorded at cost, and any dividend or interest from these investments is recorded in the income statement. Investments classified as trading securities are reported at fair value. Unrealized gains and losses on trading securities are reported in income. When investments are sold, the difference between the net proceeds from the sale and the cost of the securities is recognized as a gain or loss.

Learning objective P2:

Account for held-to-maturity securities.

Summary

Debt securities held-to-maturity are reported at cost when purchased. Interest revenue is recorded as it accrues. The cost of long-term held-to-maturity securities is adjusted for the amortization of any difference between cost and maturity value.

Learning objective P3:

Account for available-for-sale securities.

Summary

Debt and equity securities available-for-sale are recorded at cost when purchased. Available-for-sale securities are reported at their fair values with unrealized gains or losses shown in the equity section of the balance sheet. Gains and losses realized on the sale of these investments are reported in the income statement.

Learning objective P4:

Account for equity securities with significant influence.

Summary

The equity method is used when an investor has a significant influence over an investee. This usually exists when an investor owns 20% or more of the investee's voting stock but not more than 50%. The equity method means an investor records its share of investee earnings with a debit to the investment account and a credit to a revenue account. Dividends received satisfy the investor's equity claims and reduce the investment account balance.

I. **Basics of Investments**
    A. Motivation for Investments—three reasons:
        1. Companies transfer excess cash to investments to produce higher income.
        2. Some entities, such as mutual funds and pension funds, are set up to produce income from investments.
        3. Strategic reasons.
    B. Short-Term Investments
        1. *Cash equivalents* are investments that are both readily converted to known amounts of cash and mature within three months.
        2. Short-term investments (*temporary investments* or *marketable securities*)—current assets that must meet these two requirements:
            a. Intended to be converted into cash within one year or the current operating cycle, whichever is longer.
            b. Readily convertible to cash.
    C. Long-Term Investments
        1. Are not readily convertible to cash and not intended to be converted to cash in short-term.
        2. Investments in securities can include both debt and equity securities.
            a. Debt securities reflect a creditor relationship.
            b. Equity securities reflect an owner relationship.
    D. Classification and Reporting of Investments—accounting for investments in securities depends on three factors:
        1. Security type—either debt or equity.
        2. Holding intention—either short term or long term.
        3. Percentage of ownership.
    E. Classifications of investments and reporting approach:
        1. Trading securities (always short-term)—reported at value.
        2. Held-to-maturity (debt securities)—reported at *amortized cost* (subject for advanced courses).
        3. Available-for-sale (debt and non-influential equity securities)—reported at market value.
        4. Significant influence (equity securities)—reported under equity method.
        5. Controlling influence (equity securities)—reported in consolidated statements.

     F. Accounting Basics for Investments

        1. Debt Securities.

           a. Acquisition is recorded at cost (including any fees).

           b. Interest revenue recorded when earned.

           c. When the cost is greater than maturity value, the difference is amortized over remaining life of security.

        2. Equity Securities.

           a. Acquisition is recorded at cost (including any fees).

           b. Dividends received are recorded as revenue and reported on income statement.

           c. At sale, proceeds are compared to cost and any gain or loss is recorded.

II.   **Reporting of Noninfluential Investments**—most must be reported at fair value. Exact reporting depends on classification. The accounting for each classification is as follows:

     A. Trading (debt and equity)—intended to be actively managed and traded for profit.

        1. Entire portfolio is reported at fair value.

        2. *Fair value adjustment* from cost results in *unrealized gain (or loss)* which is reported on the income statement.

        3. Upon sales of individual securities, the difference between their cost and net proceeds is recognized as gain or loss. Subsequent fair value adjustments will exclude the sold securities.

     B. *Held-to-Maturity* Securities (HTM)—Debt securities a company intends and is able to hold until maturity.

        1. Classify as long-term investment when maturity date extends beyond one year or the operating cycle, whichever is longer.

        2. Record interest revenue when earned.

        3. Amortize the difference between cost and maturity value over the remaining life of the security. (Discussed in advance course.)

        4. Adjustments to fair value are *not* required.

     C. Available-for-Sale Securities (AFS)—debt and equity securities that are not intended to be held to maturity. Intent is to sell them in future.

        1. Long vs. short-term classification depends on when they are intended to be sold.

        2. Entire portfolio is reported at fair value.

        3. Unrealized gains or losses are *not* reported on income statement. It is reported in equity section of the balance sheet and is part of comprehensive income. (discussed later)

III. **Reporting of Influential Investments**

A. Equity Securities with Significant Influence—Implies investor can exert significant influence over the investee.

1. An investor who owns more than 20% (but not more than 50%) is presumed to have a significant influence over the investee.

2. Equity method is used. Under this method the investor

   a. records its share of the investee's earnings as increase to its investment and on its income statement.

   b. reduces investment by share of losses and also reports them on the income statement.

   c. does not record cash dividends received as income (share of investee's income already reported) but instead that dividend is viewed as a conversion of assets (cash increased and investment account decreased).

   d. records and reports gain or loss when investment is sold. Gain or loss is computed by comparing proceeds from sale to book value of the investment on the date of sale.

B. Equity Securities with Controlling Influence—Investor is able to exert a controlling influence over the investee (generally owns more than 50% of a company's voting stock).

1. The *equity method with consolidation* (subject for advanced course) is used.

2. The controlling investor is called the *parent company* and the investee company is called the *subsidiary*.

3. Investor also reports *consolidated financial statements* (subject for advanced course) to the public when owning such securities.

C. Summary of Accounting for Investments in Securities See Exhibit 15.8 (text p. 604).

D. Comprehensive Income—is defined as all changes in equity for a period except those due to owner investments and dividends.

1. Includes: Unrealized gains and losses on available-for-sale securities, foreign currency adjustments and pension adjustments.

2. Can be reported in financial statements:

   a. as part of the statement of stockholders' equity

   b. on the income statement

   c. in a statement of comprehensive income.

IV. **Global View—Compares U.S.GAAP to IFRS**

    A. Accounting for Noninfluential Securities—both systems are broadly similar. Differences in terminology exist.

    B. Accounting for Influential Securities—both systems are broadly similar. Differences in terminology exist.

V. **Decision Analysis—Components of Return on Total Assets**

    A. Assesses financial performance and can be separated into *two components*:

        1. Profit margin (net income divided by net sales) reflects the percentage of net income in each dollar of net sales.

        2. Total asset turnover (net sales divided by average total assets) reflects a company's ability to produce net sales from total assets.

    B. Calculated as:

$$\frac{\text{Net Income}}{\text{Average total assets}} = \frac{\text{Net Income}}{\text{Net Sales}} \times \frac{\text{Net Sales}}{\text{Average total assets}}$$

VI. **Investments in International Operations—Appendix 15A**

    A. Exchange Rates Between Currencies

        1. Price of one currency stated in terms of another currency is called a *foreign exchange rate*.

        2. These rates fluctuate due to changing economic and political conditions (include the supply and demand for currencies and expectations about future events).

    B. Sales and Purchases Listed in a Foreign Currency

        1. Companies making cash sales (or purchases) for which they receive (or pay) foreign currency must translate the transaction amounts into domestic currency. The transaction is recorded using exchange rates on the date of the event.

        2. Prior to statements, and/or at point of collection/payment, adjustments to receivables/payables resulting from change in exchange rates must be recorded. These adjustments result in *Foreign Exchange Gains/Losses*.

Problem I

The following statements are either true or false. Place a (T) in the parentheses before each true statement and an (F) before each false statement.

1. ( ) An investor who owns 20% or more of a corporation's voting stock is presumed to have significant influence over the investee.

2. ( ) Unrealized holding gains and losses on investments in equity securities available for sale are reported in the stockholders' equity section of the balance sheet.

3. ( ) The equity method is used to account for investments in equity securities available for sale.

4. ( ) When an investment in trading securities is sold and the proceeds net of any sales commission differ from cost, a gain or loss must be recorded.

5. ( ) At acquisition, the purchase of stock is recorded at cost regardless of which method is used to account for the investment.

6. ( ) The only difference between accounting for debt securities held to maturity and debt securities available for sale is that interest is not accrued on debt securities held to maturity.

7. ( ) Investments in equity securities available for sale are reported on the balance sheet at their fair values.

8. ( ) An investment in debt securities results in a creditor position for the investor.

9. ( ) An investment in equity securities results in an ownership position for the investor.

10. ( ) (Appendix 15A) A credit sale by a U.S. company to a foreign customer required to make payment in U.S. dollars may result in an exchange gain or loss to the U.S. company.

Problem II

You are given several words, phrases, or numbers to choose from in completing each of the following statements or in answering the following questions. In each case select the one that best completes the statement or answers the question and place its letter in the answer space provided.

_____ 1. On January 1, 2011, Allured Company purchased 12,000 shares of More Corporation's common stock at 60-1/4 plus a $6,000 commission. On July 1, 2011, More Corporation declared and paid dividends of $0.85 per share, and on December 31, 2011, it reported a net income of $156,000. Assuming More Corporation has 48,000 outstanding common shares and that the fair value per share at December 31, 2011, is $65, what is the carrying value of Allured's investment in More at December 31?

    a. $729,000.

    b. $757,800.

    c. $751,800.

    d. $723,000.

    e. $780,000.

2. On January 1, 2011, Allured Company purchased 12,000 shares of More Corporation's common stock at 60-1/4 plus a $6,000 commission. On July 1, 2011, More Corporation declared and paid dividends of $0.85 per share, and on December 31, 2011, it reported a net income of $156,000. Assuming More Corporation has 96,000 outstanding common shares and that the fair value per share at December 31, 2011, is $65, what is the carrying value of Allured's investment in More at December 31?

   a. $723,000.

   b. $742,500.

   c. $738,300.

   d. $780,000.

   e. $729,000.

3. (Appendix 15A) December 1, Sprocket Company made a credit sale of 340,000 francs to Blanc Company of Paris, France, payment to be received in full on February 1. On December 1, the exchange rate for francs was $0.16420. On December 31, the exchange rate was $0.15930. Sprocket's December 31 adjusting entry to record the foreign exchange gain or loss would include a:

   a. $54,162 debit to Accounts Receivable.

   b. $1,666 Credit to Foreign Exchange Gain or Loss.

   c. $1,666 debit to Accounts Receivable.

   d. $1,666 debit to Foreign Exchange Gain or Loss.

   e. No entry is made to record any foreign exchange gain or loss until actual payment is received on February 1.

4. Macon Company's total assets on December 31, 2012 and 2011 were $860,000 and $650,000, respectively. Net income for 2012 was $77,400 and $42,250 for 2011. Calculate Macon's return on total assets for 2012.

   a. 9.0%.

   b. 10.3%.

   c. 7.0%.

   d. 7.9%.

   e. 6.5%.

Problem III

Many of the important ideas and concepts discussed in chapter 15 are reflected in the following list of key terms. Test your understanding of these terms by matching the appropriate definitions with the terms. Record the number identifying the most appropriate definition in the blank space next to each term.

_____ Available-for-sale (AFS) debt securities	_____ Long-term investments	
_____ Comprehensive Income	_____ Multinational	
_____ Consolidated financial statements	_____ Parent	
_____ Equity method	_____ Return on total assets	
_____ Equity securities with controlling influence	_____ Short term investments	
_____ Equity securities with significant influence	_____ Subsidiary	
_____ Foreign exchange rate	_____ Trading Securities	
_____ Held to maturity (HTM)securities	_____ Unrealized gain (loss)	

1. Long-term investment when the investor is able to exert controlling influence over the investee; investors owning 50% or more of voting stock are presumed to exert controlling influence over the investee.

2. Long-term investment when the investor is able to exert significant influence over the investee; investors owning 20% or more (but less than 50%) of a voting stock are presumed to exert significant influence.

3. Long-term investments in debt securities held with the intent to sell them in the future.

4. Price of one currency stated in terms of another currency.

5. Investments in debt and equity securities that are not marketable or, if marketable, are not intended to be converted into cash in the short-term; also special purpose funds, other assets not used in operations.

6. Company that operates in a large number of different countries.

7. Debt securities that the company has the intent and ability to hold until they mature.

8. Measure of operating efficiency, calculated as net income as divided by average total assets.

9. Company that owns a controlling interest in another corporation (requires more than 50% of voting stock).

10. Accounting method used when the investor has "significant influence" over the investee.

11. Corporation controlled by another company (parent) when the parent owns more than 50% of the subsidiary's voting stock.

12. Financial statements that show all (combined) activities under the parent's control, including those of any subsidiaries.

13. Net change in equity for a period, excluding owner investments and distributions.

14. Debt and equity securities that management expects to convert to cash within the next 3 to 12 months (or the operating cycle if longer); also called *temporary investments* or *marketable securities*.

15. Gain (loss) not yet realized by an actual transaction or event such as a sale.

16. Investments in debt and equity securities that the company intends to actively trade for profit.

Problem IV

Complete the following by filling in the blanks.

1. If a corporation acquires _____ of another corporation's common stock, the investor is presumed to have a significant influence on the investee corporation's operations, and the investment should be accounted for according to the

   _____.

2. Debt securities held to maturity should be accounted for according to the _____,
   _____ whereas debt securities available for sale should be accounted for according to the _____.

3. (Appendix 15)Any entries to Foreign Exchange Gain or Loss on foreign currency transactions are closed to _____ and included on the

   _____.

Problem V

On January 1, 2011, Large Company paid $90,000 for 36,000 of Small Company's 90,000 outstanding common shares. Small Company paid a dividend of $20,000 on November 1, 2011, and at the end of the year reported earnings of $40,000. The fair value per share on December 31, 2011, was $2.10. On January 3, 2012, Large Company sold its interest in Small Company for $120,000.

1. What method should be used in Large Company's books to account for the investment in Small Company? _____.

2. Complete general journal entries for Large Company to record the facts presented above. Do not give explanations and skip a line between entries.

DATE	ACCOUNT TITLES AND EXPLANATION	P.R.	DEBIT	CREDIT

Problem VI

On January 1, 2011, Celestial Company paid $25,000 for 20,000 of Yardley Company's 120,000 outstanding common shares. Yardley Company paid a dividend of $.10 per share on June 1, 2011, and at the end of the year reported earnings of $500,000. The fair value per share on December 31, 2011, was $1.90. Assume that Celestial did not own any investments prior to 2011. On January 1, 2012, Celestial Company sold its interest in Yardley Company for $37,900.

1.   What method should be used by Celestial to account for its long-term investment in Yardley?
     _____.

2.   Complete general journal entries for Celestial Company to record the facts presented above. Also, prepare an entry dated January 1, 2012, to remove any balances related to the fair value adjustment. Do not give explanations and skip a line between entries.

DATE	ACCOUNT TITLES AND EXPLANATION	P.R.	DEBIT	CREDIT

Solutions for Chapter 15

Problem I

1.	T	6.	F
2.	T	7.	T
3.	F	8.	T
4.	T	9.	T
5.	T	10.	F

Problem II

1.	B
2.	D
3.	D
4.	B

Problem III

3	Available-for-sale (AFS) debt securities	5	Long-term investments
13	Comprehensive Income	6	Multinational
12	Consolidated financial statements	9	Parent
10	Equity method	8	Return on total assets
1	Equity securities with controlling influence	14	Short term investments
2	Equity securities with significant influence	11	Subsidiary
4	Foreign exchange rate	16	Trading securities
7	Held to maturity (HTM)securities	15	Unrealized gain (loss)

Problem IV

1. more than 20%, but less than 50%, equity method

2. cost method, market value method

3. Income Summary, income statement

Problem V

1. The equity method

2.
```
   2011
   Jan. 1   Long-Term Investment–Small Company ...............................   90,000.00
                 Cash ..........................................................................                90,000.00


   Nov. 1   Cash ..........................................................................   8,000.00
                 Long-Term Investment–Small Company...........................                 8,000.00


   Dec. 31  Long-Term Investment–Small Company ...............................   16,000.00
                 Earnings from Long-Term Investment–Small Company....                 16,000.00


   2012
   Jan. 3   Cash ..........................................................................   120,000.00
                 Long-Term Investment–Small Company...........................                 98,000.00
                 Gain on Sale of Long-Term Investment ...........................                 22,000.00
```

Problem VI

1. The fair value method

2. 2011

    Jan. 1   Long-Term Investment–Yardley Company............................25,000.00
                 Cash 25,000.00

    June 1   Cash 2,000.00
                 Dividend Revenue..   2,000.00

    Dec. 31 Fair Value Adjustment–Available for Sale (LT) 13,000.00
                 Unrealized Gain–Equity 13,000.00

    2012

    Jan. 1   Cash 37,900.00
                 Long-Term Investment–Yardley Company........................   25,000.00
                 Gain on Sale of Long-Term Investment 12,900.00

        1   Unrealized Gain–Equity 13,000.00
                 Fair Value Adjustment–Available for Sale........................   13,000.00

CHAPTER 16
REPORTING THE STATEMENT OF CASH FLOWS

Learning Objective C1:

Distinguish among operating, investing, and financing activities and describe how noncash investing and financing activities are disclosed.

Summary

The purpose of the statement of cash flows is to report the major cash receipts and cash payments relating to either operating, investing, or financing activities. Operating activities include the transactions and events that determine net income. Investing activities include transactions and events that mainly affect long-term assets. Financing activities include transactions and events that mainly affect long-term liabilities and equity. Noncash investing and financing activities must be disclosed in either a note or a separate schedule to the statement of cash flows. Examples are the retirement of debt by issuing equity securities and the exchange of a note payable for plant assets.

Learning Objective A1:

Analyze the statement of cash flows and apply the cash flow on total assets ratio.

Summary

To understand and predict cash flows, users stress identification of the sources and uses of cash flows by operating, investing, and financing activities. Emphasis is placed on operating cash flows since they derive from continuing operations. The cash flow on total assets ratio is defined as operating cash flows divided by average total assets. Analysis of current and past values for this ratio can reflect a company's ability to yield regular and positive cash flows. It is also viewed as a measure of earnings quality.

Learning Objective P1:

Prepare a statement of cash flows.

Summary

Preparation of a statement of cash flows involves five steps: (1) Compute the net increase or decrease in cash, (2) compute net cash provided (used) by operating activities *(using either the direct or indirect method)*, (3) compute net cash provided (used) by investing activities, (4) compute net cash provided (used) by financing activities, and (5) report the beginning and ending cash balance and prove that it is explained by net cash flows. Noncash investing and financing activities are disclosed.

Learning Objective P2:

Compute cash flows from operating activities using the indirect method.

Summary

The indirect method for reporting net cash provided (used) by operating activities starts with net income and then adjusts it for three items: (1) changes in noncash current assets and current liabilities related to operating activities, (2) revenues and expenses not providing (using) cash, and (3) gains and losses from investing and financing activities.

Learning Objective P3:

Determine cash flows from both investing and financing activities.

Summary

Cash flows from both investing and financing activities are determined by identifying the cash flow effects of transactions and events affecting each balance sheet account related to these activities. All cash flows from these activities are identified when we can explain changes in these accounts from the beginning to the end of the period.

Learning Objective P4[A] (Appendix 16A):

Illustrate use of a spreadsheet to prepare a statement of cash flows.

Summary

A spreadsheet is a useful tool in preparing a statement of cash flows. Six steps (see appendix) are applied when using the spreadsheet to prepare the statement.

Learning Objective P5[B] (Appendix 16B)

Compute cash flows from operating activities using the direct method.

Summary

The direct method for reporting net cash provided (used) by operating activities lists major classes of operating cash inflows less cash outflows to yield net cash inflow or outflow from operations.

I.   **Basics of Cash Flow Reporting**

    A. Purpose of a Statement of Cash Flows
To report all major cash receipts (inflows) and cash payments (outflows) during a period. This report classifies cash flows into operating, investing, and financing activities. It answers important questions such as:

      1. How does a company obtain its cash?

      2. Where does a company spend its cash?

      3. What explains the change in the cash balance?

    B. Importance of Cash Flows
Information about cash flows, and its sources and uses, can influence decision makers in important ways.

    C. Measurement of Cash Flows
The phrase, cash flows refers to both *cash* and *cash equivalents*. A *cash equivalent* must satisfy two criteria:

      1. Be readily convertible to a known amount of cash.

      2. Be sufficiently close to its maturity date so its market value is unaffected by interest rate changes.

    D. Classifications of Cash Flows
Cash receipts and cash payments are classified and reported in one of three categories:

      1. Operating activities include transactions and events that determine net income (with some exceptions such as unusual gains and losses). Specific examples:

        a. Cash inflows from cash sales, collections on credit sales, receipts of dividends and interest, sale of trading securities, and settlements of lawsuits.

        b. Cash outflows for payments to suppliers for goods and services, to employees for wages, to lenders for interest, to government for taxes, to charities, and to purchase trading securities.

      2. Investing activities include transactions and events that affect long-term assets, namely the purchase or sale of these assets. Specific examples:

        a. Cash inflows from selling long-term productive assets, selling available-for-sale securities, notes and held-to-maturity securities, and collecting principal on loans to others.

        b. Cash outflows from purchasing long-term productive assets, purchasing available for sale securities and held-to-maturity securities, and making loans to others.

3. Financing activities include transactions and events that affect long-term liabilities and equity:

   a. Cash inflows from owner contributions, from issuing company's own stock, from issuing bonds and notes and from issuing short and long-term debt.

   b. Cash outflows from repaying cash loans, owner's withdrawals, paying shareholder's cash dividend and purchasing treasury stock.

E. Noncash Investing and Financing Activities
Activities that do not affect cash receipts or payments but because of their importance and the *full disclosure* principle they are disclosed at the bottom of the statement of cash flows or in a note to the statement.

F. Format of the Statement of Cash Flows

   1. Lists cash flows by categories (operating, financing and investing) and identifies the net cash inflow or outflow in each category.

   2. Combines the net cash flow in each of the three categories and identifies the net change in cash for the period.

   3. Combines the net change in cash with the prior period ending cash to prove the current period ending cash.

   4. Contains a separate schedule or note disclosure of any noncash financing and investing activities.

G. Preparing the Statement of Cash Flow

   1. Five steps:

      a. Compute the net increase or decrease in cash (bottom line or target number).

      b. Compute and report net cash provided (used) by operating activities (using either the direct or indirect method).

      c. Compute and report net cash provided (used) by investing activities.

      d. Compute and report net cash provided (used) by financing activities.

      e. Compute net cash flow by combining net cash provided by operating, investing, and financing activities and then *prove it* by adding it to the beginning cash balance to show that it equals the ending cash balance.

Note: Noncash investing and financing activities are disclosed in either a note or in a separate schedule to the statement.

    2. Sources of information for preparing the statement of cash flows

        a. Comparative balance sheets.

        b. The current income statement.

        c. Other information—generally derived from analyzing noncash balance sheet accounts.

    3. Alternative approaches to preparing the statement:

        a. Analyzing the cash account.

        b. Analyzing noncash accounts.

II.   **Cash Flows from Operating Activities**

    A. Indirect and Direct Methods of Reporting—Two ways of reporting that apply *only* to the operating activities section.

        1. Direct Method—separately lists each major item of operating cash receipts and each major item of operating cash payments. Cash payments are subtracted from cash receipts to determine the net cash provided (used) by operating activities.

        2. Indirect Method—reports net income and then adjusts it for items necessary to obtain net cash provided (used) by operating activities.

        3. Note that the net cash provided (used) by operating activities is *identical* under both the direct and indirect method.

    B. Application of the Indirect Method of Reporting

        1. Reports net income and then adjusts it for three types of items necessary to obtain net cash provided (used) by operating activities.

        2. The three types of adjustments are:

            a. to reflect changes in noncash current assets and current liabilities.

            b. to income statement items involving operating activities that do not affect cash inflows or outflows.

            c. to eliminate gains and losses resulting from investing and financing activities (not part of operating activities).

        3. Adjustments for changes in current assets and current liabilities are made as follows:

            a. Decreases in noncash current assets are added to net income.

            b. Increases in noncash current assets are subtracted from net income.

            c. Increases in current liabilities are added to net income.

            d. Decreases in current liabilities are subtracted from net income.

4. Adjustments for operating items not providing or using cash are made as follows:

   a. Expenses with no cash outflows are added back to net income.

   b. Revenues with no cash inflows are subtracted from net income.

5. Adjustments for nonoperating items are made as follows:

   a. Nonoperating losses are added back to net income.

   b. Nonoperating gains are subtracted from net income.

C. Summary of Adjustments for the Indirect method—see Exhibit 16-12, page 644 of text.

III. **Cash Flows from Investing**—*identical under direct and indirect methods.* Three-stage process of analysis to determine cash provided (used) by investing activities:

A. Identify changes in investing-related accounts (all non-current assets, and the current accounts for both notes receivable and investments in securities—excluding trading securities).

B. Explain these changes to identify their cash flows effects using reconstruction analysis (reconstructed entries—not the actual entries by the preparer).

C. Report their cash flow effects.

IV. **Cash Flows from Financing**—*identical under direct and indirect methods.* Three-stage process of analysis to determine cash provided (used) by financing activities:

A. Identify changes in financing-related accounts (all non-current liabilities—including current portion of any notes and bonds, and the equity accounts).

B. Explain these changes to identify their cash flows effects using reconstruction analysis (reconstructed entries—not the actual entries by the preparer).

C. Report their cash flow effects.

V.   Global View—Compares U.S.GAAP to IFRS

A. Both systems permit the direct or indirect approach to reporting cash flows from operating activities and the application of both methods are fairly consistent under both systems. Two basic differences are:

1. U.S. GAAP requires cash inflows from interest and dividend revenue is classified as operating activities, whereas IFRS permits classification under operating or investing provided it is consistent across periods.

2. U.S. GAAP requires cash outflows for interest expense to be classified as operating activities, whereas IFRS permits classification under operating or investing provided it is consistent across periods.

B. Both systems are fairly similar in reporting cash flows from investing and financing activities.

VI.   Decision Analysis—Cash Flow Analysis

A. Analyzing Cash Sources and Uses

1. Managers stress understanding and predicting cash flows for business decisions.

2. Creditor and investor decisions are also based on a company's cash flow evaluations.

3. Operating cash flows are generally considered to be most significant because they represent results of ongoing operations.

B. Cash Flow on Total Assets

1. Similar to return on total assets except the return is analyzed based on operating cash flows rather than net income.

2. Computed by dividing cash flow from operations by average total assets.

VII.   Spreadsheet Preparation of the Statement of Cash Flows (Appendix 16A)

A spreadsheet approach may be used to organize and analyze the information to prepare a statement of cash flows by the indirect method, including the supplemental disclosures of noncash investing and financing activities.

A. The spreadsheet has four columns containing dollar amounts.

1. Columns one and four contain the beginning and ending balances of each balance sheet account.

2. Columns two and three are for reconciling the changes in each balance sheet account.

B. Separate sections on the working paper present (a) balance sheet items with debit balances; (b) balance sheet items with credit balances; (c) cash flows from operating activities, starting with net income; (d) cash flows from investing activities; (e) cash flows from financing activities; and
(f) noncash investing and financing activities.

C. Information for sections (c) - (f) is developed in four steps in the Analysis of Changes columns:

1. By adjusting net income for the changes in all noncash current asset and current liability account balances. This reconciles the changes in these accounts.

2. By eliminating from net income the effects of all noncash revenues and expenses. This begins the reconciliation of noncurrent assets.

3. By eliminating from net income any gains or losses from investing and financing activities. This involves the reconciliation of noncurrent assets and noncurrent liabilities and perhaps the recording of disclosures in sections (c) - (g).

4. By entering any remaining items, such as dividend payments, which are necessary to reconcile the changes in all balance sheet accounts.

VIII. Direct Method of Reporting Operating Cash Flows (Appendix 16B)

A. Separately list each major item or class of operating cash receipts and cash payments.

B. Classes of operating cash receipts include cash received from customers, renters, interest, and dividends.

C. Classes of operating cash payments include cash paid to suppliers, to employees and other operating expense, interest, and income taxes.

D. Subtract the cash payments from cash receipts to determine the net cash provided (used) by operating activities.

E. The items to be listed are determined by adjusting individual accrual basis income statement items to cash basis items. This is done by determining the impact from changes in their related balance sheet accounts.

F. Exhibit 16B.6 (p. 661) summarizes the common adjustments for the items making up net income to arrive at net cash provided (used) by operating activities under the direct method.

G. This is the method recommended (but not required) by the FASB.

H. When the direct method is used, the FASB requires a reconciliation of net income to net cash provided (used) by operating activities. This is operating cash flows computed using the indirect method.

CLASSIFYING ACTIVITIES IN THE STATEMENT OF CASH FLOWS

OPERATING ACTIVITIES

Cash inflows from	Cash outflows to
• Customers for cash sales	• Salaries and wages
• Collections on credit sales	• Lenders for interest
• Borrowers for interest	• Charities
• Dividends received	• Suppliers of goods and services
• Lawsuit settlements	• Government for taxes and fines

INVESTING ACTIVITIES

Cash inflows from	Cash outflows to
• Selling investments in securities	• Make loans to others
• Selling (discounting) notes	• Purchase long-term productive assets
• Collecting principal on notes	
• Selling long-term productive assets	• Purchase investments in securities

FINANCING ACTIVITIES

Cash inflows from	Cash outflows to
• Contributions by owners	• Repay cash loans
• Issuing notes and bonds	• Pay withdrawals by owners
• Issuing its own equity stock	• Pay dividends to shareholders
• Issuing short-term and long-term debt	• Purchase treasury stock

NONCASH INVESTING AND FINANCING ACTIVITIES

- Retirement of debt by issuing equity stock
- Conversion of preferred stock to common stock
- Leasing of assets in a capital lease transaction
- Purchase of a long-term asset by issuing a note or a bond
- Exchange of noncash assets for other noncash assets
- Purchase of noncash assets by issuing equity or debt

STEPS TO DETERMINE INFORMATION
STATEMENT OF CASH FLOWS

1. Find <u>change</u> in Cash—This is the target number.

2. Find cash flow from operations
   (Using direct or indirect method)

3. Find Cash Flow from   A. Financing <u>and</u>
                                                     B. Investing

   Procedure:

   In real life: Using data from comparative balance sheets, trace
   changes through ledgers and journals probably using a worksheet
   to organize, analyze, and prove data disclosed.

   In the classroom: Determine the changes in noncurrent accounts
   and notes from comparative balance sheets. Use the relevant data
   the text provides that comes from the ledgers and the journals to
   systematically analyze the data using chart and/or reconstructing
   journal entries.

4. Combine cash flows from all three activities (from 2 and 3) to find
   net cash flow and prove change in cash. (Target number
   determined in Step 1).

Note: Once the above information has been gathered, the statement
can be prepared following the required format. If the direct method
was used, GAAP requires a reconciliation of net income to cash
provided from operations.

Determining Cash Flows from Operating Activities
Direct Method
(Need income statement and balance sheet data)

1. Cash = Sales   + Decrease in
    Receipts   Accounts
    from Customers*   Receivable
                           or
                         − Increase in
                         Accounts
                         Receivable

2. Cash = Cost of   + Increase in   + Decrease in
    Payments   Goods Sold   Inventory   Accounts
    to Suppliers   or   Payable
                     − Decrease in   − Increase in
                     Inventory   Accounts
                                  Payable

3. Cash = Operating   + Increase in   + Decrease in   − Depreciation
    Payments   Expenses   Prepaid   Accrued   and Other
    for   Expenses   Liabilities   Noncash
    Operating**   or   or   Expenses
    Expenses   − Decrease in   − Increase in
                     Prepaid   Accrued
                     Expenses   Liabilities

4. Cash = Income   + Decrease in
    Payments   Taxes   Income
    for   Expense   Taxes
    Income   Payable
    Taxes   or
                     − Increase in
                     Income
                     Taxes
                     Payable

5. Cash = Interest   + Decreases in
    Payments   Expense   Interest Payable
    for   − Increase in
    Interest   Interest Payable

*use similar computations for
CR from Interest &/or Dividends
CR from Rent

**Wage expense would be taken out if CP for wages was to be reported separately. The related prepaids and payables would be considered in the computation.

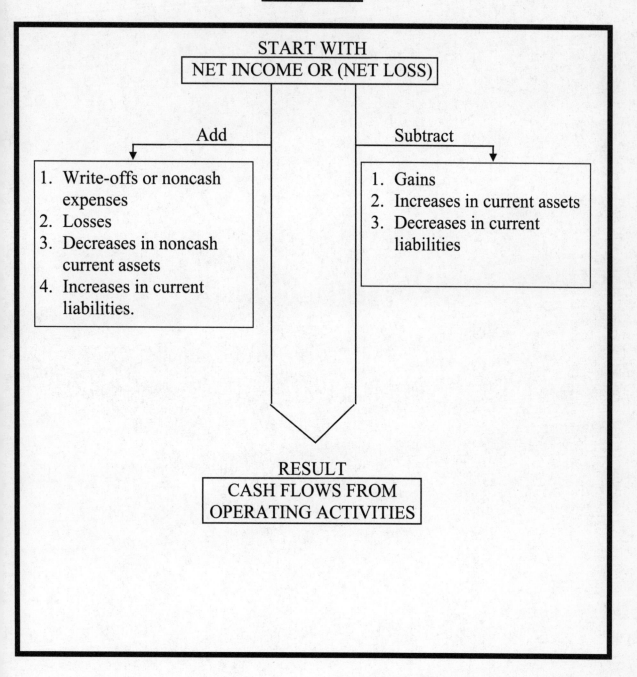

START WITH
NET INCOME OR (NET LOSS)

Add

Subtract

1. Write-offs or noncash expenses
2. Losses
3. Decreases in noncash current assets
4. Increases in current liabilities.

1. Gains
2. Increases in current assets
3. Decreases in current liabilities

RESULT
CASH FLOWS FROM
OPERATING ACTIVITIES

Problem I

The following statements are either true or false. Place a (T) in the parentheses before each true statement and an (F) before each false statement.

1. ( )   (Appendix B) The FASB encourages companies to use the direct method of presenting cash flows from operating activities.

2. ( )   A statement of cash flows should explain the differences between the beginning and ending balances of cash and cash equivalents.

3. ( )   Cash outflows to purchase items classified as cash equivalents are not shown on a statement of cash flows.

4. ( )   A payment by a company in the form of a loan is an example of a financing activity.

5. ( )   The Cash account of a company provides all of the information necessary to prepare a statement of cash flows.

6. ( )   (Appendix B) If a company purchases all merchandise for cash and the ending balance of Merchandise Inventory is unchanged from the beginning balance, then cost of goods sold equals the total cash payments for merchandise.

7. ( )   U.S. GAAP requires cash inflows from interest and dividends be classified as operating activities, whereas IFRS permits classification under operating or investing.

Problem II

You are given several words, phrases, or numbers to choose from in completing each of the following statements or in answering the following questions. In each case select the one that best completes the statement or answers the question and place its letter in the answer space provided.

_____   1.   (Appendix B) If a company purchases merchandise on account and there are some changes in the Merchandise Inventory balance during a period, what calculations are necessary to calculate cash payments for merchandise?

a. Purchases + Decrease (– Increase) in Merchandise Inventory.

b. Cost of Goods Sold + Increase (– Decrease) in Merchandise Inventory.

c. Purchases + Decrease (– Increase) in Accounts Payable.

d. Both a and b.

e. Both b and c.

_____   2.   (Appendix B) Given the following T-account (partially completed), determine the cash payment for interest.

	Interest Payable	
	12/31/09Bal.	12,000
	Interest expense	8,000
	12/31/10 Bal.	13,000

a. $7,000.

b. $4,000.

c. $8,000.

d. $12,000.

e. $20,000.

_____ 3. Bat Company purchased a plant asset that cost $30,000 by borrowing $25,000 and paying the $5,000 balance in cash. What would be reported on the statement of cash flows?

a. Cash outflow from investing activities: $5,000.

b. Cash inflow from financing activities: $25,000.

c. Cash outflow from investing activities: $30,000.

d. The transaction would only be reported on the schedule of noncash investing and financing activities.

e. Both a and b.

Problem III

Many of the important ideas and concepts discussed in Chapter 16 are reflected in the following list of key terms. Test your understanding of these terms by matching the appropriate definitions with the terms. Record the number identifying the most appropriate definition in the blank space next to each term.

_____ Cash flow on total assets   _____ Investing activities
_____ Direct method   _____ Operating activities
_____ Financing activities   _____ Statement of cash flows
_____ Indirect method

1. Transactions with a company's owners or creditors that include obtaining cash from issuing debt, repaying amounts borrowed, and obtaining cash from or distributing cash to owners.

2. Activities that involve the production or purchase of merchandise and the sale of goods and services to customers, including expenditures related to administering the business.

3. Calculation of the net cash provided (used) by operating activities that lists the major operating cash receipts, less the major operating cash payments.

4. Financial statement that reports cash inflows and outflows for an accounting period and classifies them as operating, investing, or financing activities.

5. Calculation that reports net income and then adjusts it by adding and subtracting items necessary to yield net cash provided (used) by operating activities.

6. Transactions that involve making and collecting notes receivable, purchasing and selling long-term assets, including investments other than cash equivalents.

7. Ratio of operating cash flows to average total assets; not affected by income recognition and measurement rules, reflects earnings quality.

Problem IV

Opposite each transaction, place an "X" in the box below the caption that best describes its disclosure category on a statement of cash flows or supplemental schedule in the case of noncash investing and financing activities.

Transaction	Operating Activity	Investing Activity	Financing Activity	Noncash Investing & Financing Activity
1. Paid wages and salaries.				
2. Cash sale of used equipment.				
3. Received a cash dividend.				
4. Issued a long-term bond payable for cash.				
5. Cash sale of merchandise.				
6. Purchased land in exchange for common stock.				
7. Paid a cash dividend.				
8. Paid interest expense.				
9. Purchased stock in another company for cash.				
10. Repaid a six-month note payable.				

Problem V

Analyze the information presented in each question below and determine the missing amounts. (Questions 1, 2, 3 and 5 are based on Appendix 16B)

1. Accounts receivable decreased from $25,000 at the beginning of the period to $18,000 at the end of the period. Sales revenue was $280,000. Assume all sales were on account. There were no uncollectible accounts written off during the period. How much cash was collected from customers during the period? _____

2. Merchandise inventory increased from $90,000 at the beginning of the period to $100,000 at the end of the period. Cost of goods sold was $160,000. How much merchandise inventory was purchased during the period? _____

3. The accounts payable balance decreased during the period from $30,000 to $26,000. Disregard your answer to question 2 and assume purchases of merchandise during the period totaled $120,000. Assume all purchases were on account. How much cash was paid to merchandise suppliers during the period? _____

4. The balance of accumulated depreciation increased during the period from $200,000 to $220,000. Also, machinery originally costing $10,000 with accumulated depreciation of $8,000 was sold during the period. What was the amount of the period's depreciation expense?

    _____

5. Refer back to question 1. Instead of assuming all sales revenues of $280,000 were on account, assume cash sales totaled $100,000 and credit sales totaled $180,000. How much cash was collected from customers during the period? _____

Problem VI

Iker Company's 2012 and 2011 balance sheets are presented below and its 2010 income statement is on the following page.

IKER COMPANY
Balance Sheet
December 31, 2012, and 2011
Assets

	2012		2011	
Cash...		$ 8,000		$ 5,000
Accounts receivable......................................		15,000		12,000
Merchandise inventory		30,000		33,000
Equipment...	$40,000		$38,000	
Less accumulated depreciation......................	16,000	24,000	18,000	20,000
Total assets		$77,000		$70,000

Liabilities and Stockholders' Equity

	2012	2011
Accounts payable...	$21,000	$17,000
Accrued liabilities...	4,000	5,000
Common stock, $5 par value	35,000	30,000
Retained earnings	17,000	18,000
Total liabilities and stockholders' equity	$77,000	$70,000

IKER COMPANY
Income Statement
For Year Ended December 31, 2012

Sales..		$80,000
Cost of goods sold		30,000
Gross profit on sales		50,000
Operating expenses..	$20,000	
Depreciation expense.....................................	10,000	
Loss from sale of plant assets	5,000	35,000
Net income..		$15,000

Additional information about the company's activities in 2012:

1. Sold used equipment costing $20,000 with accumulated depreciation of $12,000 for $3,000 cash.

2. Purchased equipment costing $22,000 by paying $17,000 cash and issuing 1,000 shares of common stock.

3. Paid cash dividends of $16,000.

Required:

Note: If you are responsible for Appendix 16A, complete part (a) and then (b). If you are not responsible for the appendix 16A, skip part (a) and complete only part (b).

a. A partially completed spreadsheet for Iker Company's statement of cash flows (assuming the indirect method is used) for the year ended December 31, 2012 appears below. Complete the spreadsheet.

b. Prepare the Iker Company's statement of cash flows for the year ended December 31, 2012 using the indirect method.

a.

IKER COMPANY

Spreadsheet for Statement of Cash Flows (Indirect Method)

For Year Ended December 31, 2012

	December 31, 2011	Analysis of Changes		December 31, 2012
		Debit	Credit	
Balance sheet—Debits:				
Cash	5,000			8,000
Accounts receivable	12,000			15,000
Merchandise inventory	33,000			30,000
Equipment	38,000			40,000
	88,000			93,000
Balance sheet—Credits:				
Accumulated depreciation	18,000			16,000
Accounts payable	17,000			21,000
Accrued liabilities	5,000			4,000
Common stock, $5 par value	30,000			35,000
Retained earnings	18,000			17,000
	88,000			93,000
Statement of Cash Flows				

b.

IKER COMPANY		
Statement of Cash Flows		
For Year Ended December 31, 2012		

Solutions for Chapter 16

Problem I

1.	T	4.	T
2.	T	5.	F
3.	T	6.	T
		7.	T

Problem II

1. C
2. A
3. A

Problem III

7	Cash flow on total assets	6	Investing activities
3	Direct method	2	Operating activities
1	Financing activities	4	Statement of cash flows
5	Indirect method		

Problem IV

	Transaction	*Classification*
1.	Paid wages and salaries.	Operating activity
2.	Cash sale of used equipment.	Investing activity
3.	Received a cash dividend.	Operating activity
4.	Issued a long-term bond payable for cash.	Financing activity
5.	Cash sale of merchandise.	Operating activity
6.	Purchased land in exchange for common stock.	Noncash investing and financing activity
7.	Paid a cash dividend.	Financing activity
8.	Paid interest expense.	Operating activity
9.	Purchased stock in another company for cash.	Investing activity
10.	Repaid a six-month note payable.	Financing activity

Problem V

1.	Cash collections from customers	$280,000	+	$ 25,000	–	$18,000	=	$287,000		
2.	Merchandise purchases	$160,000	+	$100,000	–	$90,000	=	$170,000		
3.	Cash payments for merchandise	$120,000	+	$ 30,000	–	$26,000	=	$124,000		
4.	Depreciation expense	$220,000	–	$200,000	+	$ 8,000	=	$ 28,000		
5.	Cash collections from customers	$100,000	+	$180,000	+	$25,000	–	$ 18,000	=	$287,000

Problem VI

a.

IKER COMPANY
Spreadsheet for Statement of Cash Flows (Indirect Method)
For Year Ended December 31, 2012

	December 31, 2011	Analysis of Changes Debit	Analysis of Changes Credit	December 31, 2012
Balance sheet—Debits:				
Cash	5,000			8,000
Accounts receivable	12,000	3,000 (b)		15,000
Merchandise inventory	33,000		3,000 (c)	30,000
Equipment	38,000	22,000 (h)	20,000 (g)	40,000
	88,000			93,000
Balance sheet—Credits:				
Accumulated depreciation	18,000	12,000 (g)	10,000 (f)	16,000
Accounts payable	17,000		4,000 (d)	21,000
Accrued liabilities	5,000	1,000 (e)		4,000
Common stock, $5 par value	30,000		5,000 (h)	35,000
Retained earnings	18,000	16,000 (i)	15,000 (f)	17,000
	88,000			93,000
Statement of Cash Flows				
Operating activities:				
Net Income		15,000 (a)		
Increase in accounts receivable			3,000 (b)	
Decrease in merchandise inventory		3,000 (c)		
Increase in accounts payable		4,000 (d)		
Decrease in accrued liabilities			1,000 (e)	
Depreciation expense		10,000 (f)		
Loss on sale of equipment		5,000 (g)		
Investing activities				
Proceeds from sale of equipment		3,000 (g)		
Payment for purchase of equipment			17,000 (h)	
Financing activities				
Payment of cash dividends			16,000 (i)	
Noncash investing and financing activities				
Issued stock to purchase equipment		5,000 (h)	5,000 (h)	
		99,000	99,000	

b.

IKER COMPANY
Statement of Cash Flows
For Year Ended December 31, 2012

Cash flows from operating activities

Net income..	$ 15,000	
Adjustments to reconcile net income to net cash provided by operating activities		
Increase in accounts receivable...	(3,000)	
Decrease in merchandise inventory	3,000	
Increase in accounts payable..	4,000	
Decrease in accrued liabilities...	(1,000)	
Depreciation expense	10,000	
Loss on sale of equipment..	5,000	
Net cash provided by operating activities..................................		$ 33,000
Cash flows from investing activities		
Cash received from sale of equipment..	3,000	
Cash paid for purchase of equipment	(17,000)	
Net cash used in investing activities..		(14,000)
Cash flows from financing activities		
Cash paid for dividends...	(16,000)	
Net cash used in financing activities		(16,000)
		3,000
Net increase in cash		3,000
Cash balance at end of 2011		5,000
Cash balance at end of 2012		$ 8,000

CHAPTER 17
ANALYSIS OF FINANCIAL STATEMENTS

Learning Objective C1:

Explain the purpose of and identify the building blocks of analysis.

Summary

The purpose of financial statement analysis is to help users make better business decisions. Internal users want information to improve company efficiency or effectiveness in providing products or services. External users want information to make better and more informed decisions in pursuing their goals. The common goals of all users are to evaluate a company's (1) past and current performance, (2) current financial position, and (3) future performance and risk. Financial statement analysis focuses on four "building blocks" of analysis: (1) liquidity and efficiency—ability to meet short-term obligations and to efficiently generate revenues; (2) solvency—ability to generate future revenues and meet long-term obligations; (3) profitability—ability to provide financial rewards sufficient to attract and retain financing; and (4) market prospects—ability to generate positive market expectations.

Learning Objective C2:

Describe standards for comparisons in analysis.

Summary

Standards for comparisons include (1) intracompany—prior performance and relations between financial items of company under analysis; (2) competitor—one or more direct competitors of the company; (3) industry—industry statistics; and (4) guidelines (rules-of-thumb) —general standards developed from past experiences and personal judgments.

Learning Objective A1:

Summarize and report results of analysis.

Summary

A financial statement analysis report is often organized around the building blocks of analysis. A good report separates interpretations and conclusions of analysis from the information underlying them. This separation enables readers to see the process and rationale of analysis. It also enables the reader to draw personal conclusions and make modifications as appropriate. An analysis report often consists of six sections: (1) executive summary; (2) analysis overview; (3) evidential matter; (4) assumptions; (5) key factors; and (6) inferences.

Learning Objective A2[A]:

Explain the form and assess the content of a complete income statement.

Summary

An income statement has of four *potential* sections: (1) continuing operations, (2) discontinued segments, (3) extraordinary items, and (4) earnings per share.

Learning Objective P1:

Explain and apply methods of horizontal analysis.

Summary

Horizontal analysis is a tool to evaluate changes in data across time. Two important tools of horizontal analysis are comparative statements and trend analysis. Comparative statements show amounts for two or more successive periods, often with changes disclosed in both absolute and percent terms. Trend analysis is used to reveal important changes occurring from one period to the next.

Learning Objective P2:

Describe and apply methods of vertical analysis.

Summary

Vertical analysis is a tool to evaluate each financial statement item or group of items in terms of a base amount. Two tools of vertical analysis are common-size statements and graphical analyses. Each item in common-size statements is expressed as a percent of a base amount. For the balance sheet, the base amount is usually total assets, and for the income statement, it is usually sales.

Learning Objective P3:

Define and apply ratio analysis.

Summary

Ratio analysis provides clues to and symptoms of underlying conditions. Ratios, properly interpreted, identify areas requiring further investigation. A ratio expresses a mathematical relation between two quantities such as a percent, rate, or proportion. Ratios can be organized into the building blocks of analysis: (1) liquidity and efficiency, (2) solvency, (3) profitability, and (4) market prospects.

I.   **Basics of Analysis**—Transforming *data* into useful information.

     A.   Purpose of Analysis
        To help users (both internal and external) make better business decisions.

        1.   Internal users (managers, officers, internal auditors, consultants, budget officers, and market researchers) make the strategic and operating decisions of a company.

        2.   External users (shareholders, lenders, directors, customers, suppliers, regulators, lawyers, brokers, and the press) rely on financial statement analysis to make decisions in pursuing their own goals.

        3.   The common goal of all users is to evaluate:

           a.   Past and current performance.

           b.   Current financial position.

           c.   Future performance and risk.

     B.   Building Blocks of Analysis
        The four areas of inquiry or building blocks are:

        1.   Liquidity and efficiency—ability to meet short-term obligations and to efficiently generate revenues.

        2.   Solvency—ability to generate future revenues and meet long-term obligations.

        3.   Profitability—ability to provide financial rewards sufficient to attract and retain financing.

        4.   Market prospects—ability to generate positive market expectations.

     C.   Information for Analysis
        Most users rely on *general purpose financial statements* that include:

        1.   Income statement

        2.   Balance sheet

        3.   Statement of stockholders' equity (or statement of retained earnings)

        4.   Statement of cash flows

        5.   Notes related to the statements

        6.   Other useful financial data—10K/other SEC filings, news releases, shareholders' meetings, forecasts, management letters, auditor's report, and analyses published in annual reports.

    D. Standards for Comparisons
    Used to determine if analysis measures suggest good, bad, or average performance. Standards (benchmarks) can include the following types of comparisons:

1. Intracompany—based on own *prior performance* and relationships between its financial items.

2. Competitor—compared to one or more direct competitors. (often best)

3. Industry—published industry statistics (available from services like Dun & Bradstreet, Standard and Poor's, and Moody's).

4. Guidelines (rules-of-thumb)—general standards developed from experience.

    E. Tools of Analysis

1. Horizontal analysis

2. Vertical analysis

3. Ratio analysis

II.   **Horizontal Analysis**—Tool to evaluate changes in financial statement data *across time*. This analysis utilizes:

    A. Comparative Statements

1. Reports where financial amounts for more than one period are placed side by side in columns on a single statement.

2. Dollar changes and percentage changes—usually shown in line items.

    a. Dollar change = Analysis period amount minus Base period amount.

    b. Percent change = (Analysis period amount minus Base period amount) divided by Base period amount multiplied by 100.

    Note: (1) When a negative amount appears in the base period and a positive amount in the analysis period (or vice versa) a meaningful percentage change cannot be computed.

          (2) When there is no value in the base period—percentage change is not computable.

          (3) When an item has a value in the base period and zero in the next period—the decrease is 100 percent.

3. Comparative Balance Sheets—balance sheets from two or more periods arranged side-by-side. Dollar and percentage changes are often shown. Analysis focuses on large changes.

4. Comparative Income Statements—also compares two or more periods presented side-by side with dollar and percentage changes.

   B. Trend analysis (also called *trend percent analysis* or *index number trend analysis*
       1. A form of horizontal analysis used to reveal patterns in data across successive periods.
       2. Involves computing trend percents (or *index number*) as follows: Analysis period amount divided by base period amount) multiplied by 100.
       3. Often aided by graphical depiction.

III. **Vertical Analysis**—(also called *common-size analysis*) Comparing financial condition and performance to a *base amount*. The analysis tools include:
   A. Common-Size Statements—reveal changes in the relative importance of each financial statement item by redefining each in terms *of common-size percents*.
       1. Base amount is commonly defined as 100%. Usually a key aggregate figure is the base (Examples: revenue—income statement base, total assets—balance sheet base).
       2. Sum of individual items is 100%.
       3. Common-size percentage equals (Analysis amount divided by Base amounts) multiplied by 100.
   B. Common-Size Graphics
       Graphical analysis (Ex. pie charts and bar charts) of common-size statements that visually highlight comparison information.

IV. **Ratio Analysis**—widely used analysis tool that express key relationships among financial statement items. Ratios are organized into the four (A to D below) building blocks of analysis:
   A. Liquidity and Efficiency
       1. *Liquidity* refers to the availability of resources to meet short-term cash requirements.
       2. *Efficiency* refers to how productive a company is in using its assets. Efficiency is usually measured relative to how much revenue is generated for a certain level of assets.
       3. Ratios in this block:
           a. Working capital—the excess of current assets less current liabilities.
           b. Current ratio—current assets divided by current liabilities; describes a company's ability to pay its short-term obligations.
           c. Acid-test ratio—similar to current ratio but focuses on quick assets (i.e., cash, short-term investments, accounts receivable, and notes receivable) rather than current assets. Calculated as quick assets divided by current liabilities.

d. Accounts receivable turnover—net sales or credit sales divided by average accounts receivable; a measure of how long it takes a company to collect its accounts.

e. Inventory turnover—cost of goods sold divided by average inventory; the number of times a company's average inventory is sold during an accounting period.

f. Days' sales uncollected—(accounts receivable divided by net credit sales) multiplied by 365 days; measures how frequently a company collects its accounts receivable.

g. Days' sales in inventory—(ending inventory divided by cost of goods sold) multiplied by 365; measures how many days it will take to convert the inventory on hand at the end of the period into accounts receivable or cash.

h. Total asset turnover—net sales divided by average total assets; describes the ability to use assets to generate sales.

B. Solvency

1. *Solvency* refers to a company's long-run financial viability and its ability to cover long-term obligations. *Capital structure* is one of the most important components of solvency analysis.

2. *Capital structure* refers to a company's sources of financing.

3. Ratios in this block:

a. Debt ratio—total liabilities divided by total assets.

b. Equity ratio—total stockholders' equity divided by total assets; compliment of debt ratio.

c. Debt-to-equity ratio—total liabilities divided by total equity.

Note: A company is considered less risky if its capital structure (equity and long-term debt) is composed more of equity. *Financial leveraging*, the inclusion of debt, can increase return to stockholders.

d. Times interest earned—income before interest expense and income taxes divided by interest expense; reflects the risk of repayments with interest to creditors.

C. Profitability

1. *Profitability* refers to a company's ability to generate an adequate *return* on invested capital.

2. *Return* is judged by assessing earnings relative to the level and sources of financing.

      3. Ratios in this block:

         a. Profit margin—net income divided by net sales; describes the ability to earn a net income from sales.

         b. Return on total assets—net income divided by average total assets; a summary measure of operating efficiency, comprises profit margin and total asset turnover.

         c. Return on common stockholders' equity—net income less preferred dividends divided by average common stockholders' equity; measures the success of a company in earning net income for its owners.

D. Market Prospects

    1. Market measures are useful for analyzing corporations with publicly traded stock.

    2. Market measures use stock price in their computation.

    3. Ratios in this block:

         a. Price-earnings ratio—market price per share of common stock divided by earnings per share; used to evaluate the profitability of alternative common stock investments.

         b. Dividend yield—annual cash dividends paid per share of stock divided by market price per share; used to compare the dividend paying performance of different investment alternatives.

E. Summary of Ratios
Exhibit 17.16 on p. 699 of text sets forth the names of each of the common ratios by category, and includes the formula and a description of what is measured by each ratio.

Chapter Outline

V.   Global View—Compares U.S. GAAP to IFRS

   A. Horizontal and vertical analyses help eliminate many differences
       between U.S. GAAP and IFRS when analyzing and interpreting
       financial statements. Percentages are consistently applied across
       and within periods. However, where reporting rules differ, users
       should exercise caution in drawing conclusions.

   B. Ratio analysis has many of the advantages and disadvantages of
       horizontal and vertical analysis as mentioned above.

VI.   Decision Analysis—Analysis Reporting

   Goal of financial statement analysis report is to reduce uncertainty
   through rigorous and sound evaluation. A good analysis report usually
   consists of six sections:

   1. Executive summary

   2. Analysis overview

   3. Evidential matter

   4. Assumptions

   5. Key factors

   6. Inferences

VII.   Sustainable Income—Appendix 17A—When a revenue and expense
   transactions are from normal, continuing operations, a simple income
   statement is adequate. When activities include events that are not
   normal, it must disclose this information by separating the income
   statement into different sections as follows (A-D):

   A. Continuing Operations
       Reports the revenues, expenses, and income generated by the
       company's continuing operations.

   B. Discontinued Segments

       1. A *business segment* is a part of a company's operations that
           serves a particular line of business or class of customers.

       2. Section reports:

           a. Income (loss) from operating each discontinued business
               segment for the current period prior to disposal (net of
               taxes).

           b. Gain or loss on disposal of each segment (net of related
               income tax effects).

C. Extraordinary Items—reports extraordinary gains and losses that are *both unusual* and *infrequent.*

1. An *unusual* gain or loss is abnormal or otherwise unrelated to the company's regular activities and environment.

2. An *infrequent* gain or loss is not expected to recur given the company's operating environment.

3. Items that are unusual or infrequent, but not both, are reported in the income statement as part of continuing operations but below the normal revenues and expenses.

D. Earnings per Share

1. Final section of income statement.

2. Reports EPS for three subcategories of income (continuing operations, discontinued segments, and extraordinary items). EPS discussed in chapter 13.

E. Changes in Accounting Principles

1. The *consistency principle* directs a company to apply the same accounting principle across periods. Changes from one accounting principles to another (Example: Lifo to Fifo) are acceptable if justified as improvements in financial reporting.

2. A footnote would describe change and why it is an improvement.

3. Requires *retrospective application* (application of new accounting principle to prior periods as if that principle had always been used).

Problem I

The following statements are ether true or false. Place a (T) in the parentheses before each true statement and an (F) before each false statement.

1. ( ) A current ratio of 2 to 1 always indicates that a company can easily meet it's current debts.

2. ( ) Accounts receivable turnover of 6.4 times in 2012 and 8.2 times in 2011 indicates that a company is collecting its accounts receivable more rapidly in 2012 than in 2011.

3. ( ) If accounts receivable is $150,000, and net credit sales is $1,000,000, days' sales uncollected is 15.

4. ( ) On a common-size income statement, the amount of net sales is assigned a value of 100%.

5. ( ) To calculate inventory turnover, cost of goods sold is divided by gross sales.

6. ( ) The ratios and turnovers of a selected group of competitive companies normally are the best bases of comparison for analyzing financial statements.

7. ( ) Return on total assets summarizes the two components of operating efficiency—profit margin and total asset turnover.

8. ( ) Current ratio, acid-test ratio, accounts receivable turnover, and inventory turnover are tools for evaluating short-term liquidity.

Problem II

You are given several words, phrases, or numbers to choose from in completing each of the following statements or in answering the following questions. In each case select the one that best completes the statement or answers the question and place its letter in the answer space provided.

_____ 1. To analyze long-term risk and capital structure, the following ratios and statistics for analysis would be used:

    a. Debt ratio.

    b. Equity ratio.

    c. Times fixed interest charges earned.

    d. Debt-to-Equity ratio.

    e. All of the above.

_____ 2. During 2011, a company's sales were $360,000. In 2012 they were $334,800 and in 2013 they were $374,400. Express the sales in trend percentages, using 2011 as the base year.

    a. 2011— 96%; 2012— 89%; 2013—100%.

    b. 2011—100%; 2012—108%; 2013— 96%.

    c. 2011—100%; 2012—100%; 2013—100%.

    d. 2011—104%; 2012—112%; 2013—100%.

    e. 2011—100%; 2012— 93%; 2013—104%.

_____ 3. Information from the 2012 income statement of Becker Company follows:

Sales	$320,000
Gross profit on sales	138,000
Operating income	32,000
Income before taxes	22,000
Net income	16,800

If the company's January 1, 2011, accounts receivable were $23,200 and its December 31, 2012, accounts receivable were $28,000, what was the company's accounts receivable turnover?

a. 7.1 times.

b. 5.4 times.

c. 12.5 times.

d. 3.9 times.

e. 10.1 times.

_____ 4. Information from the 2011 income statement of Sumner Company follows:

Sales	$300,000
Cost of goods sold:	
Inventory inventory, January 1, 2011	28,480
Purchases, net	171,040
Goods available for sale	199,520
Inventory inventory, December 31, 2011	19,520
Cost of goods sold	180,000
Gross profit on sales	120,000
Operating expenses	34,000
Income from operations	$ 86,000

Calculate the company's inventory turnover.

a. 7.5 times.

b. 9.2 times.

c. 12.5 times.

d. 8.3 times.

e. 17.9 times.

_____ 5. The Keyes Company had the following comparative income statements for 2012 and 2011:

	2012	2011
Net sales	$630,000	$552,000
Cost of goods sold	428,400	389,160
Gross profit from sales	201,600	162,840
Operating expenses	97,500	78,600
Net income	$104,100	$ 84,240

What are the cost of goods sold in common-size percentages for 2012 and 2011?

a. 110.1% in 2012; 100.0% in 2011.

b. 24.3% in 2012, 21.6% in 2011.

c. 41.2% in 2012; 46.2% in 2011.

d. 68.0% in 2012; 70.5% in 2011.

e. 147.0% in 2012; 141.8% in 2011.

Problem III

Many of the important ideas and concepts discussed in Chapter 17 are reflected in the following list of key terms. Test your understanding of these terms by matching the appropriate definitions with the terms. Record the number identifying the most appropriate definition in the blank space next to each term.

_____ Business segment	_____ Infrequent gain or loss
_____ Common-size financial statement	_____ Liquidity
_____ Comparative financial statement	_____ Market prospects
_____ Efficiency	_____ Profitability
_____ Equity ratio	_____ Ratio analysis
_____ Extraordinary gain and loss	_____ Solvency
_____ Financial reporting	_____ Unusual gain or loss
_____ Financial statement analysis	_____ Vertical analysis
_____ General-purpose financial statements	_____ Working capital
_____ Horizontal analysis	

1. Process of communicating information relevant to investors, creditors, and others in making investment, credit, and other decisions.

2. Statements published periodically for use by a variety of interested parties; includes the income statement, balance sheet, statement of changes in equity (or statement of retained earnings), statement of cash flows, and notes to these statements.

3. Statement with data for two or more successive periods placed in side-by-side columns, often with changes shown in dollar amounts and percentages.

4. Current assets minus current liabilities.

5. Statement that expresses each amount as a percentage of a base amount. In the balance sheet, the amount of total assets is usually the base amount and is expressed as 100%. In the income statement, net sales is usually the base amount.

6. Portion of total assets provided by equity, calculated as total equity divided by total assets.

7. Evaluation of each financial statement item or group of items in terms of a specific base amount.

8. Availability of resources to meet short-term cash requirements.

9. Company's productivity in using its assets; usually measured relative to how much revenue a certain level of assets generates.

10. Company's long-run financial viability and its ability to cover long-term obligations.

11. Application of analytical tools to general-purpose financial statements and related data for making business decisions.

12. Company's ability to generate an adequate return on invested capital.

13. Comparison of a company's financial condition and performance across time.

14. Expectations (both good and bad) about a company's future performance as assessed by users and other interested parties.

15. Determination of key relationships between financial statement items.

16. Part of operations that serves a line of business or class of customers and that has assets, liabilities, and operating results distinguishable from other parts.

17. Gain or loss reported separate from continuing operations because it is both unusual and infrequent.

18. Gain or loss is not expected to recur, given the operating environment of the business.

19. Gain or loss that is abnormal or unrelated to the ordinary activities and environment.

Problem IV

The sales, cost of goods sold, and gross profits from sales of the Laker Company for a five-year period are shown below:

	2009	2010	2011	2012	2013
Sales	$350,000	$385,000	$413,000	$455,000	$497,000
Cost of goods sold	250,000	280,000	305,000	345,000	375,000
Gross profit	100,000	105,000	108,000	110,000	122,000

Laker Company's sales are expressed in trend percentages below. Express its cost of goods sold and gross profit in trend percentages in the spaces provided.

	2009	2010	2011	2012	2013
Sales	100	110	118	130	142
Cost of goods sold					
Gross profit					

Comment on the situation shown by the data: _____

_____

_____

_____

_____

Problem V

Complete the following by filling in the blanks.

1. When calculating accounts receivable turnover, the preferable sales number to use is _____ (cash, credit, total) sales.

2. The acid-test ratio is calculated by dividing _____ by _____.

3. Inventory turnover is calculated by dividing _____ by _____.

4. A slower turnover of inventory _____ (will, will not) tend to increase working capital requirements.

5. The current ratio is calculated by dividing _____ by_____. It is an indication of a company's _____ to meet its current obligations.

6. Return on total assets is calculated by dividing _____ by the amount of _____.

7. Times fixed interest charges earned is calculated by dividing income before deducting _____and_____ by the amount of _____.

8. Days' sales uncollected is calculated by dividing _____ by _____and multiplying the resulting quotient by _____. Days' sales uncollected is an indication of _____ _____.

9. The price-earnings ratio for a company's common stock is calculated by dividing the _____ _____ per share of the common stock by _____.

10. Return on common stockholders' equity is calculated by dividing _____ _____ by _____ stockholders' equity.

11. Compared to companies with an average growth rate, companies in a growth industry would be expected to have a _____ (higher, lower) price-earnings ratio.

12. Days' sales in inventory is calculated by dividing _____ by _____and multiplying by 365.

Problem VI

1. Following are the condensed income statements of two companies of unequal size.

   Examine the statement amounts and write in this space (_____) the name of the company that operated more efficiently. If you cannot tell from examining the statement amounts, write "cannot tell" in the blank.

COMPANIES A AND Z
Income Statements
For Year Ended December 31, 20__

	Company A	Company Z
Sales	$325,000	$265,000
Cost of goods sold	204,750	164,300
Gross profit on sales	120,250	100,700
Selling expenses	61,750	49,025
Administrative expenses	42,250	34,450
Total operating expenses	104,000	83,475
Net income	$ 16,250	$ 17,225

2. Common-size percentages are often used in comparing the statements of companies of unequal size. Below are the condensed income statements of Companies A and Z with the income statement amounts of Company A already expressed in common-size percentages. Express the income statement amounts of Company Z in common-size percentages in the spaces provided.

COMPANIES A AND Z
Income Statements
For Year Ended December 31, 20__

	Dollar Amounts		Common-Size Percentages	
	Company A	Company Z	Company A	Company Z
Sales	$325,000	$265,000	100.0	_____
Cost of goods sold	204,750	164,300	63.0	_____
Gross profit on sales	120,250	100,700	37.0	_____
Selling expenses	61,750	49,025	19.0	_____
Administrative expenses	42,250	34,450	13.0	_____
Total operating expenses	104,000	83,475	32.0	_____
Net income	$ 16,250	$ 17,225	5.0	_____

3. After expressing the Company Z income statement amounts in common-size percentages, examine the common-size percentages of the two companies identify the name of the company that operated more efficiently. _____.

Solutions for Chapter 17

Problem I

1.	F	5.	F
2.	F	6.	T
3.	F	7.	T
4.	T	8.	T

Problem II

1. E
2. E
3. C
4. A
5. D

Problem III

16	Business segment	18	Infrequent gain or loss
5	Common-size financial statement	8	Liquidity
3	Comparative financial statement	14	Market prospects
9	Efficiency	12	Profitability
6	Equity ratio	15	Ratio analysis
17	Extraordinary gain or loss	10	Solvency
1	Financial reporting	19	Unusual gain or loss
11	Financial statement analysis	7	Vertical analysis
2	General-purpose financial statements	4	Working capital
13	Horizontal analysis		

Problem IV

	2009	2010	2011	2012	2013
Sales	100	110	118	130	142
Cost of goods sold	100	112	122	138	150
Gross profit....................................	100	105	108	110	122

Laker Company's sales increased each year throughout the five-year period, but its cost of goods sold increased more rapidly. This slowed the rate of increase in its gross profit.

Problem V

1. credit

2. quick assets, current liabilities

3. cost of goods sold, average inventory

4. will

5. current assets, current liabilities, ability

6. net income, average total assets

7. income taxes, fixed interest charges, fixed interest charges

8. accounts receivable, credit sales, the number of days in a year, collection efficiency (how frequently a company collects its accounts)

9. market price, earnings per share

10. net income less any preferred dividends, average common

11. higher

12. ending inventory, cost of goods sold

Problem VI

1. The average person cannot tell from an examination of the figures which company operated more efficiently.

2.

COMPANIES A AND Z
Income Statements
For Year Ended December 31, 20__

	Dollar Amounts		Common-Size Percentages	
	Company A	Company Z	Company A	Company Z
Sales...	$325,000	$265,000	100.0	100.0
Cost of goods sold	204,750	164,300	63.0	62.0
Gross profit on sales	120,250	100,700	37.0	38.0
Selling expenses	61,750	49,025	19.0	18.5
Administrative expenses..............	42,250	34,450	13.0	13.0
Total operating expenses	104,000	83,475	32.0	31.5
Net income..................................	$ 16,250	$ 17,225	5.0	6.5

3. Company Z

CHAPTER 18
MANAGERIAL ACCOUNTING CONCEPTS AND PRINCIPLES

Learning Objective C1:

Explain the purpose and nature of managerial accounting and the role of ethics.

Summary

The purpose of managerial accounting is to provide useful information to management and other internal decision makers. It does this collecting, managing and reporting both financial and nonfinancial information in a manner useful to internal users. Major characteristics of managerial accounting include: (1) focus on internal decision makers, (2) emphasis on planning and control, (3) flexibility, (4) timeliness, (5) reliance on forecasts and estimates, (6) focus on segments and projects, and (7) source of both monetary and nonmonetary information. Ethics are beliefs that distinguish right from wrong. Ethics can be important in reducing fraud in business operation.

Learning Objective C2:

Describe accounting concepts useful in classifying costs.

Summary

We can classify costs on the basis of their (1) behavior—fixed vs. variable, (2) traceability—direct vs. indirect, (3) controllability—controllable vs. uncontrollable, (4) relevance—sunk vs. out of pocket, and (5) function—product vs. period. A cost can be classified in more than one way, depending on the purpose for which the cost is being determined. These classifications help us to understand cost patterns, analyze performance, and plan operations.

Learning Objective C3:

Define product and period costs and explain how they impact financial statements.

Summary

Costs that are capitalized because they are expected to have future value are called product costs. Costs that are expensed are called period costs. This classification is important because it affects the amount of costs expensed in the income statement and the amount of costs assigned to inventory on the balance sheet. Product costs are commonly made up of direct materials, direct labor and overhead. Period costs include selling and administrative expenses.

Learning Objective C4:

Explain how balance sheets and income statements of manufacturing and merchandising companies differ.

Summary

The main difference is that manufacturers usually carry three inventories—raw materials, goods in process, and finished goods—instead of one inventory that merchandisers carry. The main difference between income statements of manufacturers and merchandisers is the items making up cost of goods sold. A merchandiser adds beginning merchandise inventory to cost of goods purchased, and then subtracts ending merchandise inventory to get cost of goods sold. A manufacturer adds beginning finished goods inventory to cost of goods manufactured, and then subtracts ending finished goods inventory to get cost of goods sold.

Learning Objective C5:

Explain manufacturing activities and the flow of manufacturing costs.

Summary

Manufacturing activities consists of materials, production and sales activities. The materials activity consists of the purchase and issuance of materials to production. The production activity consists of converting materials into finished goods. At this stage in the process, the materials, labor and overhead costs have been incurred and the manufacturing statement is prepared. The sales activity consists of selling some or all of finished goods available for sale. At this stage in the process, the cost of goods sold is determined.

Learning Objective C6:

Describe trends in managerial accounting.

Summary

Important trends in managerial accounting include an increased focus on satisfying customers, the impact of a global economy, and the growing presence of e-commerce and service-based businesses. The lean business model, designed to eliminate waste and satisfy customers, can be useful in responding to recent trends. Concepts such as total quality management, just-in-time production, and the value chain often aid in the application of the lean business model.

Learning Objective A1:

Compute cycle time and cycle efficiency, and explain their importance to production management.

Summary

It is important for these companies to reduce the time to produce their products and to improve manufacturing efficiency. One measure of that time is cycle time (CT), defined as Process time + Inspection time + Move time + Wait time. Process time is value-added time, the others are non-value-added time. Cycle efficiency (CE) is the ratio of value-added time to total cycle time. If CE is low, management should evaluate its production process to see if it can reduce non-value-added activities.

Learning Objective P1:

Compute cost of goods sold for a manufacturer.

Summary

A manufacturer adds beginning finished goods inventory to cost of goods manufactured, and then subtracts ending finished goods inventory to get cost of goods sold.

Learning Objective P2:

Prepare a manufacturing statement and explain its purpose and links to financial statements.

Summary

The manufacturing statement reports computation of cost of goods manufactured for the period. It begins by showing the period's costs for direct materials, direct labor and overhead and then adjusts these numbers for the beginning and ending inventories of the goods in process to yield cost of goods manufactured.

Chapter Outline

I. **Introduction to Managerial Accounting**—also called *management accounting*

   A. Purpose of Managerial Accounting—to provide financial and nonfinancial information to managers and other *internal* decision makers of an organization.

      1. *Cost of products and services*—this information is very important to managers when making *planning* and *control* decisions. This includes predicting the future costs of producing the same or similar items. Predicted costs are used in:

         a. product pricing.

         b. profitability analysis.

         c. deciding whether to make or buy a product or component.

      2. *Planning* is the process of setting goals and making plans to achieve them.

         a. *Strategic plans* usually set the *long-term* direction of a firm (considers potential opportunities such as new products, new markets and capital investments).

         b. *Medium to short-term plans* often cover a one-year period which, when translated in monetary terms, is known as the *budget*.

      3. *Control* is the process of monitoring planning decisions and evaluating the organization's activities and employees.

         a. Control includes *measurement and evaluation* of actions, processes and outcomes.

         b. Control feedback allows managers to take timely corrective actions to avoid undesirable outcomes.

   B. Nature of Managerial Accounting—illustrated by comparing the seven key differences between *managerial to financial* accounting:

      1. Users and decision makers

         a. In financial—Investors, creditors and other users external to the organization.

         b. In managerial—Managers, employees and decision makers *internal* to the organization.

2. Purpose of information

    a. In financial—Assist external users in making investment, credit and other decisions.

    b. In managerial—Assist managers in making *planning*, and *control* decisions.

3. Flexibility of practice

    a. In financial—Structured and often controlled by GAAP.

    b. In managerial—Relatively *flexible* (no GAAP constraints).

4. Timeliness of information

    a. In financial—Often available only after the audit is complete.

    b. In managerial—Available quickly without the need to wait for an audit.

5. Time dimension

    a. In financial—Focus on historical information with some predictions.

    b. In managerial—Many *projections and estimates*; historical information also presented.

6. Focus of information

    a. In financial—Emphasis on whole organization.

    b. In managerial—Emphasis on organization's projects, processes and subdivisions.

7. Nature of information

    a. In financial—Monetary information.

    b. In managerial—Mostly monetary; but also nonmonetary information.

C. Managerial Decision Making—managerial accounting information is primarily used for internal decisions about a company's activities but financial and managerial accounting are not entirely separate since both can affect people's decisions and actions.

   D. Managerial Accounting in Business—the importance of managerial accounting analytical tools has increased as a result of the following changes in the business environment:

      1. Lean business model—goal is to *eliminate waste* while "satisfying the customer" and providing a "positive return to the company". This results in *customer orientation* and is affected by the expanded competitive boundaries of the *global economy.*

      2. Lean practices, that follow an underlying philosophy of *continuous improvement*, include:

         a. Total quality management (TQM)—focuses on quality improvement and applies this standard to all aspects of business activities.

         b. Just-in-time manufacturing (JIT)—a system that acquires inventory and produces only when needed (as order received—a *demand-pull* system).

   E. Fraud and Ethics in Managerial Accounting—important factors in running business operations. Fraud involves the deliberate misuse of one's job for personal gain, through the deliberate misuse of the employer's assets.

      1. All fraud:

         a. Is done to provide direct or indirect benefit to the employee.

         b. Violates the employee's duties to his employer.

         c. Costs the employer money.

         d. Is secret.

      2. Implications for managerial accounting—fraud increases business costs and management must therefore rely on and *internal control systems* that define policy and procedures to:

         a. Urge adherence to company policies.

         b. Promote efficient operations.

         c. Ensure reliable accounting.

         d. Protect assets.

      3. Ethics are beliefs that distinguish right from wrong. The IMA (Institute for Management Accountants) has issued a code of ethics to help accountants involved in solving ethical dilemmas and provide a "road map" for resolving ethical conflicts.

II.   **Managerial Cost Concepts**—Costs can be classified based on any one or combination of the five classifications listed below. To classify it is necessary to understand costs and operations.

   A. Behavior—At a basic level, a cost can be classified as *fixed or variable or mixed*.

      1. Fixed cost—cost does not change with changes in the volume of an activity (within a certain range of activity known as an activity's *relevant range*).

      2. Variable cost—cost *changes* in proportion to changes in the volume of an activity.

      3. Mixed—combination of fixed and variable costs.

   B. Traceability—cost is traced to a *cost object* (a product, process, department or customer to which costs are assigned). Cost is classified as either a *direct or indirect cost*. To classify must identify the cost object.

      1. Direct costs—those traceable to a single cost object.

      2. Indirect costs—those that cannot be traced to a single cost object.

   C. Controllability—costs can be defined as controllable or not controllable and this classification depends on employee's responsibilities *(hierarchical levels)*.

   D. Relevance—costs classified by identifying it as either a sunk cost or an out-of-pocket cost.

      1. Sunk cost—already incurred and cannot be avoided or changed. Irrelevant to future decisions.

      2. Out-of-pocket cost—requires a future outlay of cash and is relevant for decision making.

      3. Opportunity cost—is the potential benefit lost by choosing a specific action from two or more alternatives.

   E. Function—costs classified as capitalized inventory (product) or expensed (period) as incurred.

      1. Product costs—expenditures necessary and integral to finished products. Include direct materials, direct labor, and overhead costs (indirect manufacturing costs). First assigned to inventory (on balance sheet) and flow to income statement when become part of cost of goods sold.

      2. Period costs—expenditures identified more with a time period than finished products. Include selling and general administrative expenses. Reported on income statement as expenses.

Chapter Outline

III. **Reporting Manufacturing Activities**—financial statements for manufacturing companies have some unique features resulting from their activity of producing goods from materials and labor.

  A. Manufacturer's Balance Sheet—carry several unique assets and usually reports these three inventories:

    1. Raw Materials Inventory—goods a company acquires to use in making products. Two types are:

      a. *Direct materials*—physically become part of the product and are clearly identified with specific units or batches of product.

      b. *Indirect materials*—used in support of the production process. Generally, do not become a part of a product. Exception: materials that do become part of product, but have low or insignificant cost, and traceability to product is not economically sound (application of *materiality* principle).

    2. Goods in Process Inventory—(or work in process inventory) consists of products in the process of being manufactured but not yet complete.

    3. Finished Goods Inventory—consists of completed products ready for resale.

  B. Manufacturer's Income Statement—the main difference between a merchandiser's and manufacturer's income statement is in items that make-up cost of goods sold (CGS).

    1. Merchandiser computes CGS: Beginning *merchandise* inventory plus cost of goods *purchased* minus ending *merchandise* inventory.

    2. Manufacturer computes CGS: Beginning *finished goods* inventory plus cost of goods *manufactured* minus ending *finished goods* inventory.

    3. *Cost of goods manufactured* is the sum *of direct materials, direct labor*, and *overhead costs* incurred in producing the products.

      a. Direct Materials—tangible components of a finished product; separately and readily traced through the manufacturing process to finished goods.

      b. Direct Labor—wages and salaries for direct labor that are separately and readily traced through the manufacturing process to finished goods.

      c. Indirect Labor—wages and salaries for those workers' efforts not linked to specific units or batches of product. Part of overhead costs.

      d.   Factory Overhead—consists of all manufacturing costs that are not direct materials or direct labor; costs that cannot be separately or readily traced to finished goods. Include indirect materials and indirect labor and other costs associated with the factory.

      e.   Direct materials and direct labor are also called *prime costs* (expenditures directly associated with the manufacturing of finished goods).

Direct labor costs and overhead costs are also called *conversion costs* (expenditures incurred in the process of converting raw materials to finished goods).

  C. Flow of Manufacturing Activities—the three manufacturing activities are:

    1. Materials Activities—manufacturers start a period with a beginning raw materials inventory and then acquire additional raw materials. When these purchases are added to beginning inventory, we get the total raw materials available for use in production. These raw materials are then either used in production during the period or remain on hand at the end of the period for use in future periods.

    2. Production Activities—Four factors come together in production:

      a.   Beginning goods in process inventory—consists of partly produced goods from the previous period.

      b.   Direct materials used—traceable materials added during the period.

      c.   Direct labor used—traceable labor added during the period.

      d.   Overhead used—nontraceable manufacturing costs added during the period.

Note: The production activity results in goods either finished or unfinished. Both groups represent *product costs*. The cost of finished goods make up the cost of goods manufactured for the year. Unfinished goods are identified as ending goods in process inventory.

    3. Sales Activities—Newly completed units are combined with beginning finished goods inventory to make up total finished goods available for sale. The cost of those goods that are sold during the year is reported on the income statement.

D. Manufacturing Statement (also called the schedule of manufacturing activities or the schedule of cost of goods manufactured)—reports costs of both materials and production activities. Contains information used by management for planning and control. It is not a general purpose financial statement. It is divided into four parts:

1. Direct material used—determined by adding the beginning raw materials inventory to this period's materials purchases to obtain total raw materials available for use during year and then subtracting ending raw materials inventory which was determined from a physical count.

2. Direct labor incurred—includes payroll taxes and fringe benefits and is taken directly from the direct labor account balance.

3. Overhead costs—generally lists each important factory overhead item along with its cost. If a summary number is used, a separate detailed schedule is usually prepared.

4. Computation of *cost of goods manufactured*—as follows:

   a. Total manufacturing costs (Total of 1,2 and 3 above) are added to beginning goods in process inventory to get total cost of goods in process inventory for the year.

   b. Compute *cost of goods manufactured (or completed)* for year by subtracting the cost of ending goods in process inventory (determined separately) from the total cost of goods in process for the year.

IV. **Decision Analysis—Cycle time and Cycle Efficiency**

A. Cycle time is a metric used to evaluate a company's manufacturing efficiency.

B. Cycle Time = Process time + Inspection time + Move time + Wait time.

C. Process time is considered a *value-added time* because it is the only activity in cycle time that adds value to the product from the customer's perspective.

D. Inspection time, move time, and wait time are *non-value added time*.

E. Cycle efficiency is the ratio of value-added time to total cycle time and is computed by dividing value-added time by cycle time.

Problem I

The following statements are either true or false. Place a (T) in the parentheses before each true statement and an (F) before each false statement.

1. ( ) Indirect materials are used in the manufacturing process but are not physically included in the finished product.

2. ( ) An example of a direct labor cost is the salary paid to an employee who inspects products for defects.

3. ( ) All manufacturing costs other than direct materials and direct labor costs are considered to be factory overhead.

4. ( ) Selling and administrative expenses are included among factory overhead costs because they are not manufacturing costs.

5. ( ) Product costs include the costs of direct materials and direct labor only; factory overhead is a period cost.

6. ( ) When an attitude of customer orientation is in place, a company attempts to orient its customers to accept products that the company produces, even if they do not meet the customer's needs.

7. ( ) An effective program of total quality management increases the quality of the products and services delivered to customers.

8. ( ) Under just-in-time manufacturing, a company attempts to accumulate large inventories of materials, in-process units, and finished goods to ensure being able to get products to customers just as soon as they are ordered.

9. ( ) When applying the theory of constraints, a company's managers continuously look for ways to constrain employees from activities that are inconsistent with a rigid plan set up long in advance.

10. ( ) The costs of ending raw materials and goods in process inventories are never listed separately on the balance sheet; instead, they are always combined with the costs of the finished goods inventory.

11. ( ) Manufacturing activities include materials, production and sales activities.

Problem II

You are given several words, phrases or numbers to choose from in completing each of the following statements or in answering the following questions. In each case select the one that best completes the statement or answers the question and place its letter in the answer space provided.

_____ 1. Tricorp Manufacturing Company had a $2,700 beginning inventory of raw materials. The ending balance of the Raw Materials Purchases account was $120,000, and a count of the ending inventory revealed that the cost of the materials on hand was $5,000. Direct labor cost during the period was $250,000 and total factory overhead cost was $135,000. The beginning goods in process inventory was $23,000, and the ending amount was $19,000. What was the cost of goods manufactured for the period?

    a. $371,700.

    b. $502,700.

    c. $503,300.

    d. $506,700.

    e. $509,000.

_____ 2. The production management concept that attempts to minimize inventories of raw materials, components, goods in process, and finished goods is called:

    a. Customer orientation.

    b. Total Quality Management.

    c. Just-in-time manufacturing.

    d. Theory of constraints.

    e. Continuous improvement.

_____ 3. The production management concept that requires all managers and employees at all stages of operations to strive toward higher standards and reduced number of defective units is called:

    a. Customer orientation.

    b. Total Quality Management.

    c. Just-in-time manufacturing.

    d. Theory of constraints.

    e. Continuous improvement.

_____ 4. The notion that employees understand the changing needs and wants of their customers and align their management and operating practices accordingly is called:

    a. Customer orientation.

    b. Total Quality Management.

    c. Just-in-time manufacturing.

    d. Theory of constraints.

    e. Continuous improvement.

Problem III

Many of the important ideas and concepts discussed in Chapter 18 are reflected in the following list of key terms. Test your understanding of these terms by matching the appropriate definitions with the terms. Record the number identifying the most appropriate definition in the blank space next to each term.

_____ Continuous improvement   _____ Indirect materials

_____ Control   _____ Inspection time

_____ Controllable or not controllable cost   _____ Just-in-time (JIT) manufacturing

_____ Conversion costs   _____ Lean business model

_____ Cost object   _____ Managerial accounting

_____ Customer orientation   _____ Manufacturing statement

_____ Cycle efficiency (CE)   _____ Move time

_____ Cycle time (CT)   _____ Non-value-added time

_____ Direct cost   _____ Opportunity costs

_____ Direct labor   _____ Out-of-pocket costs

_____ Direct labor costs   _____ Period costs

_____ Direct materials   _____ Planning

_____ Direct materials costs   _____ Prime costs

_____ Factory overhead   _____ Product costs

_____ Factory overhead costs   _____ Raw materials inventory

_____ Finished goods inventory   _____ Sunk costs

_____ Fixed costs   _____ Total quality management (TQM)

_____ Goods in process inventory   _____ Value-added time

_____ Indirect costs   _____ Variable costs

_____ Indirect labor   _____ Wait time

_____ Indirect labor costs

1. Costs that are capitalized as inventory which are necessary and integral to finished products. They include direct materials, direct labor and factory overhead.

2. Products that have completed the manufacturing process and are ready for sale.

3. Materials used in support of the production process but not clearly identified with units or batches of product.

4. Concept requiring that every manager and employee continually look for ways to improve operations.

5. Factory activities supporting the manufacturing process and are not direct material or direct labor.

6. Products in the process of being manufactured but not yet complete; also called _work in process inventory_.

7. Efforts of manufacturing employees who do not work specifically on converting direct materials into finished products and who are not clearly identified with specific units or batches of product.

8. Raw materials that physically become part of the product and is clearly identified with specific units or batches of product.

9. The total of process time, inspection time, move time and wait time.

10. Goods a company acquires to use to make products.

11. Expenditures incurred in the process of converting raw materials to finished goods—direct labor costs and factory overhead costs.

12. Expenditures identified more with a time period than with finished products costs; includes selling and general administrative expenses.

13. Efforts of employees who physically convert raw materials into finished products.

14. Product, process, department, or customer to which costs are assigned.

15. The ratio of value-added time to total cycle time.

16. Process of monitoring planning decisions and evaluating the organization's activities and employees.

17. Cost depending on a manager's responsibilities and whether or not he/she is in position to make decisions that impact on this cost.

18. Company's managers and employees are in tune with the changing wants and needs of consumers.

19. Concept calling for all managers and employees at all stages of operations to strive toward higher standards and a reduced number of defects.

20. All manufacturing costs that are not direct materials or direct labor.

21. Costs incurred for the benefit of one specific cost object.

22. Costs incurred for the benefit of more than one cost object.

23. Practice of eliminating waste while meeting customer needs and yielding positive company returns.

24. Potential benefit lost by choosing a specific action from two or more alternative choices.

25. Expenditures for direct materials that are separately and readily traced through the manufacturing process to finished goods.

26. Cost that does not change with changes in the volume of activity.

27. Process to acquiring or producing inventory only when needed.

28. Cost already incurred and cannot be avoided or changed.

29. Wages and salaries for direct labor that are separately and readily traced through the manufacturing process to finished goods.

30. Expenditures directly identified with the manufacturing of finished goods—include direct material costs and direct labor costs.

31. Process of setting goals and preparing to achieve them.

32. Area of accounting that serves the decision making needs of internal users (also called *management accounting*).

33. Report that summarizes the types and amounts of costs incurred in a company's manufacturing process for a period; also called a *cost of goods manufacturing statement*.

34. Cost requiring a future outlay of cash relevant to current and future decisions.

35. Cost that change in proportion to changes in the activity volume.

36. Time spent moving raw materials from storage to production and goods in process from factory location to another factory location.

37. Manufacturing workers' efforts not linked to specific units or batches of the product.

38. Time activities other than process time, which are identified as inspection time, move time and wait time.

39. Time that an order or job sits with no production applied to it: this can be due to order delays, bottlenecks in production, and poor scheduling.

40. Time spent inspecting raw materials when received, goods in process while in production and finished goods prior to shipment.

41. Time spent that adds value to the product from the customer's perspective: process time is the only time element that fits this description.

Problem IV

Complete the following by filling in the blanks.

1. When a company is managed under the concept of _____ _____, all managers and employees seek to uncover_____ in business activity.

2. A company that operates by manufacturing products only when they are needed and thereby keeping a low inventory is said to be operating with a _____ system.

3. Expenditures are necessary and integral to finished products are called _____ costs. These costs are _____as inventory.

4. Expenditures identified more with a time period than finished products are called _____ costs. These costs are _____on the income statement.

5. Increased emphasis on customers as the most important part of business that results in increased focus on quality, flexibility and on-time delivery is called _____.

6. A cost that is already incurred and cannot be avoided or changed is called a _____ cost, where as a cost that requires a future outlay of cash is called an _____ cost.

7. The potential benefit lost by taking a specific action from two or more alternative choices is called an _____ cost.

8. The manufacturer's cost of goods manufactured is the sum of _____, _____, and _____ costs incurred in producing the product.

9. The inventory accounts found on a manufacturer's balance sheet include _____ _____ and _____.

10. The cost of goods sold for a manufacturer is computed as _____ plus _____ less _____.

11. When costs are classified based on behavior, costs that remains the same irrespective of the volume of an activity are called _____costs, whereas costs that change in proportion to changes in the volume of an activity are called _____costs.

12. A metric used to evaluate a company's manufacturing efficiency is called _____ _____ and is calculated by adding _____time plus _____ time plus _____ time plus_____ time.

13. Process time is considered _____time and inspection time is considered _____ time.

14. The ratio of value-added time to total cycle time, computed by dividing value-added time by cycle time is called_____.

15. Manufacturing activities are described in a special financial report called a _____
_____ .

16. Manufacturing activities include _____,_____ , and
_____activities.

Problem V

Calculate cost of goods sold using the following information:

Finished goods inventory, December 31, 2011 ....$421,000

Goods in process inventory, December 31, 2011.........82,500

Goods in process inventory, December 31, 2012.........74,200

Cost of goods manufactured, 2012...........................850,250

Finished goods inventory, December 31, 2012 395,200

Problem VI

The following costs are incurred by Hang-Ten Company, a company that manufactures surfboards. Classify each cost as either a product or a period cost. If a product cost, using the product as the cost object, identify it as a direct or indirect cost. Use an X to mark your identification column.

	Product Cost		Period Cost
	Direct Cost	Indirect Cost	
Fiberglass			
State and federal income taxes			
Payroll taxes for production supervisor			
Amortization of patents on factory machine			
Glue			
Accident insurance on factory workers			
Wages to assembly workers			
Factory utilities			
Stains and paint			
Small tools used			
Bad debts expense			
Emblems			
Depreciation of factory building			
Advertising			
Office supplies used			

Solutions for Chapter 18

Problem I

1.	T	7.	T
2.	F	8.	F
3.	T	9.	F
4.	F	10.	F
5.	F	11.	T
6.	F		

Problem II

1.	D
2.	C
3.	B
4.	A

Problem III

Problem IV

1. Total Quality Management; waste

2. just-in-time

3. product, capitalized

4. period, expensed

5. customer orientation

6. sunk, out-of-pocket

7. opportunity

8. raw materials used, direct labor incurred and factory overhead

9. raw materials, goods-in-process, and finished goods

10. beginning finished goods inventory, cost of goods manufactured, ending finished goods inventory

11. fixed, variable

12. cycle time, process, inspection, move, wait

13. value-added, non-value added

14. cycle efficiency

15. manufacturing statement

16. materials, production, sales

Problem V

Finished goods inventory, December 31, 2011 .... $ 421,000

Plus cost of goods manufactured .... __850,250__

Cost of goods available for sale 1,271,250

Less finished goods inventory, December 31, 2012......... __395,200__

Cost of goods sold .... $ 876,050

Problem VI

	Product Cost		Period Cost
	Direct Cost	**Indirect Cost**	
Fiberglass	X		
State and federal income taxes			X
Payroll taxes for production supervisor		X	
Amortization of patents on factory machine		X	
Glue		X	
Accident insurance on factory workers		X	
Wages to assembly workers	X		
Factory utilities		X	
Stains and paint		X	
Small tools used		X	
Bad debts expense			X
Emblems	X		
Depreciation of factory building		X	
Advertising			X
Office supplies used			X

Learning Objective C1:

Describe important features of job order production.

Summary

Certain companies called *job order manufacturers* produce custom-made products for customers. These customized or special products are produced in response to a customer's orders. A job order manufacturer produces products that usually are different and, typically, produced in low volumes. The production systems of job order companies are flexible, and are not highly standardized.

Learning Objective C2:

Explain job cost sheets and how they are used in job order cost accounting.

Summary

In a job order cost accounting system, the costs of producing each job are accumulated on a separate job cost sheet. Costs of direct materials, direct labor, and manufacturing overhead are accumulated separately on the job cost sheet and then added to determine the total cost of a job. Job cost sheets for jobs in process, finished jobs, and jobs that are sold make up subsidiary records controlled by general ledger accounts.

Learning Objective A1:

Apply job order costing in pricing services.

Summary

Job order costing can usefully be applied to a service setting. The resulting job cost estimate can then be used to help determine a price for services.

Learning Objective P1:

Describe and record the flow of materials costs in job order cost accounting.

Summary

Costs of materials flow from receiving reports to materials ledger cards and then to either job cost sheets or the Indirect Materials account in the factory overhead ledger.

Learning Objective P2:

Describe and record the flow of labor costs in job order cost accounting.

Summary

Costs of labor flow from clock cards to the Factory Payroll account and then to either job cost sheets or the Indirect Labor account in the factory overhead ledger.

Learning Objective P3:

Describe and record the flow of overhead costs in job order cost accounting.

Summary

Overhead costs are accumulated in the Factory Overhead account that controls the subsidiary factory overhead ledger. Then, using a predetermined overhead application rate, overhead costs are charged to jobs.

Learning Objective P4:

Determine adjustments for overapplied and underapplied factory overhead.

Summary

At the end of each period, the Factory Overhead account usually has a residual debit (underapplied overhead) or credit (overapplied overhead) balance. If the balance is not material, it is transferred to Cost of Goods Sold, but if it is material, it is allocated to Goods in Process Inventory, Finished Goods Inventory, and Cost of Goods Sold.

I. **Job Order Cost Accounting**
    A. Cost accounting system
        1. Records manufacturing activities using a *perpetual* inventory system.
        2. Continuously updates records for costs of materials, goods in process, and finished goods inventories.
        3. Provides timely information about inventories, and manufacturing costs per unit of product.
        4. Two basic types of cost accounting systems are *job order* cost accounting and *process* cost accounting.
    B. Job Order Production—producing products individually designed to meet the needs of a specific customer (special orders).
        1. The production activities for a customized product is called a *job*.
        2. A *job lot* involves producing more than one unit of a unique product.
    C. Events in Job Order Costing
        1. Jobs can be initiated by a customer order or management decision to begin work on job before order (*jobs on speculation*).
        2. Step 1: Predict the cost to complete the job. Cost depends on the product design prepared by either the customer or the producer.
        3. Step 2: Negotiate price and decide whether to pursue the job. Price is determined on a *cost-plus basis* or producer evaluates market price and determines a *target cost* to that would allow a reasonable profit while meeting competitive market price.
        4. Step 3: Schedule production of the job. This must meet customer's needs and fit within company's production constraints.
        5. Raw materials are ordered.
        6. Production occurs as materials and labor are applied to the job.
        7. Finished job cost sheets—moved from jobs in process file to finished jobs file (subsidiary ledger controlled by Finished Goods Inventory) awaiting delivery to customers.
        8. As finished jobs are sold, file moves to permanent file supporting the cost of goods sold

D. Job Cost Sheet—separate record maintained for each job used to record costs as incurred

1. Classifies costs as direct materials, direct labor, or overhead.

2. Used by managers to monitor costs incurred to date and to predict and control costs to complete each job.

3. Accumulated job costs are kept in the goods in process inventory while goods are being produced.

4. Job cost sheets filed for all of the jobs in process make up a subsidiary ledger controlled by the Goods in Process Inventory account in the general ledger.

II. **Job Order Cost Flows and Reports**

A. Cost Flows and Documents—the three cost components and documents used to account for them are:

1. Materials Cost Flows and Documents

a. Receiving report—*Source document* used to record the quantity and cost of items received. Materials purchased are used as a debit to Raw Materials Inventory and a credit to Accounts Payable.

b. Materials ledger cards (or files)—perpetual records that are updated each time units are purchased and each time units are issued for use in production. Serves as the subsidiary ledger for the Raw Materials Inventory account.

c. Materials Requisition—document identifying the type and quantity of material needed in production. Job number is also identified on direct materials requisitions.

d. Job Cost Sheet—accumulates the cost of direct materials (from materials ledger card) as they are placed into production on a job. Recorded as a debit to Goods in Process Inventory and a credit to Raw Materials Inventory.

e. Indirect materials ledger cards in factory overhead ledger—accumulates indirect material costs as they are placed into production. This subsidiary ledger is controlled by the Factory Overhead account in the general ledger. Use of indirect materials is recorded as a debit to Factory overhead and a credit to Raw Materials Inventory.

2. Labor Cost Flows and Documents

   a. Clock cards—used by employees to record hours worked. Used to determine total labor costs for pay period. This amount is debited to Factory Payroll account and credited to Cash.

   b. Time tickets—indicate how much time employees spent on each job. Used to assign (direct) labor costs to specific jobs and (indirect) to overhead. Direct labor costs are debited to Goods in Process Inventory and credited to Factory Payroll.

   c. Job Cost Sheets—accumulates the cost of direct labor (from time tickets and related entry) as these costs are incurred.

   d. Indirect labor card in Factory Overhead Ledger—accumulates indirect labor costs (from time tickets and related entry). Entry to record indirect labor costs debits Factory Overhead and credits Factory Payroll.

3. Overhead Cost Flows and Documents

   a. Materials requisitions forms for indirect materials.

   b. Time tickets for indirect labor.

   c. Other sources include vouchers authorizing payments for items such as supplies or utilities and adjusting entries for costs such as depreciation.

   d. Factory Overhead Ledger—contains a separate account for each overhead cost. It is controlled by the Factory Overhead account in the General Ledger which accumulates costs until they are allocated to specific jobs.

   e. Job Cost Sheets—shows factory overhead costs that have been applied using the *predetermined overhead rate* (Estimated overhead costs divided by estimated factor costs).

   f. Recording Overhead Costs—debited Factory Overhead; account credited varies by overhead element and action at point the cost is incurred.

   g. Allocating Overhead Costs—debited to Goods in Process Inventory and credited to Factory Overhead as allocated to specific jobs.

    4.   Summary of Cost Flows—Summary journal entries are used to record cost flows as follows:

      a.   Into (debit) Raw Materials Inventory as acquired.

      b.   From (credit) Raw Materials Inventory to (debit) Goods In Process Inventory (direct materials) and (debit) Factory Overhead (indirect materials) as good are requisitioned. Direct material costs also accumulated on Job Cost Sheets.

      c.   Into (debit) Factory Payroll as labor is incurred.

      d.   From (credit) Factory Payroll to (debit) Goods In Process Inventory (direct labor) and (debit) Factory Overhead (indirect labor) as labor costs are analyzed. Direct labor costs also accumulated on Job Cost Sheets.

      e.   Into (debit) Factory Overhead as other overhead costs are incurred.

      f.   From (credit) Factory Overhead and into (debit) Goods In Process as overhead costs are applied using overhead rate.

      g.   From (credit) Goods In Process Inventory to (debit) Finished Goods Inventory as jobs are completed. Full cost from Job Cost Sheets.

      h.   From (credit) Finished Goods Inventory to (debit) Cost of Goods Sold as goods are sold.

      i.   Any under or over applied factory overhead cost is accounted for in an adjustment.

III.   **Adjusting Factory Overhead**—overhead applied rarely equals that incurred because a predetermined overhead rate is used in applying factory overhead costs to jobs.

    A. Factory Overhead T-Account

      1.   The debit side shows the actual amount of factory overhead incurred during the period based on bills received.

      2.   The credit side shows the amount applied during the period that was an estimate based on the predetermined overhead rate.

      3.   A debit balance in the FOH account indicated less was applied than incurred; an underapplied FOH amount.

      4.   A credit balance in the FOH account indicates more was applied than incurred; an overapplied FOH amount.

    B. Underapplied and Overapplied Overhead

      1.   Factory Overhead debit balance (underapplied amount) is credited (closed) and debited (charged) to Cost of Goods Sold.

      2.   Factory Overhead credit balance (overapplied amount) is debited (closed) and credited to Cost of Goods Sold.

IV. **Decision Analysis—Pricing for Services**

   A. Job order costing concepts and procedures are applicable to a service setting.

   B. Procedure to determine:

     1. Determine direct labor costs.

     2. Determine the overhead based on predetermined rate(s).

     3. Combine labor and overhead to obtain cost of job.
Note: service firms do not have material costs or inventory.

Tracing Product Costs
Through a Cost Accounting System

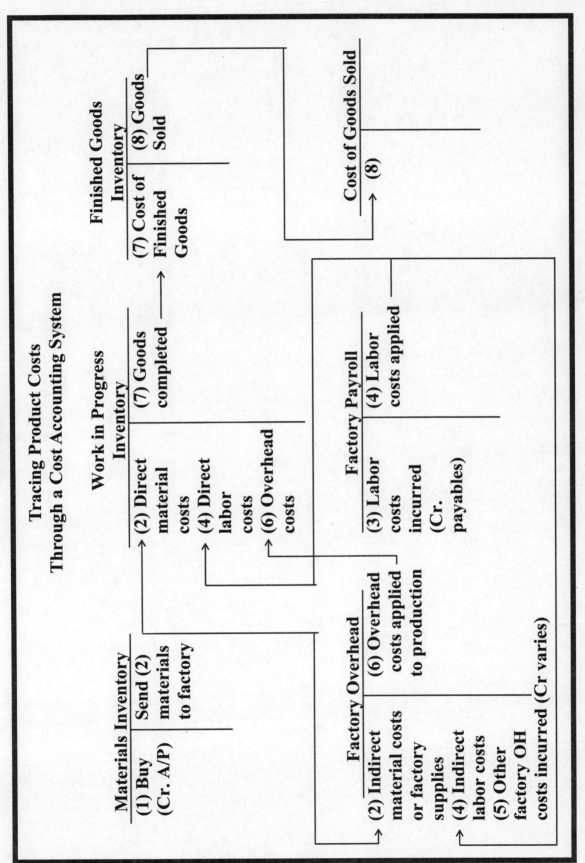

Job Cost Sheet

Customer __Build We Must, Inc.__   Job No. ____114____

Product __Bracket-H3__   Date Promised _10/1/xx_____

Quantity __200__   Dates: Started _9/1/xx_ Completed _9/20/xx____

Direct Material		Direct Labor			Cost Summary	
Mat'l. Req'n. No.	Amount	Payroll Summary Dated	Dept.	Amount	Direct Material	$ 900.00
					Direct Labor	600.00
667	$ 340.00	9/2	A	$ 70.00		
673	180.00	9/9	A	240.00	Factory Overhead	
691	200.00	9/16	B	190.00	(applied at):	
623	180.00	9/23	B	100.00		
					150% of direct labor cost	900.00
Totals	$ 900.00			$ 600.00	Total Cost	$2,400.00
					Units Finished	200
					Unit Cost	$ 12.00

Problem I

The following statements are either true or false. Place a (T) in the parentheses before each true statement and an (F) before each false statement.

1. ( ) A general accounting system records production activities using perpetual inventory.

2. ( ) The collection of job cost sheets for jobs in production serves as a subsidiary ledger for the finished goods inventory account.

3. ( ) Job costing concepts and procedures can be applied in a service business setting.

4. ( ) A job-order cost accounting system uses periodic inventory records.

5. ( ) A job cost sheet records the direct materials, direct labor, and overhead costs assigned to a specific job.

6. ( ) A materials requisition for direct materials causes entries to be recorded in a materials ledger card and a job-cost sheet.

7. ( ) Clock cards cause entries to be recorded on job cost sheets for direct labor costs.

8. ( ) The transfer of completed jobs to the finished goods inventory is recorded with a debit to the Goods in Process Inventory account and a credit to the Finished Goods Inventory account.

9. ( ) If the predetermined application rate caused too much overhead cost to be assigned to jobs during the year, the company faces a condition of overapplied overhead.

Problem II

You are given several words, phrases or numbers to choose from in completing each of the following statements or in answering the following questions. In each case select the one that best completes the statement or answers the question and place its letter in the answer space provided.

_____ 1. Which of the following source documents causes entries to be recorded on a job cost sheet?

    a. Materials ledger cards.

    b. Materials requisitions.

    c. Clock cards.

    d. Time tickets.

    e. Both materials requisitions and time tickets.

_____ 2. Which of the following journal entries would properly record the allocation of overhead costs to a specific job?

    a. Debit Factory Overhead; Credit Goods in Process Inventory.

    b. Debit Factory Overhead; Credit Finished Goods Inventory.

    c. Debit Goods in Process Inventory; Credit Factory Overhead.

    d. Debit Finished Goods Inventory; Credit Factory Overhead.

    e. None of the above.

_____ 3. Assume that the Merlin Company applies overhead to jobs by using a predetermined overhead application rate. At the end of the reporting period, the Factory Overhead account had a credit balance of $1,400, which the manager considers to be material. Overhead had been charged to jobs during the period as follows:

Jobs still in process	$ 1,800
Jobs finished but unsold	3,600
Jobs finished and sold	6,600
Total overhead applied to jobs	$12,000

Which of the following items would be included in the entry to allocate the overapplied or underapplied overhead?

a. Goods in Process—$1,800 debit.

b. Finished Goods—$420 debit.

c. Cost of Goods Sold—$6,600 credit.

d. Factory Overhead—$1,400 credit.

e. Goods in Process—$210 credit.

Problem III

Many of the important ideas and concepts discussed in Chapter 19 are reflected in the following list of key terms. Test your understanding of these terms by matching the appropriate definitions with the terms. Record the number identifying the most appropriate definition in the blank space next to each term.

_____ Clock card	_____ Job order cost accounting system
_____ Cost accounting system	_____ Job order manufacturing
_____ Finished Goods Inventory	_____ Materials ledger card
_____ General accounting system	_____ Materials requisition
_____ Goods In Process Inventory	_____ Overapplied overhead
_____ Job	_____ Predetermined overhead rate
_____ Job cost sheet	_____ Time ticket
_____ Job lot	_____ Underapplied overhead

1. Rate established prior to the beginning of a period that relates estimated overhead to another variable, such as estimated direct labor, and is used to assign overhead cost to jobs.

2. Products in the process of being manufactured but not yet complete.

3. Production of a customized product or service.

4. Perpetual record updated each time units are purchased and issued for production use.

5. Amount by which overhead incurred in a period exceeds the overhead applied to jobs with the predetermined overhead allocation rate.

6. Source document used to report how much time an employee spent working on a job or on overhead activities, and then to determine the amount of direct labor to charge to the job or to determine the amount of indirect labor to charge to overhead.

7. Production of special-order products; also called *customized production*.

8. Completed products ready to be sold by the manufacturer.

9. Separate record maintained for each job.

10. Source document that production managers use to request materials for production and that is used to assign materials costs to specific jobs or overhead.

11. A source document used to record the number of hours an employee works and to determine the total labor cost for each pay period.

12. Amount by which the overhead applied to jobs during a period with the predetermined overhead application rate exceeds the overhead incurred during the period.

13. Accounting system for manufacturing activities based on the *periodic* inventory system.

14. Production of more than one unit of a customized product or service.

15. Cost accounting system to determine the cost of producing each job or job lot.

16. Accounting system for production activities based on the *perpetual* inventory system.

Problem IV

Complete the following by filling in the blanks.

1. In a _____ accounting system, costs are accumulated by jobs, using a separate subsidiary account called a _____.

2. When raw materials are needed on a job, a _____ is prepared and signed by a _____ manager, and is given to the _____ manager.

3. When direct _____ are used in production, the materials requisition causes a _____ to be recorded in the Goods in Process Inventory account and a _____ be recorded in the Raw Materials Inventory account.

4. Materials requisitions for indirect materials cause debits to be recorded in the _____ _____ account.

5. When employees report for work and leave to go home, they complete a document called a _____ that is used to determine total labor cost. When they work on specific jobs, they complete a document called a _____ that is used to determine the direct labor cost to assign to those jobs.

6. When overhead is applied to jobs on the basis of direct labor cost, a _____ _____ rate is established by predicting the amounts of _____ and _____ for the upcoming period, and then dividing the _____ cost by the _____ cost.

7. The completion of a job is recorded in the journal with a debit to the _____ _____ account and a credit to the _____ _____ account.

8. If the residual ending balance of the Factory Overhead account is material, it is disposed of by allocating it among the costs of the _____ inventory, the _____ inventory, and _____. However, if the amount is immaterial, it may be assigned to _____.

Problem V

The Haywire Manufacturing Company produces special order products and uses a job order cost accounting system. The system provided the following information:

	March 31	April 30
Inventories:		
Raw materials...	$40,000	$ 45,000
Goods in process..	15,000	13,000
Finished goods	6,000	9,500
Information-about April activities		
Raw materials purchases..		$120,000
Factory payroll..		200,000
Factory overhead...		
Indirect materials		17,000
Indirect labor..		40,000
Other overhead costs..		135,000
Sales...		700,000
Predetermined overhead application rate based on direct labor cost..		120.0%

Calculate the following amounts for the month of April:

a. Cost of direct materials used.

b. Cost of direct labor used.

c. Cost of goods manufactured.

d. Cost of goods sold.

e. Gross profit.

Problem VI

Goode Company uses the proportional relationship between factory overhead and direct labor costs to assign factory overhead to inventories of goods in process and finished goods. The company incurred the following costs during the current year:

Direct materials used....................................	$500,000
Direct labor costs	200,000
Factory overhead costs................................	360,000

a. Determine the company's overhead rate.

b. Under the assumption that the company's $50,000 goods in process inventory had $8,000 of direct labor costs, determine the inventory's direct material costs.

c. Under the assumption that the company's $100,000 finished goods inventory had $44,000 of direct material costs, determine the inventory's direct labor cost and its factory overhead costs.

Solutions for Chapter 19

Problem I

1.	F	6.	T
2.	F	7.	F
3.	T	8.	F
4.	F	9.	T
5.	T		

Problem II

1.	E
2.	C
3.	E

Problem III

Clock card	11
Cost accounting system	16
Finished Goods Inventory	8
General accounting system	13
Goods in Process Inventory	2
Job	3
Job cost sheet	9
Job lot	14

Job order cost accounting system	15
Job order manufacturing	7
Materials ledger card	4
Materials requisition	10
Overapplied overhead	12
Predetermined overhead rate	1
Time ticket	6
Underapplied overhead	5

Problem IV

1. job order cost; job cost sheet

2. materials requisition; production; materials

3. materials; debit; credit

4. Factory Overhead

5. clock card; time ticket

6. predetermined overhead application; overhead cost; direct labor cost; overhead; direct labor.

7. Finished Goods Inventory; Goods in Process Inventory

8. goods in process; finished goods; cost of goods sold; cost of goods sold

Problem V

a. Cost of direct materials used:

Beginning raw materials inventory	$ 40,000
Plus purchases	120,000
Less indirect materials	(17,000)
Less ending raw materials inventory	(45,000)
Cost of direct materials used	$ 98,000

b. Cost of direct labor used

Total factory payroll	$ 200,000
Less indirect labor	(40,000)
Cost of direct labor used	$ 160,000

c. Cost of goods manufactured

Beginning goods in process inventory	$ 15,000
Plus direct materials	98,000
Plus direct labor	160,000
Plus overhead applied (120%)	192,000
Total cost of goods in process	$ 465,000
Less ending goods in process inventory	(13,000)
Cost of goods manufactured	$ 452,000

d. Cost of goods sold:

Beginning finished goods inventory	$ 6,000
Plus cost of goods manufactured	452,000
Less ending finished goods inventory	(9,500)
Cost of goods sold	$ 448,500

e. Gross profit

Sales	$ 700,000
Cost of goods sold	(448,500)
Gross profit	$ 251,500

Problem VI

a. Overhead rate   = Total overhead cost / Total direct labor cost
                    = $360,000 / $200,000 = 180%

b. The solution is based on the facts that the total cost is the sum of the direct materials, labor, and overhead costs, and that the overhead is 180% of the direct labor cost.

Total cost of goods in process inventory		$50,000
Deduct: Direct labor..	$8,000	
Factory overhead ($8,000 x 180%)..	14,400	22,400
Direct materials...		$27,600

c. The solution is based on the facts that the total cost is the sum of the direct materials, labor, and overhead costs, and that the overhead is 180% of the direct labor cost.

Total cost of finished goods inventory...	$100,000
Deduct: Direct materials	44.000
Direct labor and factory overhead costs..	$ 56,000

We also know that the total of the direct labor and the factory overhead equals 280% of the direct labor cost because the factory overhead equals 180% of the direct labor cost.

Direct labor costs ($56,000/280%)	$ 20,000
Factory overhead costs ($20,000) x 180%)	36,000
Direct labor and factory overhead costs..	$ 56,000

Learning Objective C1:

Explain process operations and the way they differ from job order operations.

Summary

Process operations produce large quantities of similar products or services by passing them through a series of processes, or steps, in production. Like job order operations, they combine direct materials, direct labor, and overhead in the operations. Unlike job order operations that assign the responsibility for each job to a manager, process operations assign the responsibility for each *process* to a manager.

Learning Objective C2:

Define and compute equivalent units and explain their use in process cost accounting.

Summary

Equivalent units of production measure the activity of a process as the number of units that would be completed in a period if all effort had been applied to units that were started and finished. This measure of production activity is used to compute the cost per equivalent unit and to assign costs to finished goods and goods in process inventory.

To compute equivalent units, determine the number of units that would have been finished if all materials (or labor or overhead) had been used to produce units that were started and completed during the period. The costs incurred by a process are divided by its equivalent units to yield cost per unit.

Learning Objective C3:

Define and prepare a process cost summary and describe its purposes.

Summary

A process cost summary reports on the activities of a production process or department for a period. It describes the costs charged to the department, the equivalent units of production for the department, and the costs assigned to the output. The report aims to: (1) help managers control their departments, (2) help factory managers evaluate department managers' performances, and (3) provide cost information for financial statements.

A process cost summary includes the physical flow of units, equivalent units of production, costs per equivalent unit, and cost reconciliation. It reports the units and costs to account for during the period and how they were accounted for during the period. In terms of units, the summary includes the beginning goods in process inventory and the units started during the month. These units are accounted for in terms of the goods completed and transferred out, and the ending goods in process inventory. With respect to costs, the summary includes materials, labor, and overhead costs assigned to the process during the period. It shows how these costs are assigned to goods completed and transferred out, and to ending goods in process inventory.

Learning Objective C4:

Appendix 20A—Explain and illustrate the accounting for production activity using FIFO.

Summary

The FIFO method for process costing is applied and illustrated to (1) report the physical flow of units, (2) compute the equivalent units of production, (3) compute the cost per equivalent units of production, and (4) assign and reconcile costs.

Learning Objective A1:

Compare process cost accounting and job order cost accounting.

Summary

Process and job order manufacturing operations are similar in that both combine materials, labor, and factory overhead to produce products or services. They differ in the way they are organized and managed. In job order operations, the job order cost accounting system assigns materials, labor, and overhead to specific jobs. In process operations, the process cost accounting system assigns materials, labor, and overhead to specific processes. The total costs associated with each process are then divided by the number of units passing through that process to get cost per equivalent unit. The costs per equivalent unit for all processes are added to determine the total cost per unit of a product or service.

Learning Objective A2:

Explain and illustrate a hybrid costing system.

Summary

A hybrid costing system contains features of both job order and process costing systems. Generally, certain direct materials are accounted for by individual products as in a job order costing, but direct labor and overhead costs are accounted for similar to process costing.

Learning Objective P1:

Record the flow of direct materials costs in process cost accounting.

Summary

Materials purchased are debited to a Raw Materials Inventory account. As direct materials are issued to processes, they are separately accumulated in a Goods in Process Inventory account for that process.

Learning Objective P2:

Record the flow of direct labor costs in process cost accounting.

Summary

Direct labor costs are initially debited to the Factory Payroll account. The total amount in it is then assigned to the Goods in Process Inventory account pertaining to each process.

Learning Objective P3:

Record the flow of factory overhead costs in process cost accounting.

Summary

The different factory overhead items are first accumulated in the Factory Overhead account and are then allocated, using a predetermined overhead rate, to the different processes. The allocated amount is debited to the Goods in Process Inventory account pertaining to each process.

Learning Objective P4:

Record the transfer of completed goods to Finished Goods Inventory and Cost of Goods Sold.

Summary

As units are completed and are eventually sold, their accumulated cost is transferred to Finished Goods Inventory and finally to Cost of Goods Sold.

I.   **Process Operations**—mass production of products in a continuous flow of steps

   A.   Comparing Job Order and Process Operations

      1.   Both manufacturers and service companies can use job order and process production systems.

      2.   Focus of job order operations is on the individual job or batch. Features of job order systems:

         a.   Custom orders

         b.   Heterogeneous products and services

         c.   Low production volume

         d.   High product flexibility

         e.   Low to medium standardization

      3.   Focus of process operations is on the process itself and on the standardized units produced. Features of process production systems:

         a.   Repetitive operations

         b.   Homogeneous products and services

         c.   High production volume

         d.   Low product flexibility

         e.   High standardization

   B.   Organization of Process Operations

      1.   Each process is identified as a separate production department, work station or work center.

      2.   Except for the first department or process, each receives the output (i.e., partially processed product) and the costs associated with the output of the prior department.

      3.   Last department produces the finished goods that are ready for sale and the accumulated costs are transferred to Finished Goods Inventory.

   C.   GenX Company—An Illustration

      1.   Product is produced by mixing its active ingredient with other materials, molding it into tablets, and then packaging the tablets.

II. **Process Cost Accounting**—overall objective is to determine the total cost per unit of a product or service.

   A.   Direct and Indirect Costs

      1.   Materials and labor that can be traced to a specific process are assigned to those processes as direct costs.

      2.   Materials and labor that cannot be traced to a specific process are indirect costs and assigned to overhead.

    B. Accounting for Materials Costs

      1. Record cost of materials acquired on credit for use in factory by debiting Raw Materials Inventory and crediting Accounts Payable.

      2. Assign costs of direct materials used in production by debiting the Goods in Process Inventory and crediting Raw Materials Inventory.

      3. Assign cost of indirect materials used by debiting Factory Overhead and crediting Raw Materials Inventory.

    C. Accounting for Labor Costs

      1. Record payment of factory wages by debiting Factory Payroll and crediting Cash.

      2. Assign costs of direct labor used in production by debiting the Goods in Process Inventory and crediting Factory Payroll.

      3. Assign cost of indirect labor used by debiting Factory Overhead and crediting Factory Payroll. (Factory Payroll account should now have a zero balance.)

    D. Accounting for Factory Overhead—Same steps as in chapter 19, except performed now for each individual department (or process).

      1. Record other manufacturing overhead items incurred by debiting Factory Overhead and crediting the related accounts.

      2. Compute each department's predetermined overhead rate. With increasing automation, companies are more likely to use machine hours to allocate the overhead costs.

      3. Determine amount of overhead that should be applied to each department. (predetermined rate x actual cost driver quantity.)

      4. Apply factory overhead costs to each department by debiting the Goods in Process Inventory and crediting Factory Overhead.

      5. At the end of the period, close the overapplied or underapplied balance, if immaterial in amount, to Cost of Goods Sold or if material in amount, allocate among costs of goods sold, goods in process inventory, and finished goods inventory accounts.

III.   **Computing and Using Equivalent Units of Production**—used to determine the cost per unit processed by each department.

    A. Accounting for Goods in Process

      1. Simple if a department (or process) has no beginning or ending goods in process inventory—unit cost of goods transferred out of department equals the total cost assigned to the process (direct materials, direct labor, and factory overhead) divided by the total number of units started and finished during the period.

      2.   Complex if a process has beginning or ending inventory of partially process units.

         a.   Numerator is the same (the total cost assigned to the process), but denominator must measure the entire production activity of the process during the period.

         b.   Measure of entire production is called equivalent units of production (or EUP).

         c.   EUP are the number of units that could have been started and completed given the costs incurred during the period. For example, 100 units that are 60% processed had the same costs to both start and finish 60 units.

  B. Differences Between Equivalent Units for Materials and Equivalent Units for Labor and Overhead

      1.   The addition of direct material costs during a process (i.e., which steps involve the addition of direct material) may not correspond to the addition of direct labor and overhead during the process (i.e., which steps involve direct labor and overhead).

      2.   Equivalent units must then be separately determined for:

         a.   Direct materials.

         b.   Direct labor.

         c.   Factory overhead (the same as direct labor if direct labor is used to apply overhead).

IV.   **Process Costing Illustration**—a four-step process.

  A. Step 1: Determine Physical Flow of Units

      1.   A reconciliation of physical units started in a period with physical units completed in that period.

      2.   The following totals should agree:

         a.   Units in beginning inventory plus units started during the period equals the number of units to account for.

         b.   Units transferred out during the period plus units in ending inventory equals the units accounted for.

  B. Step 2: Compute Equivalent Units of Production (EUP)

      1.   Focus is on what was done during the period.

         a.   Can be calculated using first-in, first-out basis (FIFO), weighted average, or last-in, first-out basis (LIFO).

         b.   Text assumes Gen-X uses weighted average method. (The FIFO method is illustrated in Appendix 20A).

      2.   Must convert the physical units worked on to equivalent units based on the amount of each input (direct materials, direct labor, and overhead) that has been used.

3. Under the weighted average method, the computation of equivalent units of production does not separate the units in beginning inventory from those units started this period. Instead, the units are treated as part of a large pool with an average cost per unit.

4. Equivalent Units—Direct Materials—add together the results of a two-step calculation:

   a. Units completed during the period times 100% (since the units have all required materials).

   b. Units in ending inventory times the percent of materials added during the period.

5. Equivalent Units—Direct Labor and Factory Overhead—add together the results of a two-step calculation:

   a. Units completed during the period times 100% (since the units have all required labor and overhead).

   b. Units in ending inventory times the percent of labor and overhead added during the period.

C. Step 3: Compute Cost per Equivalent Unit

1. The total of the costs in the beginning inventory and the costs added to the department during the period divided by the equivalent units of production (EUP) in the period equals the cost per equivalent unit for the period.

2. Perform the calculation separately for direct materials, direct labor, and overhead.

D. Step 4: Cost Assignment and Reconciliation

1. Similar in concept to the reconciliation of the physical flow of units (except that dollars are used instead of units).

2. The following totals should agree:

   a. Cost of beginning inventory plus cost assigned to units started during the period (i.e., amounts debited to the Goods in Process Inventory during the period) equals total costs to account for.

   b. Cost assigned to units completed during the period, plus the cost assigned to ending inventory also equals the costs accounted for (see 3 below).

3. Sources of amounts used in cost reconciliation:

   a. Cost assigned to units completed during the period equals:

      i. Direct material cost assigned during the period (equivalent units in units completed for direct material times the related equivalent cost per unit).

      ii. Direct labor cost assigned during the period (equivalent units in units completed for direct labor times the related equivalent cost per unit).

         iii. Factory overhead cost assigned during the period
             (equivalent units in units completed for factory
             overhead times the related equivalent cost per unit).

     b. Cost assigned to ending inventory equals:

         i. Direct material cost assigned during the period
            (equivalent units in ending inventory for direct
            material times the related equivalent cost per unit).

         ii. Direct labor cost assigned during the period
            (equivalent units in ending inventory for direct labor
            times the related equivalent cost per unit).

         iii. Factory overhead cost assigned during the period
             (equivalent units in ending inventory for factory
             overhead times the related equivalent cost per unit).

E. Process Cost Summary

    1. Primary managerial accounting report. Also called a
       production report.

    2. A separate Process Cost Summary is prepared for each process
       or production department.

    3. Purposes:

       a. Help managers control and monitor departments.

       b. Help factory managers evaluate department managers'
          performance.

       c. Provide cost information for financial statements.

    4. Three sections:

       a. Costs charged to production.

       b. Unit Cost Information.

       c. Cost assignment and reconciliation.

F. Transferring to Finished Goods Inventory and Cost of Goods Sold.

    1. Record cost of units transferred out by debiting Finished Goods
       Inventory and crediting Goods in Process Inventory.

    2. Record cost of goods sold by debiting Cost of Goods Sold and
       crediting Finished Goods Inventory.

G. Summary of Cost Flows—As shown in Exhibit 20.21, the flow of
    costs through accounts reflects the flow of manufacturing
    activities and products in the factory.

V.   **Decision Analysis—Hybrid Costing System**

A. Contains features of both job order and process operations.

    1. Material costs are often applied to specific jobs as in a job
       order system.

    2. Conversion costs (direct labor and factory overhead) are
       usually accounted for using a process costing system.

B. A hybrid system of processes requires a hybrid costing system.

1. Assembly line costs may be compiled using process costing.

2. Customizing the product may use a job order system.

3. The total product cost will include the assembly line cost per unit plus the cost of customizing the product.

VI. **Appendix 20A—FIFO method of process costing**

A. The objectives, concepts, and journal entries (but not amounts) are the same as for the weighted average method.

B. The computation of equivalent units of production and cost assignments are slightly different.

C. Step 1: Determine the physical flow of units.

1. The following totals should agree:

a. Units in beginning inventory plus units started during the period equal number of units to account for.

b. Units completed and transferred out (beginning inventory units plus units started and completed) during the period plus units in ending inventory equal units accounted for.

D. Step 2: Compute Equivalent Units of Production (EUP)

1. Focus is on what was done during the period.

2. Equivalent Units—Direct Materials—add together the results of a three-step calculation:

a. Units in beginning inventory times the percent of materials added during the period.

b. Units started and completed during the period times 100% (since all materials were added during the period).

c. Units in ending inventory times the percent of materials added during the period.

3. Equivalent Units—Direct Labor and Factory Overhead—add together the results of a three-step calculation:

a. Units in beginning inventory times the percent of labor and overhead added during the period.

b. Units started and completed during the period times 100% (since all labor and overhead was added during the period).

c. Units in ending inventory times the percent of labor and overhead added during the period.

E. Step 3: Compute Cost per Equivalent Unit

1. Costs assigned to the department during the period divided by the equivalent units of production in the current period equals the cost per equivalent unit for the period.

2. Perform calculation separately for direct materials, direct labor, and overhead.

F. Step 4: Cost Assignment and Reconciliation

1. Similar in concept to the reconciliation of the physical flow of units (except that dollars are used instead of units).

2. The following totals should agree:

    a. Costs of beginning inventory plus costs incurred during the period (i.e., amounts debited to the Goods in Process Inventory during the period) equals total costs to account for.

    b. Costs assigned to the completed beginning inventory units, plus costs assigned to the units started and completed during the period, plus the costs assigned to ending inventory equals the costs accounted for *(see 3 below)*.

3. Sources of amounts used in cost reconciliation:

    a. Cost of the completed beginning inventory units equals beginning balance of the Goods in Process Inventory plus the following costs to complete the beginning inventory:

        i. Direct material cost assigned during the period (equivalent units to complete beginning inventory for direct materials X the equivalent cost per unit).

        ii. Direct labor cost assigned during the period (equivalent units to complete beginning inventory for direct labor X equivalent cost per unit.

        iii. Factory overhead cost assigned during the period (equivalent units to complete beginning inventory for factory overhead X equivalent cost per unit).

    b. Cost assigned to units started and completed during the

        i. Direct material cost assigned during the period (equivalent units for units started and finished for materials X equivalent cost per unit).

        ii. Direct labor cost assigned during the period (equivalent units in ending inventory for direct labor X equivalent cost per unit).

        iii. Factory overhead cost assigned during the period (equivalent units in ending inventory for factory overhead X equivalent cost per unit).

    c. Cost assigned to ending inventory equals:

        i. Direct material cost assigned during the period (equivalent units in ending inventory for direct material X equivalent cost per unit).

        ii. Direct labor cost assigned during the period (equivalent units in ending inventory for direct labor X equivalent cost per unit).

        iii. Factory overhead cost assigned during the period (equivalent units in ending inventory for factory overhead X equivalent cost per unit).

Problem I

The following statements are either true or false. Place a (T) in the parentheses before each true statement and an (F) before each false statement.

1. ( ) In a process cost accounting system, the cost of each unique job is tracked while its production is in process.

2. ( ) In process operations, many units of identical products are fabricated by sending them through a series of processes.

3. ( ) A production department in a process system works directly on products.

4. ( ) The costs of labor efforts by maintenance workers are always considered to be overhead, even if they work full-time in only one production department.

5. ( ) Process cost accounting systems do not use predetermined overhead application rates to assign overhead costs to products.

6. ( ) With respect to providing information to be recorded in the accounts, a materials consumption report serves the same purpose as a materials requisition.

7. ( ) Determining the equivalent units of production is necessary only if a production department in a process manufacturing system has a beginning or ending goods in process inventory.

8. ( ) The term "equivalent unit" is used in process cost accounting to describe a unit of one product that has essentially the same cost as a unit of another kind of product.

9. ( ) To find the equivalent units with respect to labor added to an ending goods in process inventory, multiply the number of physical units in the inventory by the percentage of total labor that was added in the reporting period.

10. ( ) If materials are added to a process at a different rate than labor, separate equivalent finished unit calculations are required for materials and labor.

11. ( ) A process cost summary lists nothing more than the total cost incurred during the month in the production department.

12. ( ) A hybrid cost accounting system contains features of both job order and process costing.

Problem II

Select the one best answer to each of the following multiple choice questions:

_____ 1. During a recent period, the Bending Department finished and transferred 3,000 units to Finished Goods Inventory. One thousand of these units were one fourth complete at the beginning of-the period and 2,000 were started and completed during the period. During the period, another 500 units were started but were only one half completed at the end of the period. The number of equivalent finished units produced by the Bending Department during the period was:

    a. 2,000 units.

    b. 2,250 units.

    c. 2,500 units.

    d. 3,000 units.

    e. 3,250 units.

_____ 2. Carlton Company has a predetermined overhead application rate equal to 40% of direct labor cost. The ending balance of the Goods in Process Inventory account is $87,000, which includes $45,000 of direct materials. How much overhead cost was assigned to these partially completed units?

    a. $12,000.

    b. $18,000.

    c. $30,000.

    d. $42,000.

    e. Cannot be determined.

_____ 3. Town & Country Factory set the predetermined overhead application rate for production after predicting that the next year's costs would include $120,000 of overhead and $96,000 of direct labor. In May, total direct labor costs were $8,600. How much overhead cost will be debited to the Goods in Process Inventory account for this department in May?

    a. $ 6,880.

    b. $10,000.

    c. $10,750.

    d. $12,500.

    e. None of the above.

_____ 4. A company starts the month with a beginning work in process inventory consisting of 5,000 units that are 80% complete with respect to labor costs. During the month, 30,000 units were started and completed and another 8,000 units were started but only did 30% of the work to complete them. The beginning work in process balance included $3,180 for direct labor and an additional $23,000 was incurred for labor costs during the month. How much direct labor cost should be assigned to the ending goods in process?

    a. $1,453.

    b. $1,680.

    c. $3,172.

    d. $3,611.

    e. $4,842.

Problem III

Many of the important ideas and concepts discussed in Chapter 20 are reflected in the following list of key terms. Test your understanding of these terms by matching the appropriate definitions with the terms. Record the number identifying the most appropriate definition in the blank space next to each term.

_____ Equivalent units of production   _____ Process cost accounting system
_____ Job order cost accounting   _____ Process cost summary
_____ Materials consumption report   _____ Process manufacturing

1. A report that describes the costs charged to a department, its equivalent units of production achieved, and the costs assigned to its output.

2. A system of assigning direct materials, direct labor, and overhead to specific processes. The total costs associated with each process are then divided by the number of units passing through that process to determine the cost per equivalent unit.

3. The processing of products in a continuous (sequential) flow of steps; also called *process operations* or *process production*.

4. The number of units that would be completed if all effort during a period had been applied to units that were started and finished.

5. A document that summarizes the materials a department uses during a reporting period; replaces materials requisitions.

6. A cost accounting system designed to determine the cost to produce each job or job lot.

Problem IV

Complete the following by filling in the blanks.

1. Process manufacturing systems produce _____ quantities of _____ products. Each product passes through a series of _____.

2. In process cost accounting systems, production costs are first assigned to _____.

3. Even though a maintenance worker's efforts are not applied directly to products, the wage cost can be considered to be a _____ cost if those efforts occur within a single production department.

4. Each production department has a _____ Inventory account.

5. Overhead costs are often assigned to production with a _____ _____ rate.

6. If a production department has a goods in process inventory at the end of a reporting period, measurements of its activity for that period will be expressed in terms of _____ units of production.

7. The calculation of _____ units of production of direct labor is based on the concept that a takes the same amount of labor to do one-fourth the work on _____ units as a does to complete one unit.

8. A _____ summary describes the costs incurred by a production department in a reporting period.

9. The three sections of the _____ summary describe: (a) the _____ _____ to the department, (b) the _____ units produced by the department and the cost per _____ unit, and (c) the costs assigned to the _____ of the department.

10. The process cost accounting system records the transfer of completed products from the production department with a _____ to the Goods in Process Inventory account of the sending department and a _____ to the Finished Goods Inventory.

Problem V

The following table summarizes the manufacturing activities that occurred at the Boone Process Manufacturing Company during a recent month:

SUMMARY SHEET

	Raw Material	Factory Payroll	Factory Over-head	Production Department	Finished Goods	Cost of Goods Sold
Materials purchases	$10,000					
Direct materials used	(9,000)			$ 9,000		
Indirect materials used	(800)		$ 800			
Labor acquired		$5,000				
Direct labor used		(3,300)		3,300		
Indirect labor used		(1,700)	1,700			
Other overhead costs			2,450			
Overhead applied			(4,950)	4,950		
Costs transferred to:						
Finished goods				(11,450)	$11,450	
Cost of goods sold					(11,000)	$11,000

Provide the journal entries that would be made to record these events:

1. Materials purchases (all on credit).

2. Materials used.

3. Labor costs (paid with cash).

4. Labor used.

5. Other overhead costs (paid with cash).

6. Overhead costs applied to departments.

7. Transfer units from Production Dept. to Finished Goods.

8. Cost of goods sold.

Problem VI

Part A

During a recent month, the Plating Department completed 65,000 units of product and transferred them to the finished goods inventory. The beginning goods in process inventory consisted of 20,000 units that were 25% completed when the month began. Another 45,000 units were started and completed during the month. The ending goods in process inventory consisted of 12,000 units that were 45% completed.

Calculate the equivalent finished units for this department:

	Physical Units	Percent Added	Equivalent Units
Goods completed and transferred out........			
Ending goods in process............................			
Total units..			

Part B

The Plating Department applies direct labor to the product evenly throughout its process. During the month described above, it incurred $78,480 of direct labor cost. The direct labor costs incurred last period to partially complete the units in the beginning inventory totaled $6,000. The weight-average method is used.

A. Use the following equation to find the direct labor costs:

Costs of Production   **Direct Labor**

Costs of beginning goods in process   _____

Costs incurred this period   _____

Total direct labor cost   _____

B. Use the following equation to find the direct labor cost per equivalent unit:

$$\frac{\text{Direct labor cost}}{\text{Equivalent units}} = \$ \text{_____} = \$ \text{_____ per unit}$$

C. Determine the amount of direct labor cost that would be assigned to the units transferred out of the Production Department:

Units completed and transferred this period:

_____ equivalent units   x $ _____ per unit   = $ _____

D. Determine the amount of the month's direct labor cost that would be assigned to the units that are still in process in the Production Department:

Ending goods in process:

_____ equivalent units   x $ _____ per unit   = $ _____

Solutions for Chapter 20

Problem I

1.	F	7.	T
2.	T	8.	F
3.	T	9.	T
4.	F	10.	T
5.	F	11.	F
6.	T	12.	T

Problem II

1. E
2. A
3. C
4. B

Problem III

Equivalent units of production 4

Job order cost accounting 6

Materials consumption report 5

Process cost accounting system 2

Process cost summary 1

Process manufacturing 3

Problem IV

1. large; identical; processes

2. processes

3. direct

4. Goods in Process

5. predetermined overhead allocation

6. equivalent

7. equivalent; four

8. process cost

9. process cost; costs charged; equivalent; equivalent; output

10. credit; debit

Problem V

1. *Materials purchases (all on credit)*

Raw Materials Inventory	10,000	
Accounts Payable		10,000

2. *Materials used*

Goods in Process Inventory	9,000	
Factory Overhead	800	
Raw Materials Inventory		9,800

3. *Labor costs (paid with cash)*

Factory Payroll	5,000	
Cash		5,000

4. *Labor used*

Goods in Process Inventory	3,300	
Factory Overhead	1,700	
Factory Payroll		5,000

5. *Other overhead costs (paid with cash)*

Factory Overhead	2,450	
Cash		2,450

6. *Overhead applied to departments*

Goods in Process Inventory	4,950	
Factory Overhead		4,950

7. *Transfer from production to finished goods*

Finished Goods Inventory	11,450	
Goods in Process Inventory		11,450

8. *Cost of goods sold*

Cost of Goods Sold	11,000	
Finished Goods Inventory		11,000

Problem VI

Part A

	Physical Units	Percent Added	Equivalent Units
Goods started and completed.....................	65,000	100%	65,000
Ending goods in process............................	12,000	45%	5,400
Total units..	77,000		70,400

Part B

A.

Costs of Production	Direct Labor
Costs of beginning goods in process	$ 6,000
Costs incurred this period	78,480
Total direct labor cost	$84,480

B.

$$\frac{\text{Direct labor cost}}{\text{Equivalent units}} = \frac{\$84,480}{70,400} = \$1.20 \text{ per unit}$$

C.

Units completed and transferred
  65,000   equivalent units   x $1.20 per unit   = $78,000

D.

Ending goods in process:
  5,400   equivalent units   x $1.20 per unit   = $ 6,480

Learning Objective C1:

Distinguish between direct and indirect expenses and identify bases for allocating indirect expenses to departments.

Summary

Direct expenses are traced to a specific department and are incurred for the sole benefit of that department. Indirect expenses benefit more than one department. Indirect expenses are allocated to departments when computing departmental net income. Ideally, we allocate indirect expenses by using a cause-effect relation for the allocation base. When a cause-effect relation is not identifiable, each indirect expense is allocated on a basis reflecting the relative benefit received by each department.

Learning Objective C2:

Explain controllable costs and responsibility accounting.

Summary

A controllable cost is one that is influenced by a specific management level. The total expenses of operating a department often include some items the department manager does not control. Responsibility accounting systems provide information for evaluating the performance of department managers. A responsibility accounting system's performance reports for evaluating departmental managers should include only the expenses (and revenues) that each manager controls.

Learning Objective C3:

(Appendix 21-A) Explain transfer pricing and methods to set transfer prices.

Summary

Transfer prices are used to record transfers of items between divisions of the same company. Transfer prices can be based on costs are market prices, or can be negotiated by division managers.

Learning Objective C4:

(Appendix 21-B) Describe allocation of joint costs across products.

Summary

A joint cost refers to costs incurred to produce or purchase two or more products at the same time. When income statements are prepared, joint costs are usually allocated to the resulting joint products using either a physical or value basis.

Learning Objective A1:

Analyze investment centers using return on total assets, residual income and balanced scorecard.

Summary

A financial measure often used to evaluate an investment center manager is the investment center return on total assets, also called return on investment. This measure is computed as the center's net income divided by the center's average total assets. Residual income, computed as investment center net income minus a target net income is an alternative financial measure of investment center performance. A balanced scorecard uses a combination of financial and non-financial measures to evaluate performance.

Learning Objective A2:

Analyze investment centers using profit margin and investment turnover.

Summary

Return on investment can also be computed as profit margin times investment turnover. Profit margin (equal to net income/sales) measures the income earned per dollar of sales and investment turnover (equal to sales/assets) measures how efficiently a division uses its assets.

Learning Objective P1:

Assign overhead costs using two-stage cost allocation.

Summary

In the traditional two-stage cost allocation procedure, service department costs are first assigned to operating departments. Then, in the second stage, a predetermined overhead allocation rate is computed for each operating department and is used to assign overhead to output.

Learning Objective P2:

Assign overhead costs using activity-based costing.

Summary

In activity-based costing, the costs of related activities are collected and then pooled in some logical manner into activity cost pools. After all activity costs have been accumulated in an activity cost pool account, users of the activity, termed *cost objects*, are assigned a portion of the total activity cost using an a cost driver (allocation base).

Learning Objective P3:

Prepare departmental income statements and departmental contribution reports.

Summary

Each profit center (department) is assigned its expenses to yield its own income statement. These costs include its direct expenses and its share of indirect expenses. The departmental income statement lists its revenues and costs of goods sold to determine gross profit. Its operating expenses (direct and its indirect expenses allocated to the department) are deducted from gross profit to yield the departmental net income. The departmental contribution report is similar to the departmental income statement in terms of computing the gross profit for each department. Then the direct operating expenses for each department are deducted from gross profit to determine the contribution generated by each department. Indirect operating expenses are deducted *in total* from the company's combined contribution.

I. Overhead Cost Allocation Methods

   A. Two-Stage Cost Allocation

      1. First stage—assign service departments costs to various operating departments:

         a. Operating departments perform the organization's main functions.

         b. Service departments provide support to the organization's operating departments.

      2. Second stage—assign operating department costs, including those assigned from service departments, to the organization's output.

   B. Activity-Based Costing—better allocation of costs to proper users of overhead activities by focusing on activities.

      1. Two stages (see Exhibit 21.3):

         a. First stage—identify activities involved in processing the product or service and then form activity cost pools by those combining activities into sets.

         b. Second stage—compute predetermined overhead cost allocation rate for each cost pool and then assign costs to the output.

      2. Terminology

         a. Cost pool—individual activities, which are pooled in a logical manner into homogeneous groups or sets.

         b. Activity Cost driver (or cost driver)—a factor that causes the cost of an activity to go up or down. Cost drivers are used to assign activity costs to cost objects.

         c. Activity cost pool—a temporary account used to accumulate the costs a company incurs to support an identified set of activities. Includes the variable and fixed processing costs.

         d. Variable costs—pertain to resources acquired as needed (e.g. materials and labor).

         e. Fixed costs—pertain to resources acquired in advance (e.g. equipment, insurance).

         f. Cost objects—users of the activity (such as jobs or products).

      3. Comparison of Two-Stage and Activity-Based Cost Allocation

         a. Traditional cost systems:

            i. capture overhead costs by individual department (or function) in one or a more overhead accounts.

            ii. Assign overhead costs using a single allocation base (such as direct labor) or multiple allocation bases.

           iii. Allocation bases are often not closely related to the actual way costs are incurred.

b. Activity-based cost systems:

   i. Capture costs by individual activity. Activities and their costs are accumulated into activity cost pools.

   ii. Select a cost driver (allocation base) for each activity pool; use this cost driver to assign accumulated activity costs to cost objects (such as jobs or products) benefiting from the activity.

c. Benefits of activity-based costing

   i. Especially effective when the same department or departments produce many different kinds of products; complex products are assigned greater portion of overhead.

   ii. Encourages managers to focus on activities as well as the use of those activities.

   iii. Results in activity-based management—causes managers to pay closer attention to *all* activities.

II. **Departmental Accounting**—divide company into subunits (or divisions) when too large. Divisions are organized into separate departments.

A. Motivation for Departmentalization

  1. Each department placed under direction of a manager.

  2. Takes advantage of diversified skills managers possess.

  3. Promotes efficiency and effectiveness as company grows.

B. Departmental Evaluation

  1. Prepared for *internal* managers to help control operations, appraise performance, allocate resources, and plan strategy.

  2. More companies are emphasizing customer satisfaction as main responsibility of each operating department.

  3. Financial information used for evaluation depends on type of center.

   a. Profit center—incurs costs and generates revenues (e.g. selling department).

   b. Cost center—incurs cost or expenses without directly generating revenues (e.g. manufacturing department and service department).

   c. Investment center—incurs costs, generates revenues and is responsible for effectively using center assets.

  4. Basis for evaluating performance:

   a. Profit center: ability to generate more revenue than expenses.

   b. Cost center: ability to control costs within a satisfactory range.

   c. Investment center: use of center assets to generate income.

    C. Departmental Reporting and Analysis

       1. Information needed depends on focus and philosophy of management.

       2. Departmental Spreadsheet Analysis—used when separate accounts not maintained in general ledger by department.

          a. Record sales, sales returns, purchases, purchase returns in general ledger as if company not departmentalized.

          b. Identify each department's transactions and enter on spreadsheet; totals equal balance of related account.

          c. Compute gross profit by department.

III.   **Departmental Expense Allocation**—accounting challenges involve allocating expenses across operating departments.

    A. Direct Expenses—readily traced to department because incurred for sole benefit of department; no allocation required.

    B. Indirect Expenses—are:

       1. Incurred for joint benefit of more than one department; can't be readily traced to one department.

       2. Allocated across departments benefiting from them.

       3. Ideally allocated using a cause-effect relation or, if cause-effect relation cannot be identified, allocated on a basis approximating the benefit received by each department.

    C. Allocation of Indirect Expenses—no standard rule identifies the best basis; judgment required.

       1. Wages and salaries:

          a. Direct expense of the department if time spent entirely in one department; otherwise indirect.

          b. Basis for allocating when indirect:

             i. Employees—relative amount of time spent in each department.

             ii. Supervisors—number of employees (if task is managing) or sales (if job reflects on departments' sales).

       2. Rent and related expenses—portion of floor space occupied. More valuable location may charge department higher rate.

       3. Advertising—Departmental portion of total sales, or by newspaper space or TV/radio time devoted to products of each department.

       4. Equipment and machinery depreciation—relative number of hours used by each department.

          a. Direct expense of the department if the asset is used only in that department.

          b. Indirect expense when the asset is used by more than 1 department.

5. Utilities—portion of floor space occupied by departments (if used uniformly); otherwise more complicated.

6. Service Department expenses—see Exhibit 21.8 for common allocation bases.

D. Departmental Income Statements (see Exhibit 21.21)

1. Departmental income statements are prepared after all expenses have been assigned to the departments.

   a. Direct expenses are accumulated by department.

   b. Indirect expenses—all the direct and indirect expenses incurred in service departments are compiled, then allocated to operating department.

2. Four Steps to allocating costs and preparing departmental income statements.

   a. Step one – accumulate direct expenses for each service and selling department.

   b. Step two – allocate indirect expenses across all departments using allocation base identified for each expense.

   c. Step three – allocate service department expenses to operating departments—departmental expense allocation spreadsheet may be used *(review Exhibits 21.12 through 21.20)*.

   d. Step four – use departmental expense allocation spreadsheet to prepare departmental income statement and performance reports for the service and operating departments. (Exhibit 21.21)

E. Departmental Contribution to Overhead (see Exhibit 21.22)

1. Departmental income statements not always best for evaluating each profit center's performance especially when indirect expenses are a large portion of total expenses.

2. Evaluate using departmental contributions to overhead—a report of the amount of sales less direct expenses (indirect expenses are often considered "overhead").

F. Evaluating Investment Center Performance with Financial Measures

1. Assesses how well center manager has utilized center's productive assets to generate income.

2. Evaluated using performance measures that combine income and assets.

3. Return on total assets, also called return on investment, is computed as:

$$\frac{\text{Investment center net income}}{\text{Investment center average invested assets}}$$

4. Investment center residual income is computed as:

Investment center net income
− target investment center net income*
residual income

*target net income : Hurdle rate x average invested assets
hurdle rate: typically the cost to obtain financing

5. Using residual income encourages managers to accept all opportunities greater than the target net income.

G. Evaluating Investment Center Performance with Nonfinancial Measures

1. Evaluating performance solely on financial measures has limitations.

a. May forgo profitable opportunities to keep the return on investment high.

b. Residual income is less useful when comparing investment centers of different size.

c. Return on investment and residual income can encourage managers to focus too heavily on short-term financial goals.

2. Balanced Scorecard: system of performance measures, including nonfinancial measures used to assess company and division manager performance. Requires managers to think of their company from four perspectives.

a. Customer: what do they think of us

b. Internal process: which of our operations are critical

c. Innovation and learning: how can we improve

d. Financial: what do our owners think of us

e. Exhibit 21.25 lists common performance measures.

IV. **Responsibility Accounting**—evaluates a manager's performance using reports that describe a department's activities in terms of controllable costs.

A. Controllable versus Direct Costs—direct costs are readily traced to department, but may not be under control of department manager; cost is controllable if manager has power to determine (or at least strongly affect) amount incurred.

1. All costs are controllable at some level of management if the time period is sufficiently long.

2. Good judgment is required when identifying controllable costs.

B. Responsibility Accounting System

1. Responsibility accounting system assigns managers the responsibility for costs and expenses under their control.

2. Responsibility accounting budgets identify costs and expenses under the manager's control.

3. Responsibility accounting performance reports (See Exhibit 21.28):

a. Accumulate and report costs for which a manager is responsible and their budgeted amounts.

b. Management's analysis of differences between actual and budget often results in corrective actions.

c. Used by upper management to evaluate effectiveness of lower-level managers in controlling costs.

4. Recognizes that control over costs and expenses belongs to several layers of management.

V. **Decision Analysis—Investment Center Profit Margin and Investment Turnover**

A. Can further examine division performance by splitting return on investment into profit margin and investment turnover as follows:

Return on Investment = Profit Margin x Investment Turnover

$$\frac{\text{Investment Center Net Income}}{\text{Investment Center Ave. Assets}} =$$

$$\frac{\text{Investment Center Net Income}}{\text{Investment Center Sales}} \ x \ \frac{\text{Investment Center Sales}}{\text{Investment Center Ave. Assets}}$$

VI.   Appendix 21A—Transfer Pricing

A. The price used to record transfers between divisions in the same company is called a transfer price.

1. If there is no excess capacity, the internal supplier will not accept a transfer price less than the market price. This is called market based transfer pricing.

2. If there is excess capacity, the internal supplier should accept a price between the cost to manufacturer the part and the market price. This is called cost based transfer pricing.

3. Other issues to consider in determining transfer prices include:

    a. Market price may not exist

    b. Cost controls

    c. Division managers' negotiation

    d. Nonfinancial factors to consider include: quality control, reduced lead times and impact on employee morale.

VII.   Appendix 21B—Joint Costs

A. Joint Costs—costs incurred to produce or purchase two or more products at the same time; similar to indirect expense in that it's shared across more than one cost object.

1. Ignored when deciding to sell product as is or process further.

2. Allocated to different products produced from it when total cost of each product must be estimated (e.g., preparation of GAAP financial statements).

3. Allocation bases

    a. Physical basis—allocates joint costs using physical characteristics such as ratio of pounds, cubic feet or gallons of each joint product to the total pounds, cubic feet or gallons of all joint products flowing from the cost; does not reflect the extra value flowing into some products or the inferior value flowing into others. not the preferred method.

    b. Value basis—allocates joint cost in proportion to the sales value of the output produced by the process at the "split-off point".

Problem I

The following statements are either true or false. Place a (T) in the parentheses before each true statement and an (F) before each false statement.

1. ( ) Controllable costs and expenses are always the same as direct costs and expenses.

2. ( ) Costs incurred by service departments in support of selling departments are direct expenses of the selling departments.

3. ( ) Depending on the circumstances, employees' wages can be either a direct or an indirect expense.

4. ( ) A department's contribution to overhead is the excess of its revenues over its direct expenses.

5. ( ) A direct expense should not be allocated among more than one department.

6. ( ) Activity-based costing produces significant benefits in addition to providing more useful cost allocations.

7. ( ) Accounting information can be used to evaluate (a) managers who are responsible for controlling costs and expenses and (b) each department's profitability or cost effectiveness.

8. ( ) An advertising department is both a service department and a cost center.

Problem II

You are given several words, phrases or numbers to choose from in completing each of the following statements or in answering the following questions. In each case, select the one that best completes the statement or answers the question and place its letter in the answer space provided.

_____ 1. A supervisor works some of the time in Department A (which has 10 employees) and the rest of the time in Department B (which has 6 employees). In square feet of area, Department A is only half the size of Department B. If the supervisor's primary task is managing people, how and in what amounts would the supervisor's $24,000 annual salary be most logically allocated between Departments A and B?

    a. Based on the number of employees in each department, $15,000 to Department A and $9,000 to Department B.

    b. Based on a combined statistic of square footage and number of employees in each department, $10,909 to Department A and $13,091 to Department B.

    c. Based on the number of departments supervised, $12,000 to Department A and $12,000 to Department B.

    d. Based on the square footage in each department, $8,000 to Department A and $16,000 to Department B.

    e. Based on the number of employees in each department, $9,000 to Department A and $15,000 to Department B.

_____ 2. Townsend Building Company purchased a partially completed four-story building and turned it into 24 condominiums of three different categories. Five 3-bedroom units are expected to sell for $150,000 each, twelve 2-bedroom units are expected to sell for $75,000 each, and seven 1-bedroom units are expected to sell for $50,000 each. The company spent $400,000 to purchase the building and $800,000 on common construction costs. How much of these two joint costs would be assigned to each condominium in each price category?

	3-Bedroom Units	2-Bedroom Units	1-Bedroom Units
a.	$50,000	$50,000	$50,000
b.	$78,261	$52,174	$26,087
c.	$80,000	$33,333	$57,143
d.	$90,000	$45,000	$30,000
e.	None of the above.		

Problem III

Many of the important ideas and concepts discussed in Chapter 21 are reflected in the following list of key terms. Test your understanding of these terms by matching the appropriate definitions with the terms. Record the number identifying the most appropriate definition in the blank space next to each term.

_____ Activity-based costing (ABC)
_____ Activity cost pool
_____ Controllable costs
_____ Cost center
_____ Cost driver
_____ Departmental accounting system
_____ Departmental contribution to overhead
_____ Direct expenses
_____ Indirect expenses

_____ Investment center
_____ Investment center return on assets
_____ Profit center
_____ Responsibility accounting budget
_____ Responsibility accounting performance report
_____ Responsibility accounting system
_____ Uncontrollable costs

1. A variable that causes an activity's cost to go up or down; a causal factor.

2. An accounting system that provides information that management can use to evaluate the performance of a department's manager.

3. The amount by which a department's revenues exceed its direct expenses.

4. A report of expected costs and expenses under a manager's control.

5. Expenses incurred for the joint benefit of more than one department (or cost object).

6. A business unit that incurs costs and generates revenues.

7. A department that incurs costs (but generates no revenues), such as the accounting or legal department.

8. Costs that a manager has the power to control or at least strongly influence.

9. Expenses traced to a specific department that are incurred for the sole benefit of that department.

10. An accounting system that provides information useful in evaluating the profitability or cost effectiveness of a department.

11. Costs that a manager does not have the power to determine or strongly influence.

12. A cost allocation method that focuses on activities performed; traces costs to activities and then assigns them to cost objects.

13. A temporary account that accumulates costs a company incurs to support an activity.

14. A center of which a manager is responsible for revenues, costs, and asset investments.

15. A responsibility report that compares actual costs and expenses for a department with budgeted amounts.

16. A measure computed as center net income divided by average total assets for the center.

Problem IV

Complete the following by filling in the blanks.

1. A departmental expense allocation sheet can be used to allocate _____ expenses among all departments and to allocate _____ department expenses among operating departments.

2. In _____ accounting, managers are held responsible for the revenues and expenses that fall under their control.

3. Service department expenses are _____ expenses of the selling or production departments. These costs should be allocated to these departments if management believes that the allocations will provide _____ information.

4. An evaluation of a department manager's performance based on _____ costs is more useful than an evaluation based on the department's net _____ or its _____ to overhead.

5. In calculating departmental net incomes, _____ expenses can be identified easily with specific departments but _____ expenses can only be allocated to the departments on the basis of a logical or observed relationship.

6. A department's contribution to overhead is the excess of its _____ over its _____ expenses.

7. A _____ center incurs costs but does not generate revenues. A _____ center incurs costs and generates revenues.

8. When companies are too large to be managed effectively as a single unit, they are divided into _____, also called _____.

9. One hundred pounds of Material A can be purchased at a cost of $200. This material can be converted into 5 units of Product Y, which can be sold for $50 per unit and 10 units of Product Z, which can be sold for $15 per unit. If the $200 cost of Material A is allocated to Products Y and Z in proportion to their market value, Product Y will be assigned $ _____ of the cost and Product Z will be assigned $ _____.

10. Under _____ costing, products receive allocated costs on the basis of numerous cost _____. One benefit of this approach is that it results in activity-based _____. Managers pay closer attention to all activities.

Problem V

Head-to-Toe Department Store has two service departments and three selling departments. The following information is available for the three selling departments:

	Sales	Purchase Orders
Shoe department	$250,000	100
Hat department	100,000	120
Sock department	150,000	30
Total.........................	$500,000	250

The table below is the *lower part* of a departmental expense allocations spreadsheet (like the lower part of the spreadsheet in Exhibit 22.12) for Head-to-Toe. The first line summarizes the total department expense amounts of each of the five departments. The details of these total department expense amounts (that is, the direct and indirect expenses of each department) would be listed in the upper part of the spreadsheet (which is not shown).

Expense	Allocation Base	Expense Account Balance	Shipping Dept.	Processing Dept.	Shoe Dept.	Hat Dept.	Sock Dept.
Total department expenses		$225,000	$10,000	$25,000	$60,000	$75,000	$55,000
Service dept. expenses:							
Shipping	Sales						
Processing	Purchase orders						
Total expenses allocated to selling depts.							

Allocate the expenses of the two service departments' expenses to the three selling departments, and then complete the spreadsheet.

©The McGraw-Hill Companies, Inc., 2011

Problem VI

We'll Fix it is a landscape and interior design company. The owners want to better understand its costs so the amount charged to the clients for services provided will generate a profit. They decide to use activity based costing.

Cost Center	Cost	Cost Driver	Driver quantity
Professional salaries	$600,000	Professional hours	6,000
Client services and supplies	20,000	Number of clients	2,500
Cost of building and equipment	180,000	Square feet	2,000
Total overhead Costs	$800,000		

The two main areas of services provided and the related data are:

Service	Hours	Clients	Square feet
Landscape design	4,000	1,500	1,200
Interior Design	2,000	1,000	800
Total	6,000	2,500	2,000

Required:

1. Compute the cost per cost driver for each of the three cost centers.

Professional salaries

$$\frac{\text{Professional Salaries}}{\text{Professional Hours}} = \frac{\$\underline{\hspace{2cm}}}{\underline{\hspace{2cm}} \text{ hours}} = \$\underline{\hspace{2cm}} \quad \text{Per hour}$$

Client services and supplies

$$\frac{\text{Service and supplies cost}}{\text{Number of clients}} = \frac{\$\underline{\hspace{2cm}}}{\underline{\hspace{2cm}} \text{ clients}} = \$\underline{\hspace{2cm}} \quad \text{Per client}$$

Cost of Building and Equipment

$$\frac{\text{Building and Equipment costs}}{\text{Total Square Feet}} = \frac{\$\underline{\hspace{2cm}}}{\underline{\hspace{2cm}} \text{ square feet}} = \$\underline{\hspace{2cm}} \quad \text{Per sq foot}$$

2. Use the results from part 1 to allocate costs to the landscape and interior design units.

	Driver quantity	x	Cost per cost driver	=	Cost allocated
Landscape design					
Professional salaries	_____		_____		_____
Client services and supplies	_____		_____		_____
Building and equipment cost	_____		_____		_____
Total Costs Allocated	_____		_____		_____
Interior design					
Professional salaries	_____		_____		_____
Client services and supplies	_____		_____		_____
Building and equipment cost	_____		_____		_____
Total Costs Allocated	_____		_____		_____

Solutions for Chapter 21

Problem I

1.	F	5.	T
2.	F	6.	T
3.	T	7.	T
4.	T	8.	T

Problem II

1. A
2. D

Problem III

Activity-based costing (ABC)	12
Activity cost pool	13
Controllable costs	8
Cost center	7
Cost driver	1
Departmental accounting system	10
Departmental contribution to overhead	3
Direct expenses	9
Indirect expenses	5
Investment center	14
Investment center return on total assets	16
Profit center	6
Responsibility accounting budget	4
Responsibility accounting performance report	15
Responsibility accounting system	2
Uncontrollable costs	11

Problem IV

1. indirect; service

2. responsibility

3. indirect; useful

4. controllable; income or profit; contribution

5. direct; indirect

6. revenues; direct

7. cost; profit

8. departments; subunits

9. $125; $75

10. activity-based; drivers; management

Problem V

Allocations of service department costs:

Shipping

	Sales	% of Total	Cost
Shoe	$250,000	50.0	$ 5,000
Hat	100,000	20.0	2,000
Sock	150,000	30.0	3,000
Total	$500,000	100.0	$10,000

Advertising

	Purchase Orders	% of Total	Cost
Shoe	100	40.0	$10,000
Hat	120	48.0	12,000
Sock	30	12.0	3,000
Total	250	100.0	$25,000

Expense	Allocation Base	Expense Account Balance	Shipping Dept.	Processing Dept.	Shoe Dept.	Hat Dept.	Sock Dept.
Total department expenses		$225,000	$10,000	$25,000	$60,000	$75,000	$55,000
Service dept. expenses:							
Shipping	Sales		$10,000		$ 5,000	$ 2,000	$ 3,000
Processing	Purchase orders			$25,000	10,000	12,000	3,000
Total expenses allocated to selling depts.		$225,000			$75,000	$89,000	$61,000

Problem VI

Compute the cost per cost driver for each of the three cost centers.

Professional salaries

Professional Salaries	=	$600,000	=	$100	Per hour
Professional Hours		6,000 hours			

Client services and supplies

Service and supplies cost	=	$20,000	=	$ 8	Per client
Number of clients		2,500 clients			

Cost of Building and Equipment

Building and Equipment costs	=	$180,000	=	$90	Per sq foot
Total Square Feet		2,000 square feet			

	Driver quantity	x	Cost per cost driver	=	Cost allocated
Landscape design					
Professional salaries	4,000 hours	x	$100 per hr	=	$400,000
Client services and supplies	1,500 clients	x	$8 per client	=	12,000
Building and equipment cost	1,200 sq. feet	x	$90 per sq. ft	=	108,000
Total Costs Allocated					$520,000
Interior design					
Professional salaries	2,000 hours	x	$100 per hr	=	$200,000
Client services and supplies	1,000 clients	x	$8 per client	=	8,000
Building and equipment cost	800 sq. feet	x	$90 per sq. ft	=	72,000
Total Costs Allocated					$280,000

Total overhead costs allocated

Landscape Design	$520,000
Interior Design	280,000
Total Overhead	$800,000

CHAPTER 22
COST-VOLUME-PROFIT ANALYSIS

Learning Objective C1:

Describe different types of cost behavior in relation to production and sales volume.

Summary

Cost behavior is described in terms of how its amount changes in relation to volume of activity changes within a relevant range. Fixed costs remain constant to changes in volume. Total variable costs change in direct proportion to volume changes. Mixed costs display the effects of both fixed and variable components. Stepwise costs remain constant over a small volume range, then change by a lump sum and remain constant over another volume range, and so on. Curvilinear costs change in a nonlinear relation to volume changes.

Learning Objective C2:

Describe several applications of cost-volume-profit analysis.

Summary

Cost-volume-profit analysis can be used to predict what can happen under alternative strategies concerning sales volume, selling prices, variable costs, or fixed costs. Applications include "what if" analysis, computing sales for a target income, and break-even analysis.

Learning Objective A1:

Compute contribution margin and describe what it reveals about a company's cost structure.

Summary

Contribution margin per unit is a product's unit sales price less its total variable cost per unit. Contribution margin ratio is a product's contribution margin per unit divided by its sales price. Unit contribution margin is the amount received from each sale that contributes to fixed costs and income. The contribution margin ratio reveals what portion of each sales dollar is available as contribution to fixed costs and income.

Learning Objective A2:

Analyze changes in sales using the degree of operating leverage.

Summary

The extent, or relative size, of fixed costs in a company's total cost structure is known as *operating leverage*. One tool useful in assessing the effect of changes in sales on income is the degree of operating leverage, or DOL. DOL is the ratio of the contribution margin divided by pretax income. This ratio can be used to determine the expected percent change in income given a percent change in sales.

Learning Objective P1:

Determine costs estimates using the scatter diagram, high-low method and regression methods of estimating costs.

Summary

Three different methods used to estimate costs are the scatter diagram, the high-low method, and least-squares regression. All three methods use past data to estimate costs. Cost estimates from a scatter diagram are based on a visual fit of the cost line. Estimates from the high-low method are based only on costs corresponding to the lowest and highest sales. The least-squares regression method is a statistical technique and uses all data points.

Learning Objective P2:

Compute break-even point for a single product company.

Summary

A company's break-even point for a period is the sales volume at which total revenues equal total costs. To compute a break-even point in terms of sales units, we divide total fixed costs by the contribution margin per unit. To compute a break-even point in terms of sales dollars, divide total fixed costs by the contribution margin ratio.

Learning Objective P3:

Graph costs and sales for a single product company.

Summary

The costs and sales for a company can be graphically illustrated using a CVP chart. In this chart, the horizontal axis represents the number of units sold and the vertical axis represents dollars of sales or costs. Straight lines are used to depict both costs and sales on the CVP chart.

Learning Objective P4:

Compute break-even point for a multiproduct company.

Summary

CVP analysis can be applied to a multiproduct company by expressing the sales volume in terms of composite units. A composite unit consists of a specific number of units of each product in proportion to their expected sales mix. Multiproduct CVP analysis treats this composite unit as a single product.

I.   **Identifying Cost Behavior** (CVP analysis)—Cost-volume-profit analysis is a tool to predict how changes in costs and sales levels affect income; conventional CVP analysis requires that all costs must be classified as either fixed or variable with respect to production or sales volume before CVP analysis can be used.

    A. Fixed Costs

        1. A total fixed cost remains unchanged in amount when volume of activity varies from period to period within a relevant range.

        2. The fixed cost *per unit* of output decreases as volume increases (and vice versa).

        3. When production volume and cost are graphed, units of product are usually plotted on the *horizontal* axis and dollars of cost are plotted on the *vertical* axis. (Exhibit 22.1)

            a. Fixed cost is represented by a horizontal line with no slope (cost remains constant at all levels of volume within the relevant range).

            b. Intersection point of line on cost (vertical) axis is at fixed cost amount.

        4. Likely that amount of fixed cost will change when outside of relevant range.

    B. Variable Costs

        1. A total variable cost changes in proportion to changes in volume of activity.

        2. Variable cost *per unit* remains constant but the *total* amount of variable cost changes with the level of production.

        3. When production volume and cost are graphed, (Exhibit 22.1)

            a. Variable cost is represented by a straight line starting at the zero cost level.

            b. The straight line is upward (positive) sloping. The line rises as volume increases.

    C. Mixed Costs

        1. Include both fixed and variable cost components.

        2. When volume and cost are graphed,

            Mixed cost is represented by a straight line with an upward (positive) slope.

            Start of line is at fixed cost point (or amount of total cost when volume is zero) on cost (vertical) axis. As activity level increases, mixed cost line increases at an amount equal to the variable cost per unit.

        3. Mixed costs are often separated into fixed and variable components when included in a CVP analysis.

  D. Step-wise Costs

    1. Fixed within a relevant range of the current production volume. If production volume expands significantly, total costs go up by a lump-sum amount (stair-step cost).

    2. Treated as either fixed or variable cost in conventional CVP analysis; depends on width of range, and requires judgment.

  E. Curvilinear (or Nonlinear) Costs

    1. Increase at a non-constant rate as volume increases.

    2. When volume and costs are graphed, curvilinear costs appear as a curved line that starts at intersection point of cost axis and volume axis (total cost is zero when volume is zero) and increases at different rates.

II. **Measuring Cost Behavior**—After establishing that cost data are reliable and useful in predicting future costs, three methods are commonly used to analyze past cost behavior.

  A. Scatter Diagrams

    1. Display past cost and unit data in graphical form.

    2. Units are plotted on horizontal axis, cost on the vertical axis.

    3. Each point reflects the number of units for a prior period.

    4. Estimated line of cost behavior—drawn with a line that best "fits" the points visually.

       a. Intersection point of line on cost axis is at fixed cost amount.

       b. The variable cost per unit of volume equals the slope of the line.

         i. Select any two points on horizontal axis.

         ii. Draw a vertical line from each of these points to intersect the estimated line of cost behavior.

         iii. The slope of the line, or variable cost per unit is computed as follows:

$$\frac{\text{Change in Costs}}{\text{Change in volume (units)}} = \text{variable cost per unit}$$

       c. Cost equation.

         i.   Fixed cost
             + <u>Variable cost per unit x number of units</u>
                    Total Costs

         ii. Useful to predict future cost levels at different volumes.

    5. Deficiency of scatter diagram method—estimates are based on "visual fit" of cost line, subject to interpretation.

B. High-low Method

1. Estimate the cost equation by graphically connecting the two cost amounts at the highest and lowest unit volumes.

    a. Intersection point of line on cost axis is at fixed cost amount.

    b. Variable cost per unit is the slope of the line—is computed as the change in cost divided by the change in units:

$$\text{Variable cost per unit} = \frac{\text{high volume costs} - \text{low volume costs}}{\text{high volume units} - \text{low volumes units}}$$

2. To compute the estimated fixed costs, use the cost equation at the low or high volumes and total costs.

3. Cost equation may differ slightly from that determined using the scatter diagram method.

4. Deficiency of high-low method—ignores all cost points except the highest and lowest resulting in less precision.

C. Least-Squares Regression—computation details covered in advanced cost accounting courses.

1. Statistical method of identifying cost behavior.

2. Cost equation readily calculated using most spreadsheet programs. Illustrated in Appendix 22A using Excel®

3. Cost equation may differ slightly from those determined using the scatter diagram and high-low methods; superior due to use of *all* data points available.

III. **Break-Even Analysis**—special case of CVP analysis.

A. Contribution Margin

1. Requires separating costs and expenses by behavior (fixed or variable).

2. Definition—the amount by which a product's unit selling prices *exceeds* its total unit variable costs. (This excess amount contributes to covering fixed costs and generating profits on a per unit basis).

3. Contribution margin per unit (CM per unit) is computed as: Selling price per unit minus Variable cost per unit.

4. Users often use contribution margin in the form of a contribution margin ratio—the proportion of a unit's selling price that exceeds total unit variable cost. (Interpreted as what proportion of each sales dollars remains after deducting total unit variable costs).

5. Contribution margin ratio (CM %) is computed as: contribution margin per unit divided by sales price per unit.

   B. Computing Break-Even Point
       1. Break-even point
           a. Sales level at which company neither earns a profit nor
               incurs a loss.
           b. Can be expressed either in units or dollars of sales.
       2. Computation of break-even point
           a. Break-even units = $\dfrac{\text{Fixed costs}}{\text{CM per unit}}$
           b. Break-even sales dollars = $\dfrac{\text{Fixed costs}}{\text{CM\%}}$
           c. Contribution Margin Income Statement

                   Revenues
                   – Variable Costs
                   Contribution Margin
                   – Fixed Costs
                   Net Income

           d. Differs from a conventional income statement in two ways:
               i.   Classifies costs and expenses as variable and fixed.
               ii. Reports contribution margin.
   C. Preparing a Cost-Volume-Profit Chart (also called a break-even
       graph or chart)
       1. Horizontal axis—number of units produced and sold (volume).
       2. Vertical axis—dollars of sales and costs.
       3. Three steps:
           a. Plot fixed costs on vertical axis; draw horizontal line at this
               level to show that FC remains unchanged regardless of
               output volume.
           b. Draw line reflecting total costs (variable costs plus fixed
               costs) for a relevant range of volume levels.
               i.   Line starts at fixed costs on vertical axis.
               ii. Slope equals variable cost per unit; compute total costs
                    for any volume level, and connect this point with the
                    vertical axis intercept.
               iii. Stop line at productive capacity for the planning period.
           c. Draw sales line.
               i.   Line starts at origin (zero units and zero dollars of
                    sales).
               ii. Slope of line is equal to selling price per unit; compute
                    total revenues for any volume level, and connect this
                    point with the origin.
               iii. Stop line at productive capacity for the planning period.

4. The break-even point is at the intersection of total cost line and sales line.

5. On either side of break-even point, the vertical distance between sales line and total cost line at any specific sales volume reflects the profit or loss expected at that point.

   Volume levels to left of break-even point—vertical distance is amount of *loss* expected because the total *costs* line is above the total sales line.

   Volume levels to right of break-even point—vertical distance is amount of *profit* expected because the total *sales* line is above the total costs line.

D. Assumptions of Cost-Volume-Profit Analysis

   1. Usefulness depends on validity of three assumptions.

      Constant selling price per unit.

      Constant variable costs per unit.

      Constant total fixed costs.

   2. If expected cost and revenue behavior is different from three assumptions stated above, CVP analysis may still be useful.

      a. Summing of costs can offset individual deviations—Individual variable cost items may not be perfectly variable, but when summed, individual deviations can offset each other. The same can be said for fixed costs.

      b. Relevant range of operations—Assumes a specific cost is variable or fixed is more likely valid when operations are within the relevant range. (If normal range of activity changes, some costs may need reclassification.)

      c. Estimates from CVP analysis—Managers need to understand that CVP analysis provides approximate estimates about future, not precise answers, and that other qualitative factors should also be considered.

   3. Output Measures—level of production often expressed in terms of sales volume (in dollars or units), or units produced. Assume production level coincides with sales level. (Inventory levels do not change).

IV. **Applying Cost-Volume-Profit Analysis**—Useful in helping managers evaluate likely effects of strategies considered in planning business operations.

A. Computing Income from Sales and Costs

   a.   Sales   (# units sold x unit selling price)
        – Variable Costs   (# units sold x unit variable cost)
        Contribution Margin
        – Fixed Costs
        Income (pretax)

B. Computing Sales for a Target Income

1. Sales (in dollars) required for target pretax income equals:

$$\frac{\text{fixed costs} + \text{target pretax income}}{\text{CM\%}}$$

2. Sales (in units) required for target income equals

$$\frac{\text{fixed costs} + \text{target pretax income}}{\text{CM\%}}$$

C. Margin of safety can be expressed in units, dollars, or as a percent of predicted level of sales

1.

Expected Unit Sales	Expected Sales Dollars
– Break-even Unit sales	– Break-even Sales Dollars
Margin of safety (units)	Margin of Safety (dollars)

2. Margin of Safety Rate (%) = $\dfrac{\text{Margin of Safety}}{\text{Expected Sales}}$

D. Sensitivity Analysis—Knowing the effects of changing some estimates used in CVP analysis by substituting new estimated amounts (in total or per unit as appropriate) in the related formula can be helpful in making predictions.

E. Computing Multiproduct Break-Even Point—Modify basic CVP analysis when company produces and sells several products.

1. Important assumption—Sales mix of the different products is known and remains constant.

2. Sales mix is the ratio (proportion) of the sales volumes for various products.

3. To apply multiproduct CVP analysis, estimate break-even point by using a composite unit.

   a. Determine sales mix of various products.

   b. Composite Unit—a specific number of units of each product in proportion to their expected sales mix.

   c. Using sales mix, determine the selling price of a composite unit by multiplying the sales mix ratio times the selling price of each product and then adding the totals for all of the products.

   d. Compute the variable price of a composite unit in the same manner,

   e. Determine the CM per composite unit by subtracting the total variable price from the total selling price of the composite unit.

f. In break-even analysis, a composite unit is treated as a unit of a single product.

g. Break-even point in composite units is computed as:

$$\frac{\text{Fixed Cost}}{\text{CM per composite unit}}$$

h. To determine how many units of each product must be sold to break even, multiply the number of units of each product in the composite unit by the break-even point in composite units.

3. To apply multiproduct CVP analysis, estimate break-even point by using a weighted average contribution margin.

    a. Determine sales mix of various products.

    b. Using the sale mix, determine the percent contribution of each individual product. If there is a 2:2:1 product mix, then the percent contribution of the first product would be 2/5 or 40%.

    c. Compute the contribution margin per unit of each product. (sales price per unit less variable cost per unit.

    d. Multiply the contribution margin per unit for each unit x the respective percentage of the sales mix.

    e. Total the individual amounts to compute the weighted average contribution margin.

    f. Divide fixed costs by the weighted average contribution margin to compute the break-even point in units.

V. **Decision Analysis—Degree of Operating Leverage**—Useful tool in assessing the effect of changes in the level of sales on income.

A. Operating leverage is the extent, or relative size, of fixed costs in the total cost structure.

B. Degree of operating leverage (DOL) is computed as:

$$\frac{\text{Total Contribution margin (dollars)}}{\text{pretax income}}$$

C. Use DOL to measure the effect of changes in the level of sales on pretax income by multiplying DOL by the percentage change in sales.

Problem I

The following statements are either true or false. Place a (T) in the parentheses before each true statement and an (F) before each false statement.

1. ( ) An example of a step-wise cost is a sales representative's compensation that consists of a constant salary amount and a commission based on the amount sold.

2. ( ) In traditional cost-volume-profit analysis, the level of activity is described in terms of sales volume (either in units or dollars).

3. ( ) Traditional cost-volume-profit analysis is based on an assumption that all costs behave as if they are either truly fixed or variable.

4. ( ) A scatter diagram plots past cost and sales volume points on a graph.

5. ( ) The high-low method of finding the estimated line of cost behavior is preferable because it takes into consideration every point on the scatter diagram.

6. ( ) The break-even point in units can be calculated by dividing expected fixed costs by the expected contribution margin ratio.

7. ( ) A loss is represented on a CVP chart by the vertical distance between the sales line and total cost line to the right of the break-even point.

8. ( ) The margin of safety is the excess of current sales over expected sales.

9. ( ) Cost-volume-profit analysis is not helpful for planning changes in business operations because the values assumed for the various factors must remain constant.

10. ( ) A multiproduct break-even analysis treats a composite unit as a unit of a single product.

Problem II

You are given several words, phrases or numbers to choose from in completing each of the following statements or in answering the following questions. In each case, select the one that best completes the statement or answers the question and place its letter in the answer space provided.

_____ 1. Assume that two points from the estimated line of cost behavior from a scatter diagram are as follows:

	Units Axis	Cost Axis
Point A............................	14,000	$18,200
Point B	42,000	28,000

Rounded to the nearest whole cent, the variable cost per unit is:

a. $2.86

b. $1.50

c. $0.35

d. $0.23

e. Cannot be determined.

_____ 2. Functional Design Furniture Company sells a product for $80 per unit and incurs $55 of variable costs per unit sold. If fixed costs are $8,500 per month, what is the break-even sales volume in terms of dollars?

    a. $340

    b. $5,037

    c. $12,364

    d. $27,200

    e. $680,000

_____ 3. Greenside Up Company has monthly fixed costs of $11,700 and a 25% contribution margin ratio. Management has set a goal of earning a monthly after-tax income of $8,000. In order to have an $8,000 net income, the company must earn a pretax income of $12,000 and pay $4,000 in taxes. What level of sales is necessary to achieve their goal?

    a. $30,800.

    b. $58,800.

    c. $78,800.

    d. $94,800.

    e. $126,800.

_____ 4. Slice Master Corp. expects to sell 7,200 units of its product in July for $15 each. Fixed costs for the month are expected to be $43,200 and budgeted variable costs are $7 per unit. What margin of safety (in dollars) does Slice Master expect for July?

    a. $12,000

    b. $27,000

    c. $78,545

    d. $81,000

    e. None of the above.

Problem III

Many of the important ideas and concepts discussed in Chapter 22 are reflected in the following list of key terms. Test your understanding of these terms by matching the appropriate definitions with the terms. Record the number identifying the most appropriate definition in the blank space next to each term.

_____ Break-even point
_____ Composite unit
_____ Contribution margin per unit
_____ Contribution margin ratio
_____ Cost-volume-profit (CVP) analysis
_____ Curvilinear cost
_____ Cost-volume-profit (CVP) chart
_____ Degree of operating leverage (DOL)
_____ Estimated line of cost behavior

_____ High-low method
_____ Least-squares regression
_____ Margin of safety
_____ Mixed cost
_____ Operating leverage
_____ Relevant range of operations
_____ Sales mix
_____ Scatter diagram
_____ Step-wise cost

1. The contribution margin per unit expressed as a percent of the product's selling price.

2. A graph used to display data about past cost behavior and sales as points on a diagram.

3. The extent, or relative size, of fixed costs in the total cost structure.

4. The ratio of contribution margin divided by pretax income; used to assess the effect on income of changes in sales.

5. The amount that the sale of one unit contributes toward recovering fixed costs and earning profit; defined as sales price per unit minus variable expense per unit.

6. A procedure that yields an estimated line of cost behavior by graphically connecting costs associated with the highest and lowest sales volume.

7. A statistical method for deriving an estimated line of cost behavior that is more precise than the high-low method and a scatter diagram.

8. A cost that behaves like a combination of fixed and variable costs.

9. A planning method that includes predicting the volume of activity, the costs to be incurred, sales earned, and profits received.

10. A line drawn on a graph to visually fit the relation between cost and sales.

11. A company's normal operating range; excludes extremely high and low volumes not likely to occur.

12. A cost that changes with volume but not at a constant rate.

13. A cost that remains fixed over limited ranges of volumes but changes by a lump sum when volume changes occur outside these limited ranges.

14. The excess of expected sales over the level of break-even sales.

15. The output level at which sales equals fixed plus variable costs (where income equals zero).

16. A graphic representation of cost-volume-profit relations.

17. The ratio of sales volumes for the various products sold by a company.

18. Consists of a specific number of units of each product in proportion to their expected sales mix.

Problem IV

Complete the following by filling in the blanks.

1. The total amount of a _____ cost changes with production volume and in the same proportion. An example of this kind of cost is _____ _____.

2. The total amount of a _____ cost remains constant at all levels of production within the relevant range. The per unit cost decreases as the number of units _____.

3. An example of a fixed cost is _____.

4. The _____ method of deriving an estimated line of cost behavior produces a straight line that most precisely fits the actual cost behavior experienced by the company.

5. The high-low method of deriving an estimated line of cost behavior is deficient because it considers only the points with the _____ and _____ costs, and ignores all the-other points.

6. In preparing a scatter diagram of costs and volume, the horizontal axis is used to represent _____ _____ and the vertical axis is used to represent _____.

7. When aggregated, deviations in individual variable costs may _____ each other and allow management to plot the total variable cost as a _____ on a CVP chart.

8. A contribution margin income statement is different than a conventional income statement in that _____ are subtracted from revenues to determine _____.

9. A company has fixed costs of $100,000 per year, a break-even sales volume of 4,000 units, and a selling price of $55 per unit. The variable cost is $ _____ per unit.

Problem V

The Lanier Company incurs $60,000 of annual fixed costs in manufacturing and selling a product that it sells for $15 per unit. The variable costs of manufacturing and selling the product are $9 per unit.

1. The contribution margin per unit is $_____.

2. The contribution margin ratio for the product is:

$$\frac{\$\rule{2cm}{0.15mm}}{\$\rule{2cm}{0.15mm}} = \rule{2cm}{0.15mm}\%$$

3. The break-even point in units is:

$$\frac{\$\rule{2cm}{0.15mm}}{\$\rule{2cm}{0.15mm}} = \rule{2cm}{0.15mm} \text{ units}$$

4. The break-even point in dollars is:

$ \underline{\hspace{3cm}} = \$ \underline{\hspace{4cm}}$

$\underline{\hspace{3cm}}\%$

5. Assume that Lanier has projected sales for the year to be $200,000?

    a. Determine the margin of safety in dollars.

$ \underline{\hspace{4cm}} - \$ \underline{\hspace{4cm}} = \$ \underline{\hspace{4cm}}$

    b. Compute the margin of safety rate.

$ \underline{\hspace{3cm}} = \underline{\hspace{3cm}}\%$

$ \underline{\hspace{3cm}}$

6. The Lanier Company's management wants to earn an annual pretax net income of $50,000. Determine the dollar sales volume that the company must achieve to reach this target income level.

$ \underline{\hspace{4cm}}$

7. Assume that Lanier Company has a 30% income tax rate. Determine the amount of after-tax income that the Lanier Company would earn from a $420,000 sales volume.

$ \underline{\hspace{4cm}}$

Problem VI

The Bowen Company sells 2 products, Product A and Product B in the ratio of 5:3. The selling price of each unit of Product A is $10 and of Product B is $8. The variable costs per unit of Product A are $7 and of Product B is $5. Fixed costs are $120,000.

1. The selling price per composite unit is:

    Product A: _____ units x $ _____ = $ _____
    Product B: _____ units x $ _____ = + _____
    $ _____

2. The variable cost per composite unit is:

    Product A: _____ units x $ _____ = $ _____
    Product B: _____ units x $ _____ = + _____
    $ _____

3. The break-even point in composite units is:

    $ _____
    ———————— = _____ units
    $

4. The number of units of Product A and Product B that must be sold to break-even are:

    Product A: _____ x _____ = _____ units
    Product B: _____ x _____ = _____ units

5. If Bowen want to earn a pretax net income of $30,000?

    The number of composite units to sell to earn a net income of $30,000 is:

    $ _____
    ———————— = _____ units
    $

    The number of units of Product A and Product B to earn a net income of $30,000 are:

    Product A: _____ x _____ = _____ units
    Product B: _____ x _____ = _____ units

Solutions for Chapter 22

Problem I

1.	F	6	F
2.	T	7.	F
3.	T	8.	F
4.	T	9.	F
5.	F	10.	T

Problem II

1. C
2. D
3. D
4. B

Problem III

Problem IV

1. variable; direct material cost or direct labor cost

2. fixed; increases

3. rent or property taxes

4. least-squares regression

5. highest; lowest

6. units; total costs

7. offset; straight line

8. variable costs, contribution margin

9. $30

Problem V

1. Contribution margin = $15 − $9 = $6

2. $\dfrac{\text{Contribution Margin}}{\text{Selling Price per Unit}} = \dfrac{\$6}{\$15} = 40.0\%$

3. $\dfrac{\text{Fixed Costs}}{\text{Contribution Margin per unit}} = \dfrac{\$60,000}{\$6} = 10,000 \text{ units}$

4. $\dfrac{\text{Fixed Costs}}{\text{Contribution Margin Ratio}} = \dfrac{\$60,000}{40.0\%} = \$150,000$

5. a.

Expected Sales	$200,000
Less Break-even Sales	150,000
Margin of Safety	$ 50,000

   b. $\dfrac{\text{Margin of Safety}}{\text{Expected Sales}} = \dfrac{\$50,000}{\$200,000} = 25.0\%$

6. $\dfrac{\text{Fixed costs} + \text{Target Net Income}}{\text{Contribution Margin Ratio}} = \dfrac{\$60,000 + \$50,000}{40\%} = \$275,000$

7.

Sales		$420,000
Less variable costs	(420,000 x 60%)	252,000
Contribution Margin		$168,000
Less fixed costs		60,000
Pretax Income		$108,000
Less Income Tax Expense	(108,000 x 30%)	32,400
Net Income		$ 75,600

Problem VI

1. The selling price per composite unit is:

Product A:	5	units	x	$ 10	=	$	50
Product B:	3	units	x	$ 8	=	+	24
						$	74

2. The variable cost per composite unit is:

Product A:	5	units	x	$ 7	=	$	35
Product B:	3	units	x	$ 5	=	+	15
						$	50

3. The break-even point in composite units is:

$$\frac{\$120,000}{\$24} = 5,000 \text{ units}$$

4. The variable cost per composite unit is:

Product A:	5	x	5,000 units	=	25,000	units
Product B:	3	x	5,000 units	=	15,000	units

5. If Bowen want to earn a pretax net income of $30,000?

The number of composite units to sell to earn a net income of $30,000 is:

$$\frac{\text{fixed costs} + \text{net income}}{\text{Composite CM}} = \frac{\$120,000 + \$30,000}{\$24} = 6,250 \text{ units}$$

The number of units of Product A and Product B to earn a net income of $30,000 are:

Product A:	5	x	6,250 units	=	31,250	units
Product B:	3	x	6,250 units	=	18,750	units

CHAPTER 23
MASTER BUDGETS AND PLANNING

Learning Objective C1:

Describe the importance and benefits of budgeting.

Summary

Planning is a management responsibility of critical importance to business success. Budgeting is the process management uses to formalize its plans. Budgeting promotes management analysis and focuses its attention on the future. Budgeting also provides a basis for evaluating performance, serves as a source of motivation, is a means of coordinating activities, and communicates management's plans and instructions to employees. Budgeting is a detailed activity that requires administration. At least three aspects are important: budget committee, budget reporting, and budget timing. A budget committee oversees the budget preparation. The budget period pertains to the time period for which the budget is prepared such as a year or month.

Learning Objective C2:

Explain the process of budget administration and the process of preparing it.

Summary

A master budget is a formal overall plan for a company. It consists of plans for business operations and capital expenditures, plus the financial results of those activities. The budgeting process begins with a sales budget. Based on expected sales volume, companies can budget purchases, selling expenses, and administrative expenses. Next, the capital expenditures budget is prepared, followed by the cash budget and budgeted financial statements. Manufacturers also must budget production quantities, materials purchases, labor costs, and overhead.

Learning Objective A1:

Analyze expense planning using activity-based budgeting.

Summary

Activity-based budgeting requires management to identify activities performed by departments, plan necessary activity levels, identify resources required to perform these activities, and budget the resources.

Learning Objective P1:

Prepare each component of a master budget and link each to the budgeting process.

Summary

The term *master budget* refers to a collection of individual component budgets. Each component budget is designed to guide persons responsible for activities covered by that component. A master budget must reflect the components of a company and their interaction in pursuit of company goals.

Learning Objective P2:

Link both operating and capital expenditures budgets to budgeted financial statements.

Summary

The operating budgets, capital expenditures budget, and cash budget contain much of the information to prepare a budgeted income statement for the budget period and a budgeted balance sheet at the end of the budget period. Budgeted financial statements show the expected financial consequences of the planned activities described in the budgets.

Learning Objective P3 (Appendix):

Prepare production and manufacturing budgets.

Summary

A manufacturer must prepare a *production budget* instead of a purchase budget. A *manufacturing budget* shows the budgeted production costs for direct materials, direct labor, and overhead.

Chapter Outline

I.   **Budget Process**—Process of planning future business activities.

    A. Strategic Budgeting

       1. Budget—Formal statement of a company's future short term financial plans.

       2. All managers should be involved.

       3. Relevant focus of budgeting analysis is future.

       4. Focus on future is important because daily operations may divert management's attention from planning.

       5. Good budgeting system formalizes planning process and demands relevant input; makes planning an explicit management responsibility.

    B. Benchmarking Budgets

       1. Control function requires management to evaluate (benchmark) business operations against some norm.

       2. Evaluation involves comparing actual results against:

          a. Past performance or

          b. Expected (budgeted) performance.

       3. Evaluation assists management in identifying problems and taking corrective actions if necessary.

       4. Evaluation using expected performance is usually superior to using past performance when deciding if actual results trigger need for corrective action.

          a. Past performance fails to take into account changes that may affect current and future activities.

             i.   Changes in economic conditions.

             ii.   Shifts in competitive advantages within the industry.

             iii. New product developments.

             iv. Increased or decreased advertising.

             v.   Technological advances and innovations.

          b. Budgeted performance levels anticipate and adjust for changes in important company, industry and economic factors.

          c. Budgets provide management an effective control and monitoring system.

    C. Budgeting and Human Behavior

       1. Budgeting provides standards for evaluating performance and can affect the attitudes of employees evaluated by them.

       2. Three guidelines to ensure positive effect on employees' attitudes.

          a. Employees affected by budget should be involved in its preparation to increase commitment to meeting it (participatory budgeting).

       b.   Budgeted levels of performance must be realistic (goals must be attainable) to avoid discouraging employees.

       c.   Evaluation should be made carefully and allow affected employees to explain reasons for apparent performance deficiencies.

   3.   Management must be aware of negative outcomes

       a.   Employees may understate the sales budget and/or overstate the expense budget to allow a budgetary slack in meeting targets.

       b.   Pressure to meet budgeted results may lead to unethical or fraudulent behavior.

       c.   Some employees may spend budgeted amounts even on unnecessary times to make sure their budgets are not reduced in the next period.

D. Budget as a Management Tool

   1.   Activities of all departments should contribute to meeting company's overall goals.

   2.   Careful coordination required; budgeting achieves coordination.

E. Budgeting Communication

   1.   Written budget clearly documents management plans and specific action plans to all employees.

   2.   Informal communication of business plans can create uncertainty and confusion.

II.   **Budget Administration**—Proper administration required of this important and detailed activity.

A. Budget Committee

   1.   Without active employee involvement, risk that employees will feel as if budget fails to reflect their special problems and needs.

   2.   Budget figures and estimates more useful if developed through bottom-up process.

   3.   Central guidance also needed; budget committee (made up of department heads and other executives) supplies guidance, and helps to ensure budgeted amounts are realistic and coordinated.

   4.   Budget committee should identify any departmental budget figures that do not reflect efficient performance; originating department should justify or adjust figures.

   5.   Ongoing communication should continue to ensure all parties accept budget as reasonable, attainable, and desirable.

    B. Budget Reporting

      1. Usually coincides with the accounting period.

      2. Most companies prepare annual budgets; usually separated into monthly or quarterly budgets.

      3. Short-term budgets allow quick performance evaluation and corrective action; reports compare actual results to budgets.

      4. Variances are differences between actual and budgeted amounts; management examines variances to identify areas for improvement.

    C. Budget Timing—Many companies apply continuous budgeting by preparing rolling budgets; as each budget period passes:

      1. New monthly or quarterly budgets are prepared to replace those that have lapsed.

      2. Entire set of budgets for months or quarters that remain is revised.

      3. Management is continuously planning ahead.

III. **The Master Budget**—Formal, comprehensive plan for a company's future.

    A. Contains several individual budgets that are linked with each other to provide a coordinated plan for the company.

      1. Typically includes individual budgets for sales, purchases or production, various expenses, capital expenditures and cash.

      2. Sequence required; certain budgets cannot be prepared until other budgets are complete.

      3. Undesirable outcomes might be revealed at any stage in budgeting process; changes must be made to prior budgets and previous steps repeated.

    B. Operating Budgets—Four major types.

      1. Sales budget

          a. First step in preparing master budget.

          b. Requires careful analysis of forecasted economic and market conditions, business capacity, proposed selling expenses, and predictions of unit sales.

          c. Participatory budgeting approach ensures greater commitment to goals, and draws on knowledge and experience of people involved in activity.

          d. More detailed than simple projections of total sales; includes forecasts of both units sales and unit prices for various products, regions, departments, and sales representatives.

2. Merchandise Purchases Budget (Production and Manufacturing Budgets in Appendix 23A)

   a. Whether company manufacturers or purchases product sold, budgeted future sales volume is primary factor in inventory management decisions.

   b. Budgets for just-in-time inventory systems cover short periods to order just enough merchandise or materials to satisfy immediate sales demand; inventory is held to a minimum (zero in ideal situations).

   c. Other companies keep enough inventory on hand to reduce risk of running short (called safety stock); provides protection against lost sales caused by unfulfilled customer demands or delays in shipments from suppliers.

   d. Merchandisers—Sales budget used as basis for merchandise purchases budget.

      i. Inventory units to be purchased is determined by

             Expected unit sales
         + <u>Budgeted ending inventory units</u>
             Total inventory units required
         − <u>Budgeted beginning inventory units</u>
             Inventory units to be purchased

      ii. The budgeted cost of merchandise purchases is computed as:

             Inventory units to be purchased
         x <u>Budgeted cost per unit</u>
             Budgeted cost of merchandise purchases

   e. Manufacturers (Appendix 23A)—A manufacturer will prepare a production budgeted instead of a purchases budget. Sales budget used as basis for production budget.

      i. Units to be produced is determined by:

             Expected unit sales
         + <u>Budgeted ending inventory units</u>
             Required units of available production
         − <u>Budgeted beginning inventory units</u>
             Units to be produced

      ii. The production budgeted is used as basis for three manufacturing budgets.

    iii. Direct Materials Budget:

        Units to be produced
      x <u>Material requirements per unit</u>
        Materials needed for production
     + <u>Desired ending inventory of direct materials</u>
        Total required materials
     − <u>Beginning inventory of direct materials</u>
        Direct materials to be purchased
     x <u>Materials price per unit of materials</u>
        Budgeted cost of direct materials purchases

    iv. Direct Labor Budget:

        Units to be produced
     x <u>Labor requirement per unit (hours)</u>
        Total direct labor hours needed
     + <u>Labor rate per hour</u>
        Labor dollars

    v. Factory Overhead Budget:

        Units to be produced
     x <u>Variable overhead rate</u>
        Budgeted variable overhead
     + <u>Budgeted fixed overhead</u>
        Budgeted total overhead

3. Selling Expense Budget
   a. Reports amounts of variable and fixed selling expenses expected during budget period.
   b. Created to provide sufficient selling expenses to meet sales goals reflected in sales budget.
4. General and Administrative Expense Budget
   a. Plan showing predicted operating expenses not included in selling expenses budget.
   b. Consists of items variable or fixed in terms of sales volume.
   c. Interest expense and income tax expense cannot be planned at this stage of budgeting process.

C. Capital Expenditures Budget
   1. Includes amounts to be received from plant asset disposals, and to be spent on purchasing additional plant assets; assumes proposed production program is carried out.
   2. Affected by long-range plans for business instead of short-term sales budgets.

      3. Capital budgeting is process of evaluating and planning for capital (plant and equipment) expenditures, which involve long-run commitments of large amounts.

      4. Major effect on predicted cash flows and company's need for debt or equity financing; often linked with company's ability to take on more debt.

  D. Financial Budgets

      1. Cash Budget—shows expected cash inflows and outflows during budget period

         Beginning cash balance
       + <u>Budgeted cash receipts</u>
         Total available cash
       – <u>Budgeted cash expenditures</u>
         Preliminary cash balance

        a. May include planned receipts from short-term loans (if expected preliminary cash balance is inadequate), or use of cash to repay loans or acquire short-term investments (if preliminary cash balance is in excess of requirements).

        b. Budgeted cash receipts include:

          i. Expected cash sales.

          ii. Expected cash collections of accounts receivable.

          iii. Other expected cash receipts such as interest revenue, sale of assets, etc.

        c. Budgeted cash disbursements include:

          i. Budgeted cash disbursements from selling expense budget and general and administrative expense budget.

          ii. Expected cash disbursements for interest expense and income taxes.

          iii. Expected cash purchases for a merchandiser.

          iv. Expected direct materials, direct labor and overhead payments for a manufacturer.

          v. Expected cash payments on accounts payable.

          vi. Other expected cash payments such as owner's withdrawals or dividends, repayment of notes, etc.

      2. Budgeted Income Statement

        a. Managerial accounting report showing predicted amounts of sales and expenses.

        b. Information comes from already prepared budgets.

        c. Income tax expense predicted at this level.

3. Budgeted Balance Sheet

    a. Final step in preparing master budget.

    b. Shows predicted amounts for assets, liabilities, and stockholders' equity as of end of budget period.

    c. Prepared using information from other budgets (see notes to budgeted balance sheet for sources of amounts).

IV. **Decision Analysis—Activity-Based Budgeting (ABB)**—budget system based on expected activities.

  A. Traditional budgets are based on figures from previous year, adjusted for changes in operating conditions.

  B. Activity-based budgeting requires management to list activities and to understand the resources required to perform these activities.

    1. Helps management assess how much expenses will increase with increases in activity levels.

    2. Helps management reduce costs by eliminating non-value-added activities.

Problem I

The following statements are either true or false. Place a (T) in the parentheses before each true statement and an (F) before each false statement.

1. ( ) A company that has a formal budgeting process has clearly established that planning for the future is an important management responsibility.

2. ( ) Because budgets are based on many predictions of the future, a performance evaluation is more likely to be useful if it compares actual performance for the most recent period with actual performance from earlier periods instead of comparing the most recent period's performance with budgeted amounts.

3. ( ) As a control over its management, the production department should not be allowed to participate in preparing its own budget; otherwise, the department is likely to manipulate the budgeted amounts so that the goals will be easy to meet.

4. ( ) If a company prepares a budget each month covering the next twelve one-month periods, it is using continuous budgeting.

5. ( ) The production budget should be the first budget prepared for a manufacturing company.

6. ( ) The final document developed in preparing the master budget is the budgeted balance sheet.

7. ( ) A production budget does not include budgeted production costs. These costs are included in the manufacturing budget.

8. ( ) Because interest and income tax expense are the responsibility of a company's top management, they are included in the general and administrative expense budget.

9. ( ) The capital expenditures budget is used to plan cash receipts and disbursements with the goal of ensuring that the company has sufficient cash available to meet future operating needs.

10. ( ) Cash budgets show how much money is to be received from or expended on each activity and when the receipts and expenditures are to occur.

Problem II

You are given several words, phrases or numbers to choose from in completing each of the following statements or in answering the following questions. In each case, select the one that best completes the statement or answers the question and place its letter in the answer space provided.

_____ 1. Playland has budgeted sales of $34,000 during September. The store expects to begin September with an $18,700 inventory and end the month with a $16,500 inventory. Playland's cost of goods sold averages 60% of sales. Determine budgeted purchases for September.

    a. $11,400.

    b. $18,200.

    c. $19,080.

    d. $22,600.

    e. $31,800.

_____ 2. Fabricon Company sells a product called the Streamer. Management predicts that the June 30 inventory will consist of 12,000 Streamers. In addition, management predicts that sales for the next three quarters will reach these levels:

Third quarter	26,500 units
Fourth quarter	57,000 units
First quarter (next year)	24,600 units

Management's policy states that the company should begin each quarter with a merchandise inventory equal to 40% of the next quarter's budgeted sales.

How many units should Fabricon purchase in the third and fourth quarters to meet this policy?

	Third Quarter	Fourth Quarter
a.	37,300	44,040
b.	25,100	69,200
c.	67,800	11,640
d.	30,400	75,300
e.	79,200	5,160

_____ 3. High Flying Kite Company has the following sales budget:

January	$ 7,000
February....................	11,000
March........................	26,000
April.........................	35,000

The company budgets cost of goods sold to be 60% of sales. Management's policy states that the company should begin each month with a merchandise inventory equal to 40% of that month's budgeted cost of goods sold. All purchases are on credit and 20% of the purchases in any month is paid for during the same month, 50% is paid during the first month after the purchase; and the remaining 30% is paid in the second month after the purchase.

The budgeted balance of accounts payable at the end of March should be:

a. $14,208.

b. $17,268.

c. $17,760.

d. $19,308.

e. $24,100.

Problem III

Many of the important ideas and concepts discussed in Chapter 23 are reflected in the following list of key terms. Test your understanding of these terms by matching the appropriate definitions with the terms. Record the number identifying the most appropriate definition in the blank space next to each term.

_____ Activity based budgeting (ABB)   _____ Manufacturing budget
_____ Budget   _____ Master budget
_____ Budgeted balance sheet   _____ Merchandise purchases budget
_____ Budgeted income statement   _____ Production budget
_____ Budgeting   _____ Rolling budgets
_____ Capital expenditures budget   _____ Safety stock
_____ Cash budget   _____ Sales budget
_____ Continuous budgeting   _____ Selling expense budget
_____ General and administrative expense budget

1. A plan that shows the predicted costs for direct materials, direct labor, and overhead to be incurred in manufacturing units in the production budget.

2. The practice of preparing budgets for a selected number of future periods and revising those budgets as each period is completed.

3. An accounting report that presents predicted amounts of the company's revenues and expenses for the budget period.

4. A comprehensive business plan that includes specific plans for expected sales, product units to be produced, merchandise (or materials) to be purchased, expenses to be incurred, plant assets to be purchased, and amounts of cash to be borrowed or loans to be repaid, as well as a budgeted income statement and balance sheet.

5. A plan that lists the types and amounts of selling expenses expected in the budget period.

6. A plan showing the units of goods to be sold or services to be provided; the starting point in the budgeting process for most departments.

7. A plan that lists dollar amounts to be both received from disposal of plant assets and spent to purchase plant assets.

8. A plan that shows the units to be produced each period.

9. A plan that shows the expected cash inflows and outflows during the budget period, including receipts from loans needed to maintain a minimum cash balance and repayments of such loans.

10. A plan that shows predicted operating expenses not included in the selling expenses budget.

11. A formal statement of future plans, usually expressed in monetary terms.

12. An accounting report that presents predicted amounts of the company's assets, liabilities, and equity balances as of the end of the budget period.

13. The process of planning future business actions and expressing them as formal plans.

14. A new set of budgets a firm adds for the next period (with revisions) to replace the ones that have lapsed.

15. Quantity of inventory or materials over the minimum needed to satisfy budgeted demand.

16. A plan that shows the units or costs of merchandise to be purchased by a merchandising company during the budget period.

17. A budget system based on expected activities.

Problem IV

Complete the following by filling in the blanks.

1. The purpose of the _____ committee is to provide central guidance for the budgeting process for the entire company. This group is especially important when the company uses a _____ approach to budgeting in order to increase employees' commitment to the process.

2. One benefit from budgeting is that it causes management to_____. _____, and _____ on the future.

3. Another benefit from budgeting is that it provides a basis for evaluating _____ that is superior to comparisons with past results.

4. A budget provides a means of _____ business activities so that all parts of the company are working toward the same goals.

5. When a company follows the practice of _____ budgeting, management continuously plans for the future. This process produces what are called _____ budgets.

6. In the process of developing a master budget, the first step is the preparation of the _____ budget. The final document to be prepared is the _____.

7. The _____ budget consists of plans based on the relationship between sales predictions and merchandise inventory management goals.

8. After preparing the _____ budget, but before preparing the manufacturing budget, the management of a manufacturing company must develop a _____ budget.

9. A company's planned _____ receipts and _____ disbursements are described in the _____ budget.

10. A company's management cannot predict the amount of _____ expense that will be incurred until the cash budget is prepared.

11. A company's management cannot predict the amount of _____ expense that will be incurred until the budgeted _____ is nearly completed.

12. A company's planned purchases and disposals of plant and equipment are described in its _____ budget.

Problem V

Woody Company had the following budgeted cash receipts and cash disbursements from operations for the third quarter of the current year:

	Receipts	Disbursements
July	$100,000	$ 80,000
August	65,000	89,950
September	115,000	110,000

According to a credit agreement with the company's bank, Woody Company promises to have a minimum cash balance of $15,000 at the end of each month. In return, the bank has agreed that the company can borrow up to $50,000 with interest of 12% per year. Interest must be paid on the last day of each month. The interest is calculated on the beginning balance of the bank loan for the month. In addition, to the extent possible, the principal amount borrowed from the bank must be repaid on the last day of each month. The company is expected to have a cash balance of $15,000 and a bank loan balance of $5,000 on July 1.

Required:

Prepare monthly cash budgets for the third quarter.

WOODY COMPANY
Cash Budget
Third Quarter

	July	August	September
Beginning cash balance			
Cash receipts			
Total			
Cash disbursements			
Interest expense:			
July ( )			
August ( )			
September ( )			
Preliminary balance			
Additional loan from bank			
Repayment of loan to bank			
Ending cash balance			
Ending bank loan balance			

Problem VI

Made-Rite Company had the following information available to prepare the manufacturing budgets for the first quarter of the year:

Expected Sales

Month	Units	Selling price
January	500	$50
February	500	$50
March	600	$50
April	600	$50

Production Budget
Management wants a budgeted ending finished goods inventory equal to 20% of the following month's expected sales.

Direct Materials
Each unit requires 2 pounds of direct materials and each pound has a budgeted cost of $5. Management wants to purchase enough materials to meet the expected production plus have an amount equal to 10% of the following month's materials requirements.

Direct Labor
Each unit requires 30 minutes of direct labor at a cost of $12 per hour.

Factory Overhead
The variable overhead rate is $2 per direct labor hour and fixed overhead is $3,000 per month.

Required:

Prepare the following budgets for the first quarter:

Sales Budget

	January	February	March	Quarter #1
Expected Sales				
X Selling price per unit				
Total budgeted sales				

Production Budget

	January	February	March	Quarter #1
Total Budgeted Sales				
+ budgeted ending inventory				
Required Units				
Less: beginning inventory (units)				
Units to be Produced				

Direct Materials Budget

	January	February	March	Quarter #1
Units to be produced				
x materials required per unit				
Materials need for production				
Add budgeted ending inventory				
Total material requirements				
Less: beginning inventory				
Materials to be purchased				
X materials price per unit				
Budgeted direct materials purchases				

Direct Labor Budget

	January	February	March	Quarter #1
Units to be produced				
x direct labor hours per unit				
Total labor hours needed				
x labor rate per hour				
Direct labor dollars				

Factory Overhead Budget

	January	February	March	Quarter #1
Direct labor hours				
x variable overhead rate (per DLH)				
Budgeted variable overhead				
Budgeted Fixed overhead				
Budgeted total factory overhead				

Solutions for Chapter 23

Problem I

1.	T	6.	T
2.	F	7.	T
3.	F	8.	F
4.	T	9.	F
5.	F	10.	T

Problem II

1. B
2. A
3. B

Problem III

Activity based budgeting (ABB)	17	Manufacturing budget	1
Budget	11	Master budget	4
Budgeted balance sheet	12	Merchandise purchases budget	16
Budgeted income statement	3	Production budget	8
Budgeting	13	Rolling budgets	14
Capital expenditures budget	7	Safety stock	15
Cash budget	9	Sales budget	6
Continuous budgeting	2	Selling expense budget	5
General and administrative expense budget	10		

Problem IV

1. budget; bottom-up or participating

2. study; research; focus

3. performance

4. coordinating

5. continuous; rolling

6. sales; budgeted balance sheet

7. merchandise purchases

8. sales; production

9. cash; cash; cash

10. interest

11. income taxes; income statement

12 capital expenditures

Problem V

WOODY COMPANY
Cash Budget
Third Quarter

	July	August	September
Beginning cash balance	$15,000	$29,950	$15,000
Cash receipts....................................	100,000	65,000	115,000
Total...	115,000	94,650	130,000
Cash disbursements	(80,000)	(89,950)	(110,000)
Interest expense			
July ($5,000 x 1%)	(50)		
August (none)...........................			
September ($10,000 x 1%)........			(100)
Preliminary balance	34,950	5,000	19,900
Additional loan from bank.............		10,000	
Repayment of loan to bank............	(5,000)		(4,900)
Ending cash balance	$29,950	$15,000	$15,000
Ending bank loan balance...............	$ 0	$10,000	$ 5,100

Problem VI

Sales Budget

	January	February	March	Quarter #1	April
Expected Sales	500	500	600	1,600	600
X Selling price per unit	$ 50	$ 50	$ 50	$ 50	$ 50
Total budgeted sales	$ 25,000	$25,000	$30,000	$80,000	$30,000

Production Budget

	January	February	March	Quarter #1	April
Total Budgeted Sales	500	500	600	1,600	600
+ budgeted ending inventory	100	120	120	120	140
Required Units	600	620	720	1,720	740
Less: beginning inventory (units)	100	100	120	100	120
Units to be Produced	500	520	600	1,620	620

Direct Materials Budget

	January	February	March	Quarter #1	April
Units to be produced	500	520	600	1,620	620
x materials required per unit	2	2	2	2	2
Materials need for production	1,000	1,040	1,200	3,240	1,240
Add budgeted ending inventory	104	120	124	124	
Total material requirements	1,104	1,160	1,324	3,364	
Less: beginning inventory	100*	104	120	100	
Materials to be purchased	1,004	1,056	1,204	3,264	
X materials price per unit	$ 5	$ 5	$ 5	$ 5	
Budgeted direct materials purchases	$5,020	$5,280	$6,020	$16,320	

* January units to be produced of $500 x 20% = 100 units of beginning inventory

Direct Labor Budget

	January	February	March	Quarter #1
Units to be produced	500	520	600	1,620
x direct labor hours per unit	0.5	0.5	0.5	0.5
Total labor hours needed	250	260	300	810
x labor rate per hour	$ 12	$ 12	$ 12	$ 12
Direct labor dollars	$3,000	$3,120	$3,600	$9,720

Factory Overhead Budget

	January	February	March	Quarter #1
Direct labor hours	250	260	300	810
x variable overhead rate (per DLH)	$ 2	$ 2	$ 2	$ 2
Budgeted variable overhead	$ 500	$ 520	$ 600	$ 1,620
Budgeted Fixed overhead	3,000	3,000	3,000	9,000
Budgeted total factory overhead	$3,500	$3,520	$ 3,600	$10,620

Learning Objective C1:

Define standard costs and explain how standard cost information is useful for management by exception.

Standard costs are the normal costs that should be incurred to produce a product or perform a service. They should be based on a careful examination of the processes used to produce a product or perform a service as well as the quantities and prices that should be incurred in carrying out those processes. On a performance report, standard costs (which are flexible budget amounts) are compared to actual costs and the differences are presented as variances. Standard cost accounting provides management information about costs that differ from budgeted (expected) amounts. Performance reports disclose the costs or areas of operations that have significant variances from budgeted amounts. This allows managers to focus attention on the exceptions and less attention on areas proceeding normally.

Learning Objective C2:

Describe variances and what they reveal about performance.

Summary

Management can use variances to monitor and control activities. Total cost variances can be broken into price and quantity variances to direct management's attention to those responsible for quantities used or prices paid.

Learning Objective A1:

Analyze changes in sales from expected amounts.

Summary

Actual sales can differ from budgeted sales, and managers can investigate this difference by computing both the sales price and sales volume variances. The *sales price variance* refers to that portion of total variance resulting from a difference between actual and budgeted selling prices. The *sales volume variance* refers to that portion of total variance resulting from a difference between actual and budgeted sales quantities.

Learning Objective P1:

Prepare a flexible budget and interpret a flexible budget performance report.

Summary

A flexible budget expresses variable costs in per unit terms so it can be used to develop budgeted amounts for any volume level within the relevant range. Thus, managers compute budgeted amounts for evaluation after a period for the volume that actually occurred. To prepare a flexible budget, we express each variable cost as a constant amount per unit of sales (or as a percent of sales dollars). In contrast, the budgeted amount of each fixed cost is expressed as a total amount expected to occur at any sales volume within the relevant range. The flexible budget is then determined using these computations and amounts for fixed and variable costs at the expected sales volume.

Learning Objective P2:

Compute material and labor variances.

Summary

Materials and labor variances are due to differences between the actual costs incurred and the budgeted costs. The price (or rate) variance is computed by comparing the actual cost with the flexible budget amount that should have been incurred to acquire the actual quantity of resources. The quantity (or efficiency) variance is computed by comparing the flexible budget amount that should have been incurred to acquire the actual quantity of resources with the flexible budget amount that should have been incurred to acquire the standard quantity of resources.

Learning Objective P3:

Compute overhead variances.

Summary

Overhead variances are due to differences between the actual overhead costs incurred and the overhead applied to production. An overhead spending variance arises when the actual amount incurred differs from the budgeted amount of overhead. An overhead efficiency (or volume) variance arises when the flexible overhead budget amount differs from the overhead applied to production. It is important to realize that overhead is assigned using an overhead allocation base, meaning that an efficiency variance (in the case of variable overhead) is a result of the overhead application base being used more or less efficiently than planned.

Learning Objective P4[A]:

Prepare journal entries for standard costs and account for price and quantity variances.

Summary

When a company records standard costs in its accounts, the standard costs of materials, labor, and overhead are debited to the Goods in Process Inventory account. Based on an analysis of the material, labor, and overhead costs, each quantity variance, price variance, volume variance, and controllable variance is recorded in a separate account. At the end of the period, if the variances are material, they are allocated among the balances of the Goods in Process Inventory, Finished Goods Inventory, and Cost of Goods Sold accounts. If they are not material, they are simply debited or credited to the Cost of Goods Sold account.

Chapter Outline

Section 1—Flexible Budgets

I.   Budgetary Process

A. Budgetary Control and Reporting
1. Budgetary control—management's use of budgets to monitor and control the company's operations.
2. Budget reports
    a. Contain relevant information that compares actual results to planned activities.
    b. Sometimes viewed as progress reports (or report cards) on management's performance in achieving planned objectives.
3. Budgetary control process involves at least four steps.
    a. Develop budget from planned objectives.
    b. Compare actual results to budgeted amounts and analyze differences.
    c. Take corrective and strategic actions.
    d. Establish new planned objectives and prepare new budget.

B. Fixed Budget Performance Report
1. In fixed budgetary control system, master budget is based on single prediction for sales volume (or other activity level).
2. Fixed budget (also called static budget) is based on a single predicted amount of sales or production volume.
3. Fixed budget performance report compares actual results with results expected under the fixed budget (that predicted a certain sales volume or other activity level).
4. Differences between budgeted and actual results are designated as variances.
    a. Favorable variance (F)—actual revenue is greater than budgeted revenue, or actual cost is lower than budgeted cost.
    b. Unfavorable variance (U)—Actual revenue is lower than budgeted revenue, or actual cost is greater than budgeted cost.

C. Budget Reports for Evaluation
1. Primary use of budget reports is to help management monitor and control operations.
2. Fixed budget reports show variances from budget, but manager doesn't know if a change in sales volume (or other activity level) is cause for variances, or if other factors have influenced the amounts.
3. Major limitation of fixed budget performance report is inability of fixed budget reports to adjust for changes in activity levels.

II.   **Flexible Budget Reports**—Superior alternative to fixed budget reports.

  A. Purpose of Flexible Budgets

    1. Flexible budget (also called variable budget) is based on predicted amounts of revenues and expenses corresponding to actual level of output.

    2. Useful both before and after the period's activities are complete.

    3. Flexible budgets prepared before the period are based on several levels of activities. Include both best case and worst case scenarios.

    4. Flexible budgets prepared after the period help managers evaluate past performance.

    5. Especially useful because it reflects the different levels of activities in different amounts of revenues and costs.

        a. Comparisons of actual results with budgeted performance are more likely to identify reasons for any differences.

        b. Helps managers to focus attention on problem areas and to implement corrective actions.

  B. Preparation of Flexible Budgets

    1. Designed to reveal effects of volume of activity on revenue and costs.

    2. Must rely on distinctions between fixed and variable costs.

        a. Variable costs imply that cost per unit of activity remains constant; total amount of variable cost changes in direct proportion to a change in level of activity.

        b. Total amount of fixed cost remains unchanged regardless of changes in level of activity within relevant (normal) operating range.

        c. Note that some costs are neither strictly variable nor strictly fixed; however, assumption here is that all costs can be reasonably classified as either variable or fixed within a relevant range.

    3. When numbers making up a flexible budget are created:

        a. Each variable cost is expressed as either a constant amount per unit of sales or as a percent of sales dollar.

        b. Budgeted amount of fixed cost is expressed as the total amount expected to occur at any sales volume within the relevant range.

    4. Layout follows a contribution margin format

        a. Sales are followed by variable costs, and then by fixed costs—difference between sales and variable costs equals contribution margin.

        b. First column (see Exhibit 24.3) shows flexible budget amounts of variable costs per unit, and second column shows fixed costs for any volume of sales in relevant range.

        c. Third, fourth, and fifth columns show flexible budget amounts computed for specified sales volumes (three different sales volumes used in this example).

      C. Flexible Budget Performance Report

         1. Lists differences between actual performance and budgeted performance based on actual sales volume (or other level of activity).

         2. Helps direct management's attention to those costs or revenues that differ substantially from budgeted amounts; areas where corrective actions may help management control operations.

         3. Used for variance analysis.

            a. Actual and budgeted sales *volumes* are the same; as such, any variance in total dollar sales must have resulted from a selling price that was different than expected.

            b. Difference between actual quantity of input used and budgeted quantity can be described as a quantity variance.

            c. Difference between actual price per unit of input and budgeted price per unit of input can be described as a price variance.

Section 2—Standard Costs

I.   **Standard Costs**—Actual costs are amounts paid in past transactions; a measure of comparison is usually needed to decide whether actual cost amounts are reasonable or excessive, and standard costs offer one basis for comparison.

      A. Standard costs are preset costs for delivering a product or service expected under normal conditions.

         1. Used by management to assess the reasonableness of actual costs incurred for producing the product or service.

         2. When actual costs vary from standard costs, management follows up to identify potential problems and take corrective action.

         3. Management by exception: managers focus attention on most significant differences and give less attention where performance is reasonably close to standard.

II.   **Materials and Labor Standards**

      A. Identifying Standard Costs

         1. Managerial accountants, engineers, personnel administrators, and other managers help set standard costs.

            a. To set direct labor costs—conduct time and motion studies for each labor operation in the process of providing product or service; sets standard labor time required for each operation under normal conditions.

            b. To set direct material costs—study quantity, grade, and cost of each material used.

2. Regardless, actual costs frequently differ from standard costs; differences often due to more than one factor.

   a. Actual quantity used (of direct labor or direct materials) may differ from standard.

   b. Actual price paid per unit (of direct labor or direct materials) may differ from standard.

B. Setting Standard Costs

1. Due to inefficiencies and waste, materials may be lost as part of process.

   a. An ideal standard is the quantity of material required if process was 100% efficient without any loss or waste.

   b. A practical standard is the quantity of material required under normal application of process; allowance for loss included in standard.

2. A standard cost card shows the standard costs of direct materials, direct labor, and overhead for one unit of product or service.

III.   **Cost Variances**—Cost variance (or simply variance) is difference between actual and standard costs; can be favorable (if actual cost is less than standard cost) or unfavorable (if actual cost is more than standard cost). Note that short-term favorable variances can lead to long-term unfavorable variances.

A. Cost Variance Analysis

1. Variances are commonly identified from performance reports.

2. Management examines circumstances to determine factors causing the variance; analysis, evaluation, and explanation involved.

3. Results of efforts should allow assignment of responsibility for the variance; actions can then be taken to correct problems.

4. Four steps involved in proper management of variance analysis.

   a. Preparation of standard cost performance report.

   b. Computation and analysis of variances.

   c. Identification of questions and their explanations.

   d. Corrective and strategic action.

B. Cost Variance Computation—Cost variance (CV) equals difference between actual cost (AC) and standard cost (SC).

1.   Actual quantity (AQ)   Standard quantity (SQ)
    x <u>Actual price (AP)</u>   x <u>Standard price (SP)</u>
       Actual Cost (AC)   Standard Cost (SC)

2. Actual quantity is input (material or labor) used in manufacturing the quantity of output, and Standard Quantity is the input expected for the quantity of output.

3. Actual Price is amount paid for acquiring the input (material or labor), and Standard Price is the expected price.

4. Two main factors cause a cost variance

    a. Price variance caused by difference between actual price paid and standard price.

    b. Quantity (or usage or efficiency) variance caused by difference between the actual quantities of materials or hours used and the standard quantity.

5. Price variance and quantity variance can be determined by formulas.

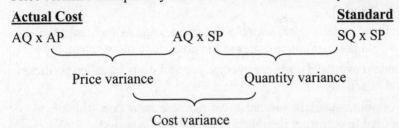

Actual Cost   **Standard**

AQ x AP   AQ x SP   SQ x SP

Price variance   Quantity variance

Cost variance

6. Alternative price variance and quantity variance formulas can also be used.

    a. Price variance = (Actual price – Standard price) x Actual quantity.

        $PV = (AP - SP)$ x AQ.

    b. Quantity variance = (Actual quantity – Standard quantity) x Standard price.

        $QV = (AQ - SQ)$ x SP.

C. Materials and Labor Variances

1. Material cost variances may be due to price and/or quantity factors.

    a. A materials price variance results when company pays different amount per unit than standard price; purchasing department usually responsible.

    b. A material quantity or usage variance results when company uses a quantity that differs from the standard quantity allowed to produce the actual amount of output; production department usually responsible. Can also be fault of purchasing department if the purchase of inferior materials caused excess use of materials.

2. Labor cost variances may be due to rate (price) and/or efficiency (quantity) factors.

    a. Labor rate (price) variance results when wage rate paid to employees differs from standard rate; personnel administrator usually responsible.

    b. Labor efficiency (quantity) variances results when labor hours used differ from the standard quantity of hours allowed to produce the actual amount of output; production department usually responsible.

    c. Labor rate and efficiency variances may be due to use of workers with different skill levels.

IV. **Overhead Standards and Variances**—A predetermined overhead rate is used to assign standard overhead costs to products or services produced; predetermined rate often based on relation between standard overhead and standard labor cost, standard labor hours, standard machine hours, or another measure of production.

A. Setting Overhead Standards

   1. Standard overhead costs are amounts expected to occur at a certain level of activity.

   2. Overhead includes both variable and fixed costs; as such, average overhead cost per unit changes as the predicted volume changes.

   3. Standard overhead costs are average per unit costs based on predicted level of activity.

   4. To establish standard overhead cost rate, use same cost structure as that used to construct flexible budget at end of a period.

      a. Management selects a level of activity (volume) and predicts total overhead costs.

      b. Many factors affect predicted activity level.

         i. Level of 100% of capacity rarely used.

         ii. Factors that cause activity level to be less than full capacity include difficulties in scheduling work, equipment under repair or maintenance, and insufficient product demand.

         iii. Total overhead costs predicted are divided by allocation base to get standard rate.

B. Total Overhead Cost Variance.

   1. Cost accounting system applies overhead using predetermined overhead rate when standard costs are used.

   2. At end of period, the difference between total overhead cost applied to products and total overhead cost actually incurred is called the overhead cost variance.

   3. Actual overhead costs incurred (AOI)
      – Standard overhead applied (SOA)
      Overhead Cost Variance (OCV)

   4. The standard overhead applied is based on the predetermined overhead rate and the standard number of hours that should have been used, based on the actual production output.

   5. To help identify factors causing the overhead cost variance managers will analyze the variance separately for controllable and volume variances.

      a. The controllable variance is the difference between the actual overhead costs incurred and the budgeted overhead costs based on a flexible budget; named because it refers to activities usually under management control.

      b.   The volume variance is the difference between the budged fixed overhead (at predicted capacity) and the applied fixed overhead).

          i.   Occurs when there is a difference between the actual volume of production and the standard volume of production.

          ii.   The budgeted fixed overhead is the same value regardless of the volume of production.

          iii.   The applied overhead is based on the standard direct labor hours allowed for the actual volume of production.

          iv.   When a company operates at a capacity different from what is expected, the volume variance will be differ from zero.

   6.   Analyzing controllable and volume variances

      a.   An unfavorable volume means the company did not reach its expected operating level—a favorable variance implies the company operated at a greater than expected operating level.

      b.   Main purpose of the volume variance to identify what portion of the total overhead variance is cause by failing to meet the expected production level.

      c.   Often the reasons the failing to meet expected operating levels are due to factors (e.g. customer demand) beyond employees' control.

   7.   Overhead Variance Reports

      a.   Help managers isolate the reasons for a controllable variance.

      b.   Provides information about specific overhead costs and how they differ from budgeted amounts.

V.   **Decision Analysis—Sales Variances**—Similar to computation and analysis of cost variances.

   A.   Sales price variance and sales volume variance can be computed.

   B.   Managers use sales variances for planning and control purposes.

      1.   Question why sales were higher/lower than expected.

      2.   Evaluate and reward salespeople.

   C.   When multiple products sold:

      1.   Sales mix variance is difference between actual and budgeted sales mix of products.

      2.   Sales quantity variance is difference between total actual and total budgeted quantity of units sold.

Appendix 24A

I.   **Expanded Overhead Variances**

    A. Computing Overhead Cost Variances—*assume predetermined rate is based on relation between standard overhead and standard labor hours.*

       1. Variable overhead cost variances can be determined by formulas.

          a. Formulas:

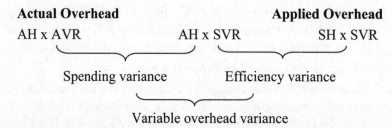

             AH = actual hours, AVR = actual variable overhead rate, SH = standard hours, and SVR = standard variable overhead rate.

          b. Variable overhead spending variance results when amount paid to acquire overhead items differs from standard price.

          c. Variable overhead efficiency variance results when standard direct labor hours (the assumed allocation base) expected for actual production are different from actual direct labor hours used; reflects on the cost-effectiveness in using the overhead allocation base such as direct labor hours.

       2. Fixed overhead cost variances can be determined by formulas that include only the fixed portion of overhead.

          a. Formulas:

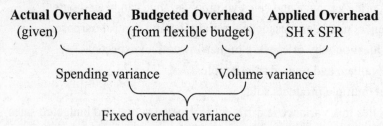

             SH = standard hours, and SFR = standard fixed overhead rate

          b. Fixed overhead spending variance results when amount paid to acquire overhead items differs from standard price.

          c. Fixed overhead volume variance results when actual volume of production differs from standard volume of production.

          d. Budgeted fixed overhead amount remains same regardless of expected volume, and is computed based on standard direct labor hours allowed for the expected production volume.

II.   **Standard Cost Accounting System**

    A. Standard cost systems also record standard costs and variances in accounts.

          a. Recordkeeping simplified.

          b. Helpful in report preparation.

      1. Record standard materials costs incurred:

         Goods in Process Inventory   SQ x SP
         Direct Materials Price Variance
         Direct Materials Quantity Variance
            Raw Materials Inventory   AQ x AP

         (the variances are debited if unfavorable or credited if favorable)

      2. Record standard labor cost of goods manufactured:

         Goods in Process Inventory   SQ x SP
         Direct Labor Rate Variance
         Direct Labor Efficiency Variance
            Factory Payroll   AQ x AP

         (the variances are debited if unfavorable or credited if favorable)

      3. Assign standard predetermined overhead to cost of goods manufactured:

         Goods in Process Inventory   SQ x SPR
         Volume Variance
         Variable Overhead Spending Variance
         Variable Overhead Efficiency Variance
            Factory Overhead   actual

         (the variances are debited if unfavorable or credited if favorable)

      4. Accumulate balances in the different variance accounts until end of accounting period; to close, add to or subtract from the manufacturing costs recorded in the period.

         a. If variance is considered immaterial, add to, or subtract from balance of Cost of Goods Sold.

         b. If variance considered material, add to, or subtract from balances of Goods in Process Inventory, Finished Goods Inventory, and Cost of Goods Sold.

         c. Recorded costs will equal actual costs in the period; must use actual costs in external financial statements prepared according to GAAP (generally accepted accounting principles.

Problem I

The following statements are either true or false. Place a (T) In the parentheses before each true statement and an (F) before each false statement.

1. ( ) A fixed budget performance report always compares actual costs with budgeted amounts based on the actual operating level.

2. ( ) The same costs are fixed or variable in all businesses. For example, office supply costs are always variable.

3. ( ) A flexible budget performance report compares actual costs with budgeted amounts based on the actual operating level.

4. ( ) Standard costs are determined by averaging historical costs that occurred when the company operated within a normal operating range.

5. ( ) A variance is favorable if actual cost is below standard cost.

6. ( ) A variance is favorable if actual revenue is below standard revenue.

7. ( ) A company's standard direct material cost for producing 10 units of a product is $200 but the actual direct material cost was $180. We can safely conclude that the $20 variance must have resulted because the materials price was lower than standard.

8. ( ) An unfavorable overhead volume variance is caused by the fact that the plant did not reach the operating level that was expected when the predetermined overhead application rate was selected.

9. ( ) A general journal entry to record a standard material cost in the Goods in Process Inventory account and an unfavorable material quantity variance would include a debit to Direct Material Quantity Variance.

10. ( ) When variances are recorded in separate accounts, they are closed directly to the Cost of Goods Sold account at the end of the accounting period only if their balances are immaterial.

Problem II

You are given several words, phrases or numbers to choose from in completing each of the following statements or in answering the following questions. In each case, select the one that best completes the statement or answers the question and place its letter in the answer space provided.

_____ 1. Bubbling Waters Company manufactures and sells hot tubs. Which one of the following costs is likely to be fixed?

    a. Fiberglass materials.

    b. Installation costs.

    c. Direct labor.

    d. Monthly rent expense for the factory building.

    e. None of the above.

This information describes the results experienced by a manufacturing company:

Standard direct materials (10 lbs. @ $4/lb.)...	$40/unit
Actual direct materials used............................	11,340 lbs.
Direct materials cost variance (favorable)......	$2,400
Actual finished units manufactured................	1,080

What is the actual cost of direct materials for the period?

a. $40,800.

b. $42,960.

c. $43,200.

d. $45,600.

e. $47,760.

3. Wimberley Company's fixed budget for 26,000 units is shown below. Note that only direct materials, direct labor, and selling expenses are considered variable costs. What is the budgeted income from operations for 28,000 units?

Sales.................................		$124,800
Cost of goods sold:		
Direct materials...........	$24,700	
Direct labor.................	26,000	
Depreciation................	1,600	
Supervisory salaries....	6,200	(58,500)
Gross profit.......................		$ 66,300
Selling expenses		
Sales commissions......	$10,400	
Packaging expense......	2,600	(13,000)
Administrative expenses:.		
Administrative salaries	$ 5,200	
Insurance expense.......	1,300	
Office rent expense.....	3,900	(10,400)
Income from operations...		$ 42,900

a. $46,200.

b. $47,100.

c. $47,600.

d. $48,000.

e. $53,500.

Problem III

Many of the important ideas and concepts discussed in Chapter 24 are reflected in the following list of key terms. Test your understanding of these terms by matching the appropriate definitions with the terms. Record the number identifying the most appropriate definition on in the blank space next to each term.

_____ Budgetary control	_____ Management by exception
_____ Budget report	_____ Overhead cost variance
_____ Controllable variance	_____ Price variance
_____ Cost variance	_____ Quantity variance
_____ Efficiency variance	_____ Spending variance
_____ Favorable variance	_____ Standard costs
_____ Fixed budget	_____ Unfavorable variance
_____ Fixed budget performance report	_____ Variance analysis
_____ Flexible budget	_____ Volume variance
_____ Flexible budget performance report	

1. The difference between two dollar amounts of fixed overhead cost; one amount is the total budgeted overhead cost, and the other is the overhead cost allocated to products using the predetermined fixed overhead rate.

2. Management process to focus on significant variances and give less attention to the areas where performance is close to the standard.

3. The difference between the total overhead cost applied to products and the total overhead cost actually incurred.

4. A process of examining differences between actual and budgeted revenues or costs and describing them in terms of price and quantity differences.

5. A planning budget based on a single predicted amount of volume; unsuitable for evaluations if the actual volume differs from the predicted volume.

6. A difference between actual and budgeted revenue or cost caused by the difference between the actual price per unit and the budgeted price per unit.

7. Combination of both overhead spending variances (variable and fixed) and the variable overhead efficiency variance.

8. A report that compares actual revenues and costs with their variable budgeted amounts based on the actual sales volume (or other level of activity) and identifies the differences as variances.

9. The difference between the actual incurred cost and the standard cost.

10. A report that compares actual revenue and costs with fixed budgeted amounts and identifies the differences as favorable or unfavorable variances.

11. The difference between actual and budgeted revenue or cost caused by the difference between the actual number of units and the budgeted number of units.

12. A budget prepared (using actual volume) after a period is complete that helps managers evaluate past performance; uses fixed and variable costs in determining total costs.

13. The costs that should be incurred under normal conditions to produce a product or component or to perform a service.

14. The difference in actual revenues or expenses from the budgeted value that contributes to a higher income.

15. The difference between the actual price of an item and its standard price.

16. Report comparing actual results to planned objectives; sometimes used as a progress report.

17. The difference in revenues or costs, when the actual value is compared to the budgeted value, that contributes to a lower income.

18. Management use of budgets to monitor and control company operations.

19. The difference between the actual quantity of an input and the standard quantity of that input.

Problem IV

Complete the following by filling in the blanks.

1. A _____ report compares budgeted and actual results.

2. A _____ budget performance report compares actual and budgeted results based on the actual sales volume or level of activity.

3. The portion of the total direct materials cost variance caused by a difference between the actual and the budgeted price per unit is called the _____ variance. The portion caused by a difference between the actual and the budgeted number of units used is called the _____ variance.

4. To prepare a flexible budget, management needs to express each _____ cost as a constant amount per unit of sales. Each _____ cost is expressed as the total amount expected to be incurred.

5. Flexible budgets are prepared _____ an operating period is completed.

6. A _____ budget is based on a prediction of a single sales volume.

7. A fixed budget is used to set the standard _____ application rate. When actual costs are known, they should be compared with a flexible budget showing amounts based on the _____ level of activity instead of the original prediction.

8. _____ costs should be incurred under _____ conditions to produce a product (or component) or to perform a service.

9. Standard costs are established with accounting, engineering, personnel, and other studies made _____ the product is produced or the service is provided.

10. A cost variance is favorable when actual costs are _____ than the standard. A cost variance is unfavorable when actual costs are _____ than the standard.

11. The _____ variance is found by multiplying the difference between actual quantity and standard quantity by the _____ price.

12. The _____ variance is found by multiplying the difference between actual price and standard price by the _____ quantity.

13. When overhead costs differ from standard, the variance can be divided into a _____ _____ variance and a _____ variance.

14. When management by _____ is used, attention is directed to
_____ variances and managers _____
analyzing situations with results close to the expected amounts.

15. A(n) _____ cost variance is recorded in the accounts with a debit
and a(n) _____ cost variance is recorded with a credit.

Problem V

A company purchased 500 pounds of material for $45,000 and used it to produce 240 units of product. The standards for this material are 2.0 pounds of material per unit of product. The standard cost is $100 per pound. Calculate the total cost variance, the material price variance, and the material quantity variance.

Materials Variances _____

Units produced.. _____ units
X std. quantity of materials per unit.............. _____ X _____ pounds per unit
Standard quantity of materials .... _____ pounds

AQ	lbs	AQ	lbs	SQ	lbs
X AP	_____	X SP	_____	X SP	_____

Price Variance   Quantity Variance

$ _____ ___ U or F $ _____ ___ U or F

Total Materials Variance

$ _____ ___ U or F

Problem VI

During a recent month, a company operated at 75% of its 10,000 unit capacity, producing 7,500 units, and incurring a total of $38,000 in overhead costs.

Before the period started, the management planned to operate at 90% of capacity by producing 9,000 units. Overhead cost was budgeted to be $45,000 at this level. This total consisted of $27,000 of variable cost and $18,000 of fixed cost. Complete the calculations listed below:

Standard predetermined overhead application rate per unit:

Budgeted overhead at 90%   x $ _____ = $ _____ per unit
Budgeted units at 90%   _____ units

Budgeted variable overhead cost per unit:

Budgeted variable cost at 90%   x $ _____ = $ _____ per unit
Budgeted units at 90%   _____ units

Overhead cost assigned to output at the predetermined rate:

$ _____ x _____ = $ _____
   (overhead rate)   (units produced)

Overhead budgeted with a flexible budget at the actual level of 7,500 units, or 75% of capacity:

$ _____ x 7,500 units   = $ _____
   (variable cost per unit)
Budgeted fixed overhead cost   = _____
Total overhead budgeted at 75% of capacity = $ _____

The overhead volume variance:

Total overhead budgeted at 75% of capacity   = $ _____
Overhead cost assigned to output at   = _____
 the predetermined rate:
Variance (favorable/unfavorable)   = $ _____ _____

The overhead controllable variance:

Actual overhead cost   = $ _____
Total overhead budgeted at 75% of capacity   = _____
Variance (favorable/unfavorable)   = $ _____ _____

Problem VII

Spartan Company makes a product that has the following standards:

Standards

Cost Element	Standard quantity	Standard Price
Direct Materials	3 pounds	$ 5 per pound
Direct labor	2 hours	$15 per hour

The following budgeted overhead amounts are for an expected production of 10,000 units using direct labor 20,000 hours. Factory overhead is applied on the basis of direct labor hours.

Variable overhead	$ 60,000
Fixed Overhead	40,000
Total Overhead	$ 100,000

Actual Results

Units produced	8,000	units
Direct materials purchased and used	$129,600	(27,000 pounds at $4.80 per pound)
Direct labor hours and rate	$231,000	(16,500 hours at $14.00 per hour)
Factory overhead:		
Variable Overhead	$ 51,000	
Fixed Overhead	41,000	
Total Overhead	$ 92,000	

Required:

1. Compute the standard predetermined variable and fixed overhead rates.

Standard variable overhead rate (SVR):

$$\frac{\text{Budgeted Variable overhead for 10,000 units}}{\text{Budged Direct Labor hours for 10,000 units}} = \frac{\$ _____}{\text{hours}} = _____ \text{ Per hr}$$

Standard fixed overhead rate (SFR):

$$\frac{\text{Budgeted Fixed overhead for 10,000 units}}{\text{Budged Direct Labor hours for 10,000 units}} = \frac{\$ _____}{\text{hours}} = _____ \text{ Per hr}$$

2. Compute the standard cost for one unit of product:

Direct Materials _____ lbs per unit X _____ per lb = $_____
Direct Labor _____ hrs per unit X _____ per hr = _____
Variable Overhead _____ hrs per unit X _____ per hr = _____
Fixed Overhead _____ hrs per unit X _____ per hr = _____
    Standard cost of one unit of product   = $_____

3. Prepare a flexible budget for production costs for the following range of output: 6,000, 8,000, 10,000, and 12,000 units.

		6,000	8,000	Expected level	12,000
Units:		6,000	8,000	10,000	12,000
	Unit Cost				
Direct Materials	$ 15			$ 150,000	
Direct Labor	30			300,000	
Variable Overhead	6			60,000	
Total Variable Costs	$ 51			$ 510,000	
Fixed Costs				40,000	
Total production costs		$	$	$ 550,000	$

4. Prepare a flexible budget report for the actual level of production achieved. The company expected to make 10,000 units but only made $8,000 units.

	Budgeted	Actual	Difference	F or U
Actual level of activity	8,000 units	8,000 units		
Direct Materials				
Direct Labor				
Variable Overhead				
Total Variable Costs				
Fixed Costs				
Total production costs	$	$		

5. Compute the Direct Materials Variances

Units produced.. _____ units
X std. quantity of materials per unit..............   X _____ pounds per unit
Standard quantity of materials ....   _____ Pounds

AQ	lbs	AQ	lbs	SQ	lbs
X AP	_____	X SP	_____	X SP	_____

Price Variance   Quantity Variance

$ _____ ___ *U or F* $ _____ ___ *U or F*

Total Materials Variance

$ _____ ___ *U or F*

6. Compute the Direct Labor Variances

Units produced.. _____ units
X std. quantity of hours per unit..............   X _____ hours per unit
Standard quantity of hours ....   _____ hours

AQ	hrs	AQ	hrs	SQ	hrs
X AP	_____	X SP	_____	X SP	_____

Rate Variance   Efficiency Variance

$ _____ ___ *U or F* $ _____ ___ *U or F*

Total Direct Labor Variance

$ _____ ___ *U or F*

7. Compute the Variable Overhead Variances

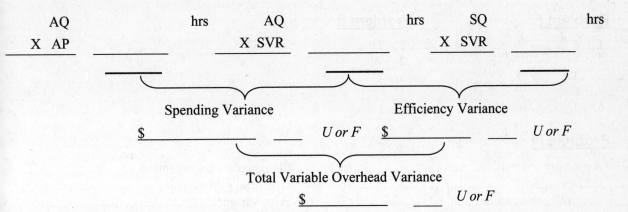

AQ	hrs	AQ	hrs	SQ	hrs
X AP		X SVR		X SVR	

Spending Variance   Efficiency Variance

$ _____ ___ *U or F* $ _____ ___ *U or F*

Total Variable Overhead Variance

$ _____ ___ *U or F*

8. Compute the Fixed Overhead Variances

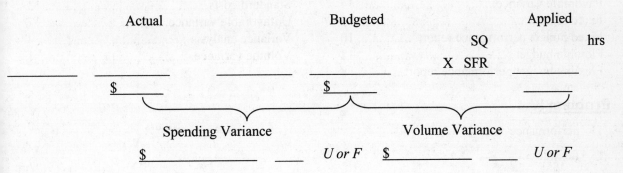

Actual	Budgeted	Applied
		SQ hrs
		X SFR
$	$	

Spending Variance   Volume Variance

$ _____ ___ *U or F* $ _____ ___ *U or F*

Solutions for Chapter 24

Problem I

1.	F	6.	F
2.	F	7.	F
3.	T	8.	T
4.	F	9.	T
5.	T	10.	T

Problem II

1. D
2. A
3. C

Problem III

Budgetary control. 18
Budget report. 16
Controllable variance................................... 7
Cost variance 9
Efficiency variance. 19
Favorable variance..................................... 14
Fixed budget 5
Fixed budget performance report. 10
Flexible budget 12
Flexible budget performance report 8

Management by exception............................ 2
Overhead cost variance................................. 3
Price variance 6
Quantity variance 11
Spending variance. 15
Standard costs.. 13
Unfavorable variance................................... 17
Variance analysis... 4
Volume variance.. 1

Problem IV

1. performance

2. flexible

3. price; quantity

4. variable; fixed.

5. after

6. fixed

7. predetermined overhead; actual

8. Standard; normal

9. before

10. less; greater

11. quantity; standard

12. price; actual

13. volume; controllable

14. exception; significant; postpone

15. unfavorable; favorable

Problem V

A company purchased 500 pounds of material for $45,000 and used it to produce 240 units of product. The standards for this material are 2.0 pounds of material per unit of product. The standard cost is $100 per pound. Calculate the total cost variance, the material price variance, and the material quantity variance.

Materials Variances

Units produced...	240	units
X std. quantity of materials per unit..............	X 2	pounds per unit
Standard quantity of materials	480	pounds

Actual price per lb. = $45,000 total cost / 500 lbs. = $90 per lb.

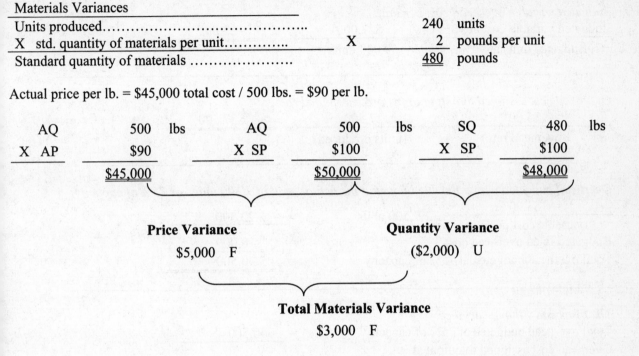

AQ	500	lbs	AQ	500	lbs	SQ	480	lbs
X AP	$90		X SP	$100		X SP	$100	
	$45,000			$50,000			$48,000	

Price Variance

$5,000 F

Quantity Variance

($2,000) U

Total Materials Variance

$3,000 F

Problem VI

Standard predetermined overhead application rate per unit:

$$\frac{\text{Budgeted overhead at 90\%}}{\text{Budgeted units at 90\%}} \text{ x } \frac{\$45,000}{9,000 \text{ units}} = \frac{\$5.00}{} \text{ per unit}$$

Budgeted variable overhead cost per unit:

$$\frac{\text{Budgeted variable cost at 90\%}}{\text{Budgeted units at 90\%}} \text{ x } \frac{\$27,000}{9,000 \text{ units}} = \frac{\$3.00}{} \text{ per unit}$$

Overhead cost assigned to output at the predetermined rate:

$$\frac{\$5.00}{\text{(overhead rate)}} \text{ x } \frac{7,500}{\text{(units produced)}} = \frac{\$37,500}{}$$

Overhead budgeted with a flexible budget at the actual level of 7,500 units, or 75% of capacity:

$\dfrac{\$3.00}{\text{(variable cost per unit)}}$ x 7,500 units	= $ 22,500
Budgeted fixed overhead cost	= 18,000
Total overhead budgeted at 75% of capacity	= $ 40,500

The overhead volume variance:

Total overhead budgeted at 75% of capacity	= $40,500
Overhead cost assigned to output at the predetermined rate:	= 37,500
Variance (favorable/unfavorable)	= $ 3,000 unfavorable

The overhead controllable variance:

Actual overhead cost	= $ 38,000
Total overhead budgeted at 75% of capacity	= 40,500
Variance (favorable/unfavorable)	= $ (2,500) favorable

Problem VII

1. Compute the standard predetermined variable and fixed overhead rates.

Standard variable overhead rate (SVR):

$$\frac{\text{Budgeted Variable overhead for 10,000 units}}{\text{Budged Direct Labor hours for 10,000 units}} = \frac{\$60,000}{20,000 \text{ hours}} = \underline{\$3} \quad \text{Per hr}$$

Standard fixed overhead rate (SFR):

$$\frac{\text{Budgeted Fixed overhead for 10,000 units}}{\text{Budged Direct Labor hours for 10,000 units}} = \frac{\$40,000}{20,000 \text{ hours}} = \underline{\$2} \quad \text{Per hr}$$

2. Compute the standard cost for one unit of product:

Direct Materials	3	lbs per unit	X	$ 5	per lb	=	$ 15
Direct Labor	2	hrs per unit	X	$15	per hr	=	30
Variable Overhead	2	hrs per unit	X	$ 3	per hr	=	6
Fixed Overhead	2	hrs per unit	X	$ 2	per hr	=	4
	Standard cost of one units					=	$ 55

3. Prepare a flexible budget for production costs for the following range of output: 6,000, 8,000, 10,000, and 12,000 units.

Units:	Unit Cost	6,000	8,000	Expected level 10,000	12,000
Direct Materials	$ 15	$ 90,000	$ 120,000	$ 150,000	$180,000
Direct Labor	30	180,000	240,000	300,000	360,000
Variable Overhead	6	36,000	48,000	60,000	72,000
Total Variable Costs	$ 51	$ 206,000	$ 408,000	$ 510,000	$612,000
Fixed Costs		40,000	40,000	40,000	40,000
Total production costs		$ 246,000	$ 448,000	$ 550,000	$652,000

4. Prepare a flexible budget report for the actual level of production achieved. The company expected to make 10,000 units but only made $8,000 units.

	Budgeted	Actual	Difference	F or U
Actual level of activity	**8,000 units**	**8,000 units**		
Direct Materials	$ 120,000	$ 129,600	($9,600)	U
Direct Labor	240,000	231,000	9,000	F
Variable Overhead	48,000	51,000	(3,000)	U
Fixed Costs	40,000	41,000	(1,000)	U
Total production costs	$ 448,000	$ 452,600	($4,600)	U

5. Compute the Direct Materials Variances

Units produced..	8,000	units	
X std. quantity of materials per unit..............	X 3	pounds per unit	
Standard quantity of materials	24,000	Pounds	

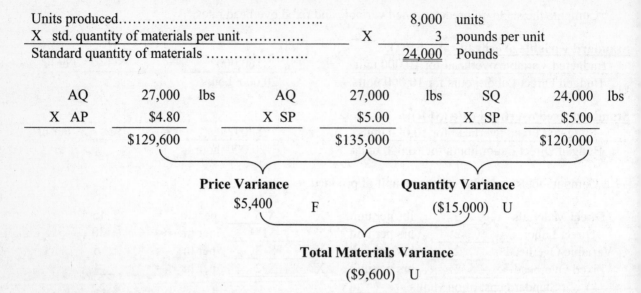

AQ	27,000	lbs	AQ	27,000	lbs	SQ	24,000	lbs
X AP	$4.80		X SP	$5.00		X SP	$5.00	
	$129,600			$135,000			$120,000	

Price Variance
$5,400   F

Quantity Variance
($15,000)   U

Total Materials Variance
($9,600)   U

6. Compute the Direct Labor Variances

Units produced..	8,000	units	
X std. quantity of hours per unit..............	X 2	hours per unit	
Standard quantity of hours	16,000	hours	

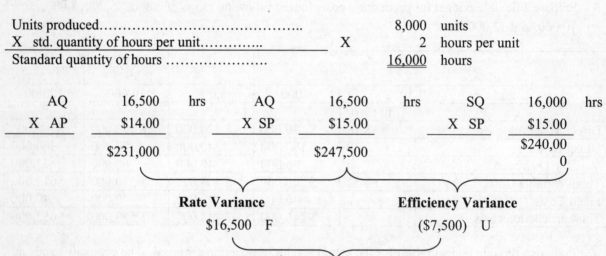

AQ	16,500	hrs	AQ	16,500	hrs	SQ	16,000	hrs
X AP	$14.00		X SP	$15.00		X SP	$15.00	
	$231,000			$247,500			$240,000	

Rate Variance
$16,500   F

Efficiency Variance
($7,500)   U

Total Direct Labor Variance
$9,000   F

7. Compute the Variable Overhead Variances

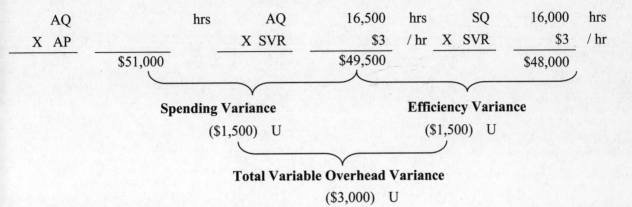

AQ	hrs	AQ	16,500	hrs	SQ	16,000	hrs
X AP		X SVR	$3	/ hr	X SVR	$3	/ hr
$51,000			$49,500			$48,000	

Spending Variance
($1,500)   U

Efficiency Variance
($1,500)   U

Total Variable Overhead Variance
($3,000)   U

8. Compute the Fixed Overhead Variances

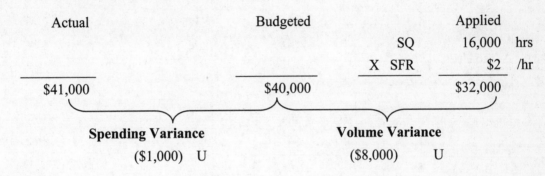

Actual		Budgeted			Applied	
				SQ	16,000	hrs
				X SFR	$2	/hr
$41,000		$40,000			$32,000	

Spending Variance
($1,000)   U

Volume Variance
($8,000)   U

CHAPTER 25
CAPITAL BUDGETING AND MANAGERIAL DECISIONS

Learning Objective C1:

Describe the importance of relevant costs for short-term decisions.

Summary

A company must rely on relevant costs pertaining to alternative courses of action rather than historical costs. Out-of-pocket expenses and opportunity costs are relevant because these are avoidable; sunk costs are irrelevant because they result from past decisions and are therefore unavoidable. Managers must also consider the relevant benefits associated with alternative decisions.

Learning Objective A1:

Evaluate short-term managerial decisions using relevant costs.

Summary

Relevant costs are useful in making decisions such as to accept additional business, make or buy, and sell as is or process further. For example, the relevant factors in deciding whether to produce and sell additional units are incremental costs and incremental revenues from the additional volume.

Learning Objective A2:

Analyze a capital investment project using break-even time.

Summary

Break-even time (BET) is a method for evaluating capital investments by restating future cash flows in terms of their present values (discounting the cash flows) and then calculating the payback period using these present values of cash flows.

Learning Objective P1:

Compute payback period and describe its use.

Summary

One way to compare potential investments is to compute and compare their payback periods. The payback period is an estimate of the expected time before the cumulative net cash inflow from the investment equals its initial cost. A payback period analysis fails to reflect risk of cash flows, differences in the timing of cash flows within the payback period, and cash flows that occur after the payback period.

Learning Objective P2:

Compute accounting rate of return and explain its use.

Summary

A project's accounting rate of return is computed by dividing the expected annual after-tax net income by the average amount of investment in the project. When the net cash flows are received evenly throughout each period and straight-line depreciation is used, the average investment is computed as the average of the investment's initial book value and its salvage value.

Learning Objective P3:

Compute net present value and describe its use.

Summary

An investment's net present value is determined by predicting the future cash flows it is expected to generate, discounting them at a rate that represents an acceptable return, and then by subtracting the investment's initial cost from the sum of the present values. This technique can deal with any pattern of expected cash flows and applies a superior concept of return on investment.

Learning Objective P4:

Compute internal rate of return and explain its use.

Summary

The internal rate of return (IRR) is the discount rate that results in a zero net present value. When the cash flows are equal, we can compute the present value factor corresponding to the IRR by dividing the initial investment by the annual cash flows. We then use the annuity tables to determine the discount rate corresponding to this present value factor.

Fundamental Accounting Principles, 20/e

Chapter Outline

Section 1—Capital Budgeting

Capital budgeting is the process of analyzing alternative long-term investments and deciding which assets to acquired or sell. Fundamental goal of capital budgeting decisions is to earn a satisfactory rate of return. Such decisions require careful analysis, and are the most difficult and risky decisions made by managers. Difficult because of need to make predictions of events that will occur well into the future. Risky because outcome is uncertain, large amounts of money are involved, long-term commitment is required, and decision may be difficult or impossible to reverse. Several techniques are used to make capital budgeting decisions.

I. **Methods Not Using Time Value of Money**—Investments are expected to produce cash inflows and cash outflows; net cash flow equals cash inflows minus cash outflows. Simple analysis methods do not consider the time value of money.

   A. Payback Period

   1. Payback period is the time period expected to recover the initial investment amount. That is, the time it will take the investment to generate enough net cash flow to return (or pay back) the cash initially invested to buy it.

   2. Managers prefer investments with shorter payback periods.

       a. Shorter payback period reduces risk of an unprofitable investment over the long run.

       b. Company's risk due to potentially inaccurate long-term predictions of future cash flows is reduced.

   3. To compute payback period, exclude all non-cash revenue and expenses from computation.

       a. When annual cash flows are even in amount,

       $$\text{Payback Period} \ = \ \frac{\text{Cost of Investment}}{\text{Annual net cash flows}}$$

       b. When annual cash flows are unequal, payback period is computed using the cumulative total of net cash flows (starting with the negative cash flow resulting from the initial investment); when cumulative net cash flow changes from positive to negative, the investment is fully recovered. (see Exhibit 25.3)

   4. Payback period should not be only consideration in evaluating investments; two factors are ignored.

       a. Differences in the timing of net cash flows within the payback period are not reflected. Investments that provide cash more quickly are more desirable.

       b. All cash flows after the point where its costs are fully recovered are ignored.

B. Accounting Rate of Return *(or return on average investment)*

1. Accounting Rate of Return $= \dfrac{\text{After-tax net income}}{\text{Average investment amount}}$

2. Accrual basis after-tax net income is used.

3. Compute the average investment:

   a. If net cash flows are received evenly throughout the year then average investment for any one year is computed as average of beginning and ending book values.

   b. Average investment (or average book value for asset's entire life) is then computed by taking the average of the individual yearly averages.

   c. If use of straight-line depreciation is assumed, average book value equals sum of beginning and ending book values divided by two.

   d. If investment has salvage value, the average amount invested when using straight-line depreciation is computed as sum of beginning book value and salvage value divided by two.

4. Risk of an investment should be considered.

   a. Investment's return is satisfactory or unsatisfactory only when related to returns from other investments with similar lives and risk.

   b. Capital investment with least risk, shortest payback period, and highest return for the longest time is often identified as best; analysis can be challenging because different investments often yield different rankings depending on measure used.

5. Accounting rate of return method is readily computed, often used in evaluating investment opportunities, yet usefulness is often limited.

   a. Amount invested is based on book values for future periods not predicted market values.

   b. If asset's net incomes may vary from year to year, then average annual net incomes must be used; method fails to distinguish between two investments with same average annual net income when one investment yields higher amounts in early years and the other in later years.

II.   **Methods Using Time Value of Money**—Net present value and internal rate of return methods consider time value of money.

A. Net Present Value *(see also Appendix B near end of textbook)*

1. To compute NPV, discount the future net cash flows from the investment at the required rate of return, and then subtract the initial amount invested.

a. The discount is the interest and to discount means to deduct interest from the future cash flows.

b. The required rate of return also called the hurdle rate or the cost of capital that the company must pay to its long-term creditors and shareholders.

c. Each annual net cash flow is multiplied by the related present value of 1 factor or discount factor. (Obtain from Table B.1 in Appendix B.)

i. Discount factors assume that net cash flows are received at the end of each year.

ii. Rate of return required by the company and number of years until cash flow is received are used to determine discount factors.

d. Initial amount invested includes all costs incurred to get asset in proper location and ready to use.

2. Net Present Value Decision Rule

a. Computed by subtracting the amount of the investment from the sum of present values of annual net cash flows.

b. If the net present value is greater than or equal to $0, then asset is expected to recover its cost and provide a return at least as high as that required; project is accepted.

c. If net present value is negative, project is rejected.

3. NPV analysis can be used when comparing several investment opportunities; if investment opportunities have same cost and same risk, the one with highest positive net present value is preferred.

4. When annual net cash flows are equal in amount, NPV calculation can be simplified.

a. Individual annual present value of $1 factors can be summed, and the total multiplied by annual net cash flow to get total present value of net cash flows.

b. To simplify the computation, the present value of an annuity of $1 table may be used.

c. Calculator with compound interest function or a spreadsheet program can be used.

5. NPV analysis can also be applied when net cash flows are unequal. (Use procedures and decision-rules above.)

6. If salvage value is expected at end of useful life, treat as an additional net cash flow received at end the of asset's life.

7. Accelerated depreciation methods do not change basics of NPV analysis, but can change results; using accelerated depreciation for tax reporting affects net present value of asset's cash flows

   a. Accelerated depreciation produces larger depreciation deductions in early years of asset's life and smaller ones in later years; large net cash inflows are produced in early years and smaller ones in later years.

   b. Tax savings from depreciation is called depreciation tax shield.

   c. Early cash flows are more valuable than later ones; as such, being able to use accelerated depreciation for tax reporting makes investment more desirable.

8. NPV is of limited value for comparison purposes if initial investment differs substantially across projects.

9. When a company can't fund all positive net present value projects, they can be compared using the profitability index

   a. Profitability Index = $\dfrac{\text{Net present value of cash flows}}{\text{Cost of investment}}$

   b. A higher profitability index makes the project more desirable.

10. When the projects being compared have different risks, the NPVs of individual projects should be computed using different discount rates; the greater the risk, the higher the discount rate.

B. Internal Rate of Return

1. IRR is a rate used to evaluate acceptability of an investment; it equals the rate that yields a NPV of zero for an investment.

2. If the total present value of a project's net cash flows is computed using the IRR as the discount rate, it will equal the initial investment.

3. Two step process in computing IRR (equal cash flows)

   a. Step 1: Compute the present value factor for the project by dividing the amount invested by net cash flows.

   b. Step 2: Find discount rate (IRR) yielding the PV factor.

      i. An annuity table (see Appendix B) can be used to determine the discount rate that relates to this present value factor given the life of the project.

      ii. If the present value factor in the table does not exactly equal the one computed, the procedure set forth in Exhibit 25.9 can be used to estimate the IRR.

4. When cash flows are unequal, trial and error must be used; select any reasonable discount rate and compute the NPV.

   a. If amount is positive, recompute NPV using higher discount rate; if amount is negative, recompute NPV using lower discount rate.

   b. Continue steps until two consecutive computations result in NPVs that have different signs (positive and negative); IRR lies between these two discount rates; value can be estimated.

   c. Spreadsheet software and calculators can also be used to compute the IRR. (See Appendix 25A)

5. Compare IRR with hurdle rate (or minimum acceptable rate of return); if IRR exceeds hurdle rate, accept project.

   a. Choice of hurdle rate is subjective, depending on the risk involved.

   b. If project financed from borrowed funds, hurdle rate should exceed interest rate paid on borrowed funds; return on investment must cover interest and provide additional profit to reward company for risk.

   c. If project is internally financed, hurdle rate is often based on actual returns from comparable projects.

   d. If evaluating multiple projects, rank by extent to which IRR exceeds hurdle rate.

6. IRR is not subject to limitations of NPV when comparing projects with different amounts invested; IRR is expressed as percent rather than an absolute dollar value using NPV.

C. Comparison of Capital Budgeting Methods *(see Exhibit 25.10)*

1. Payback period and accounting rate of return do not consider time value of money; NPV and IRR do.

2. Payback period method is simple; sometimes used when limited cash to invest and a number of projects to choose from. Gives manager an estimate of how soon the initial investment can be recovered.

3. Accounting rate of return is a percent computed using accrual income instead of cash flows, and is an average rate for the entire investment period; annual returns are not reflected.

4. NPV:

   a. Considers all estimated cash flows of project; can be applied to equal and unequal cash flows.

   b. Can reflect changes in level of risk over life of project.

   c. Comparisons of projects of unequal sizes is more difficult.

　　　　5.　IRR:

　　　　　　a.　Considers all estimated cash flows of project.

　　　　　　b.　Readily computed when cash flows are equal, but requires trial and error estimation when cash flows are unequal.

　　　　　　c.　Allows comparisons of projects with different investment amounts.

　　　　　　d.　Does not reflect changes in risk over life of project.

Section 2—Managerial Decisions

Emphasis is on use of quantitative measures to make important short-term decisions. Costs and other factors relevant to decision must be identified.

I.　Decisions and Information

　　A.　Decision Making

　　　　1.　Five steps involved in managerial decision making.

　　　　　　a.　Define task and goal.

　　　　　　b.　Identify alternative courses of action.

　　　　　　c.　Collect relevant information.

　　　　　　d.　Select course of action.

　　　　　　e.　Analyze and assess the decision.

　　　　2.　Both managerial and financial accounting information play important role in making decisions.

　　　　　　a.　Accounting system provides primarily financial information such as performance reports and budget analyses.

　　　　　　b.　Non-financial information is also relevant, such as environmental effects, political sensitivities, and social responsibility.

　　B.　Relevant Costs

　　　　1.　Most financial measures from cost accounting systems are based on historical amounts; however, relevant costs, or avoidable costs, are especially useful. Three types of costs:

　　　　　　a.　Sunk cost arises from a past decision; cannot be avoided or changed, and not relevant to future decisions.

　　　　　　b.　Out-of-pocket cost requires future outlay of cash and results from result of management's decisions; is relevant.

　　　　　　c.　Opportunity cost is a potential benefit lost by taking specific action when two or more alternative choices are available; consideration is important.

　　　　2.　Relevant benefits are additional or incremental revenue generated by selecting a particular course of action over another; relevant to decision-making.

II.   **Managerial Decision Scenarios**—consider each decision task discussed below independent from the others.

    A. Additional Business

       1. Effect on net income must be considered when deciding whether to accept or reject an order; reject if loss results.

       2. Historical costs are not relevant to this decision.

       3. Incremental or additional costs (also called differential costs) are additional costs incurred if company pursues certain course of action; relevant to this decision.

       4. Minimum acceptable price per unit can be determined by dividing incremental cost by the number of units in the order.

       5. Incremental costs of additional volume are relevant.

       6. If additional volume approaches or exceeds existing available capacity of factory, incremental costs required to expand capacity are then relevant.

       7. Accepting order may cause existing sales to decline; the contribution margin lost from the decline in sales is an opportunity cost and is relevant (if future cash flows over several time periods are affected, net present value should be computed).

       8. Note – Allocated overhead costs, which are historical costs, should not automatically be considered; only incremental costs to be incurred are relevant.

    B. Make or Buy

       1. When determining whether to make or buy a component of a product, only incremental costs are relevant.

       2. Only incremental overhead costs are relevant; an incremental overhead rate should be determined.

       3. If the incremental costs of making the component exceed the purchase price paid to buy the component, decision rule would be to buy; however, several other factors should be considered.

          a. Product quality.

          b. Timeliness of delivery (especially in JIT settings).

          c. Reactions of customers and suppliers.

          d. Other intangibles (employee morale and workload).

          e. Must also consider if making the part will require incremental fixed costs to expand plant capacity.

       4. Make or buy decision for component parts can also be used for decisions about the outsourcing of services.

C. Scrap or Rework
1. Costs already incurred in manufacturing units of product not meeting quality are sunk costs; are entirely irrelevant in any decision on whether to sell to substandard units as scrap or rework so meet quality standards.
2. Incremental revenues, incremental costs of reworking defects, and opportunity costs (the contribution margin lost if sales of other units are given up) are all relevant.

D. Sell or Process
1. Partially completed products can be sold as is or processed further and then sold.
2. Compute incremental revenue from further processing (amount of revenue after further processing less revenue from selling the products as partially completed)
3. Compute incremental cost from further processing.
4. Process further and sell if incremental revenue from further processing exceeds related incremental costs.

E. Sales Mix Selection
1. When more that one product is sold, some are likely to be more profitable than others; management should concentrate sales efforts on more profitable products.
2. If production facilities or other factors are limited, an increase in production and sale of one product usually requires reduction in production and sale of others.
3. The most profitable combination, or sales mix, of products should be determined.
4. Determine the contribution margin of each product, the facilities required to produce these products and any constraints on facilities and markets for the products.
5. If all products require same facilities and the market for products is unlimited, the product with the highest contribution margin should be produced.
6. If each product requires different facilities, there is no excess capacity and the market for products is unlimited, determine contribution margin per unit of the constraint (the factor that limits capacity, such as machine time required); produce the product with the highest contribution margin per unit of the constraint.
7. If market demand is not sufficient for company to sell all that it produces, production of any given product should not exceed limitation of market demand; spare capacity should be used to produce product with highest contribution margin (or contribution margin per unit of the constraint, if applicable).

F. Segment Elimination

1. If segment of company is performing poorly, management must consider eliminating it.

2. Decision should not be based on net income (loss) or its contribution to overhead.

3. Need to look at avoidable and unavoidable expenses:

    a. Avoidable (or escapable) expenses are costs or expenses that would not be incurred if the segment is eliminated.

    b. Unavoidable (or inescapable) expenses are costs or expenses that would continue even if the segment is eliminated.

4. Decision rule – Segment is candidate for elimination if its revenues are less than its avoidable expenses.

5. Should also assess impact of elimination on other segments.

    a. An unprofitable segment might contribute to another segment's revenue and expenses.

    b. A profitable segment might be eliminated if its space, assets and staff can be more profitably used by another segment or new segment.

G. Keep or Replace Equipment

1. Must decide whether the reduction in variable manufacturing costs over its life is greater than the net purchase price of the new equipment.

    a. Net purchase price is the cost of the new equipment less any trade in allowance given or cash receipt for the old equipment.

    b. Book value of the old equipment is not considered. It is a sunk cost.

H. Qualitative Decision Factors

1. Management should not rely solely on financial data to make managerial decisions.

2. Various qualitative factors should also be considered.

III. **Decision Analysis—Break-Even Time (BET)**—A variation of the payback period method—overcomes the limitation

A. The future cash flows are restated in terms of their present values;

B. The payback period is computed using these present values.

C. Break-even time (BET) is useful measure; managers know when to expect cash flows to yield net positive returns.

D. If BET is less than estimated life of investment, positive net present value can be expected from investment.

E. To compare and rank alternative investment projects, choose the project with the lowest break-even time.

Problem I

The following statements are either true or false. Place a (T) in the parentheses before each true statement and an (F) before each false statement.

1. ( ) Capital budgeting decisions involve uncertain outcomes and long-term commitments. Therefore, management does not need to carefully analyze the factors affecting these decisions.

2. ( ) Management's estimate of an investment's payback period is significantly affected by predicted future net cash flows.

3. ( ) In general, an investment with a longer payback period is preferred over an investment with a shorter payback period.

4. ( ) When comparing asset purchase proposals, an opportunity with a higher expected rate of return on average investment is always preferred over an opportunity with a lower expected rate of return.

5. ( ) When average investment returns are used to select between capital investments, the one with the least risk, the shortest payback period, and the highest return for the longest time is often identified as the best.

6. ( ) An analysis of alternative capital investments based on net present values is not affected by the asset's salvage values and management's choice of tax depreciation methods.

7. ( ) When performing a net present value analysis, management compares the asset's cost with the sum of the unadjusted predicted future cash flows from the asset.

8. ( ) The net present value of a project can be significantly affected by the pattern of the cash flows to be received over the project's life.

9. ( ) When a company considers accepting an order for additional units that will not reduce its normal sales activity, the order should be accepted only if the revenue from the sale exceeds the average cost of producing the product.

10. ( ) A company should always purchase components of its product if the purchase prices are less than the incremental costs of making those components.

11. ( ) Assets' historical costs are sunk costs and are irrelevant to decisions about what to do with those assets in the future.

12. ( ) If a company decides to make a component instead of buying it, an opportunity cost is incurred equal to the net value of the products that could have been produced with the capacity committed to making the component.

13. ( ) In selecting a sales mix, management needs to have good measures of the company's production and market constraints and the contribution margins generated by its products.

14. ( ) When a department's elimination is being considered, its revenues should be compared with its avoidable expenses.

Problem II

You are given several words, phrases or numbers to choose from in completing each of the following statements or in answering the following questions. In each case, select the one that best completes the statement or answers the question and place its letter in the answer space provided.

_____ 1. Hansen Company is considering buying a machine for $24,000. It has a predicted salvage value of $4,000. Annual depreciation over its five-year life will be $4,000 each year. The company expects sales of the machine's product to generate an after-tax annual net income of $4,200. The cash flows are expected to be received evenly throughout each year. The machine's accounting rate of return is:

  a. $12,000.

  b. $14,000.

  c. 1.4286%.

  d. 30%.

  e. 35%.

_____ 2. The Motoroma Company is considering making an investment that will have an initial cost of $240,000 and that is expected to generate the following cash flows:

> Year 1............. $120,000
> Year 2.............   140,000
> Year 3.............   40,000

Management wants to earn no less than 12% on this investment. What is its net present value?

  a. $ 7,228.

  b. $ 60,000.

  c. $126,212.

  d. $247,228.

  e. $300,000.

_____ 3. Concordia Corporation operates a process that can produce 40 bells per hour or 60 whistles per hour. The annual capacity of the process is 2,400 hours. The market demand is 50,000 bells per year and 90,000 whistles per year. Use the following additional information to find the most profitable sales mix for the company:

	Bells	Whistles
Selling price per unit..............	$1.20	$1.00
Variable costs per unit	0.70	0.60
Contribution margin per unit .	$0.50	$0.40

	Bells	Whistles
a.	50,000	69,000
b.	96,000	(none)
c.	(none)	144,000
d.	36,000	90,000
e.	None of the above	

_____ 4. Schroeder Department Store has clothing, housewares, and cosmetics departments. Net income (or loss) for the departments is $13,000, $(1,000) loss, and $10,000, respectively. Operating expenses for the housewares department are $15,000, of which 40% are unavoidable. Should Schroeder automatically eliminate the housewares department? Why or why not?

   a. Yes, because it incurred a net loss of $1,000.

   b. Yes, because the store would save $9,000 of avoidable expenses.

   c. Yes, because its unavoidable expenses of $6,000 are less than its avoidable expenses of $9,000.

   d. No, because its revenues of $14,000 are greater than its unavoidable expenses of $6,000.

   e. No, because its revenues of $14,000 are greater than its avoidable expenses of $9,000.

Problem III

Many of the important ideas and concepts discussed in Chapter 25 are reflected in the following list of key terms. Test your understanding of these terms by matching the appropriate definitions with the terms. Record the number identifying the most appropriate definition in the blank space next to each term.

_____ Accounting rate of return   _____ Internal rate of return (IRR)
_____ Avoidable expense   _____ Net present value (NPV)
_____ Break-even time (BET)   _____ Payback period (PBP)
_____ Capital budgeting   _____ Relevant benefits
_____ Hurdle rate   _____ Unavoidable expense
_____ Incremental cost

1. An additional cost incurred only if a company pursues a specific course of action.

2. A dollar amount estimate of an asset's value that is used to evaluate the acceptability of an investment; computed by discounting future cash flows from the investment at a satisfactory rate and then subtracting the initial cost of the investment.

3. A time based measurement used to evaluate the acceptability of an investment; equals the time expected to pass before an investment's net cash flows equal its initial cost.

4. An expense (or cost) that is not relevant for business decisions; an expense that would continue even if a department, product or service is eliminated.

5. The process of analyzing alternative investments and deciding which assets to acquire or sell.

6. Expense (or cost) that is relevant for decision making; an expense that is not incurred if a department, product or service is eliminated.

7. Additional or incremental revenue generated by selecting a particular course of action over another.

8. A time-based measurement used to evaluate the acceptability of an investment; equals the time expected to pass before the present value of the net cash flows from an investment equals its initial cost.

9. A rate used to evaluate the acceptability of an investment; equals the after-tax periodic income from a project divided by the average investment in the asset; also called *rate of return on average investment*.

10. A minimum acceptable rate of return (set by management) for an investment.

11. A rate used to evaluate the acceptability of an investment; equals the rate that yields a net present value of zero for an investment.

Problem IV

Complete the following by filling in the blanks.

1. The _____ should not be the only factor considered when choosing between possible investments with different lives because it does not include all cash flows in the analysis.

2. A _____ payback period is desirable because the more quickly cash is received, the more quickly it is available for other uses.

3. The annual net cash flow from selling a machine's product can be calculated _____ as net income plus the annual _____ expense for the machine.

4. _____ budgeting is the process of analyzing alternative investments and deciding which _____ to acquire or sell.

5. An _____ cost is the potential _____ of one alternative that are lost by choosing another.

6. An _____ cost requires a current outlay of _____. It is usually an _____ cost.

7. A _____ cost cannot be avoided or changed in any way because it arises from a _____ decision. These _____ costs are _____ to future decisions.

8. In making a decision about accepting additional business, management should not consider the average costs of the product. Instead, they should analyze the _____ costs that would be incurred.

9. Management would normally not invest in a proposed project that has a _____ net present value.

10. In analyzing a decision between making or buying a component of a product, management must compare the purchase price with the _____ costs of making the component.

11. Because of differences in _____, it is not possible to say with certainty that the return on a particular investment is either good or bad without relating it to the returns from other investments.

12. As a general rule, a department can be considered a candidate for elimination if its _____ are _____ than its _____ expenses.

13. _____ expenses are avoided by eliminating a department, but _____ expenses continue.

Problem V

A company is considering whether to purchase a new machine that would cost $50,000, have a four-year life and no salvage value. It would be depreciated with the straight-line method. Revenues are assumed to occur near the end of each year. The company would expect to generate income over the next four years as shown below:

Sales..		$210,000
Costs:		
Materials, labor, and overhead other than depreciation on the new machine	$115,000	
Depreciation on the new machine	12,500	
Selling and administrative expenses	65,000	192,500
Operating income...		$ 17,500
Income taxes		7,000
Net income...		$ 10,500

1. This machine is expected to produce an annual net cash flow of
   $_____.

2. The expected payback period on this machine is:

   $$\frac{\text{Cost of Asset}}{\text{Annual Net Cash Flow}} = \frac{\$\rule{3cm}{0.4pt}}{\$\rule{3cm}{0.4pt}} = \rule{3cm}{0.4pt} \text{ years}$$

3. The expected average investment in this machine is:

   $$\frac{\text{First year's beginning book value} + \text{Final year's ending book value}}{2} =$$

   $$\$\rule{5cm}{0.4pt} + \$\rule{5cm}{0.4pt} = \$\rule{3cm}{0.4pt}$$

4. The expected rate of return on the average investment in this machine is:

   $$\frac{\text{Annual after-tax net income}}{\text{Average investment}} = \frac{\$\rule{3cm}{0.4pt}}{\$\rule{3cm}{0.4pt}} = \rule{3cm}{0.4pt} \%$$

5. If the company has a 10% minimum desired compounded rate of return on capital investments, the net present value of the expected cash flows from this machine discounted at 10% is:

Present value of cash flows (3.1699 x $_____)	$_____
Less: amount to be invested..	_____
Net present value...	$_____

Solutions for Chapter 25

Problem I

1.	F	8.	T
2.	T	9.	F
3.	F	10.	F
4.	F	11.	T
5.	T	12.	T
6.	F	13.	T
7.	F	14.	T

Problem II

1. D
2. A
3. D
4. E

Problem III

Accounting rate of return.	9	Internal rate of return (IRR).	11
Avoidable expense.	6	Net present value (NPV)	2
Break-even time (BET)	8	Payback period (PBP)	3
Capital budgeting	5	Relevant benefits.	7
Hurdle rate.	10	Unavoidable expense	4
Incremental cost	1		

Problem IV

1. payback period

2. short

3. indirectly; depreciation

4. Capital; assets

5. opportunity; benefits

6. out-of-pocket; cash; incremental

7. sunk; past; sunk; irrelevant

8. incremental

9. negative

10. incremental

11. risk

12. revenues; less; avoidable

13. Avoidable; unavoidable

Problem V

1. Expected annual net cash flow can be calculated directly as:

Sales..	$ 210,000
Operating costs	(115,000)
Selling and admin. expenses..............	(65,000)
Income taxes..	(7,000)
Annual cash flow...............................	$ 23,000

The same amount can be calculated indirectly:

Net income...	$ 10,500
Plus: depreciation	12,500
Annual cash flow...............................	$ 23,000

2. The expected payback period on this machine is:

$$\frac{\$50,000}{\$23,000} = 2.2 \text{ years}$$

3. The expected average investment in this machine is:

$$\frac{\$50,000 + \$0}{2} = \$25,000$$

4. The expected rate of return on the average investment in this machine is:

$$\frac{\$10,500}{\$25,000} = 42\%$$

5.

Present value of cash flows (3.1699 x $23,000)	$72,908
Less: amount to be invested..	50,000
Net present value...	$22,908

APPENDIX B
PRESENT AND FUTURE VALUES

Learning Objective C1:

Describe the earning of interest and the concepts of present and future values.

Summary

Interest is the payment by a borrower to the owner of an asset for its use. Present and future value computations are a way for us to estimate the interest component of holding assets or liabilities over a period of time.

Learning Objective P1:

Apply present value concepts to a single amount by using interest tables.

Summary

The present value of a single amount received at a future date is the amount that can be invested now at the specified interest rate to yield that future value.

Learning Objective P2:

Apply future value concepts to a single amount by using interest tables.

Summary

The future value of a single amount invested at a specified rate of interest is the amount that would accumulate by the future date.

Learning Objective P3:

Apply present value concepts to an annuity by using interest tables.

Summary

The present value of an annuity is the amount that can be invested now at the specified interest rate to yield that series of equal periodic payments.

Learning Objective P4:

Apply future value concepts to an annuity by using interest tables.

Summary

The future value of an annuity invested at a specified rate of interest is the amount that would accumulate by the date of the final payment.

Appendix Outline

I.   Present Value and Future Value Concepts

    A. As time passes, certain assets and liabilities that are held grow.

    B. Growth is due to interest.

    C. Present and future value computations are a way for us to measure or estimate the interest component of holding assets or liabilities over time.

II.   Present Value of a Single Amount

    A. The present value of a single amount received at a future date is the amount that can be invested now at the specified interest rate to yield that future value.

    B. A table of present values for a single amount shows the present values of $1 for a variety of interest rates and a variety of time periods that will pass before the $1 is received.

III. Future Value of a Single Amount

    A. The future value of a single amount invested at a specified rate of interest is the amount that would accumulate by the future date.

    B. A table of future values of a single amount shows the future values of $1 invested now at a variety of interest rates for a variety of time periods.

IV.   Present Value of an Annuity

    A. An *ordinary annuity* is defined as equal end-of-period payments at equal intervals.

    B. The present value of an annuity is the amount that can be invested now at the specified interest rate to yield that series of equal periodic payments.

    C. A table of present values for an annuity shows the present values of annuities where the amount of each payment is $1 for different numbers of periods and a variety of interest rates.

V.   Future Value of an Annuity

    A. The future value of an annuity invested at a specified rate of interest is the amount that would accumulate by the date of the final payment.

    B. A table of future values for an annuity shows the future values of annuities where the amount of each payment is $1 for different numbers of periods and a variety of interest rates.

Problem I

The following statements are either true or false. Place a (T) in the parentheses before each true statement and an (F) before each false statement.

1. ( ) In discounting, the number of periods must be expressed in terms of 6-month periods if interest is compounded semiannually.

2. ( ) One way to calculate the present value of an annuity is to find the present value of each payment and add them together.

3. ( ) A table for the future values of 1 can be used to solve all problems that can be solved using a table for the present values of 1.

4. ( ) Erlich Enterprises should be willing to pay $100,000 for an investment that will return $20,000 annually for 8 years if the company requires a 12% return. (Use the tables to get your answer.)

Problem II

You are given several words, phrases, or numbers to choose from in completing each of the following statements or in answering the following questions. In each case select the one that best completes the statement or answers the question and place its letter in the answer space provided. Use the tables in your text as necessary to answer the questions.

_____ 1. Ralph Norton has $300 deducted from his monthly paycheck and deposited in a retirement fund that earns an annual interest rate of 12%. If Norton follows this plan for 1 year, how much will be accumulated in the account on the date of the last deposit? (Round to the nearest whole dollar.)

        a. $3,600.

        b. $4,032.

        c. $3,805.

        d. $7,240.

        e. $4,056.

_____ 2. Maxine Hansen is setting up a fund for a future business. She makes an initial investment of $15,000 and plans to make semiannual contributions of $2,500 to the fund. The fund is expected to earn an annual interest rate of 8%, compounded semiannually. How much will be in the fund after five years?

        a. $52,218.

        b. $36,706.

        c. $68,600.

        d. $45,332.

        e. $51,373.

_____ 3. Tricorp Company is considering an investment that is expected to return $320,000 after four years. If Tricorp demands a 15% return, what is the most that it will be willing to pay for this investment?

        a. $320,000.

        b. $177,696.

        c. $182,976.

        d. $ 45,216.

        e. $278,272.

_____ 4. Tom Snap can invest $6.05 for 17 years, after which he will be paid $10. What annual rate of interest will he earn?

  a. 15%.

  b. 9%.

  c. 7%.

  d. 5%.

  e. 3%.

Problem III

Complete the following by filling in the blanks. Use the tables in Appendix C to find the answers.

1. Leila Turner expects to invest $0.83 at a 7% annual rate of interest and receive $2 at the end of the investment. Turner must wait _____ years before she receives payment.

2. Jim Ables expects to invest $5 for 35 years and receive $102.07 at the end of that time. He will earn interest at a rate of _____% on this investment.

Solutions for Appendix B

Problem I

1. T

2. T

3. T

4. F

Problem II

1. C

2. A

3. C

4. E

Problem III

1. Table E-1 show that when the interest rate = 7% and the present value of 1 = 0.4150 ($0.83/$2), the number of periods = 13.

2. Table E-2 shows that when the number of periods = 35 and the future value of 1 = 20.4140 ($102.07/$5), the interest rate = 9%.